"These nineteenth- and early-twentieth-century biographies, now republished by Chelsea House, reveal an unsuspected significance. Not only are a good many of them substantively valuable (and by no means entirely superseded), but they also evoke a sense of the period, an intimacy with the attitudes and assumptions of their times."
—*Professor Daniel Aaron*

Edgar A Poe

EDGAR ALLAN POE
GEORGE E. WOODBERRY

INTRODUCTION BY
R.W.B. LEWIS

American Men and Women of Letters Series

GENERAL EDITOR
PROFESSOR DANIEL AARON
HARVARD UNIVERSITY

CHELSEA HOUSE

LONGWOOD PUBLIC LIBRARY

Copyright © 1980, 1997, by Chelsea House Publishers, a division of Main Line Book Co.
All rights reserved. Printed and bound in the United States of America.

3 5 7 9 8 6 4 2

Library of Congress Cataloging-in-Publication Data

Woodberry, George Edward, 1855-1930.
    Edgar Allen Poe / George E. Woodberry : introduction by R.W.B. Lewis.
    p.   cm. -- (American men and women of letters series)
    Previously published: New York: Chelsea House, 1980.
    Includes index.
    ISBN 0-7910-4538-2 (hc)
    1. Poe, Edgar Allen Poe, 1809-1849--Biography. 2. Authors, American--19th
Century--Biography. I.Title. II. Series: American men and women of letters.
PS2631.W65 1997
818'.309--dc21
(B)   96-51456
                                                                       CIP

CONTENTS

GENERAL INTRODUCTION, DANIEL AARON . . . ix
INTRODUCTION, R. W. B. LEWIS xi
AUTHOR'S PREFACE 1885, GEORGE E. WOODBERRY . xxvii

CHAPTER I.
PARENTAGE 1

CHAPTER II.
EDUCATION 15

CHAPTER III.
WANDERINGS 30

CHAPTER IV.
AT THE SOUTH 63

CHAPTER V.
IN PHILADELPHIA 104

CHAPTER VI.
IN NEW YORK 201

CHAPTER VII.
THE END OF THE PLAY 278

General Introduction

THE VISITABLE PAST
Daniel Aaron

THE TWENTY-FIVE BIOGRAPHIES of American worthies reissued in this Chelsea House series restore an all but forgotten chapter in the annals of American literary culture. Some of the authors of these volumes—journalists, scholars, writers, professional men—would be considered amateurs by today's standards, but they enjoyed certain advantages not open to their modern counterparts. In some cases they were blood relations or old friends of the men and women they wrote about, or at least near enough to them in time to catch the contemporary essence often missing in the more carefully researched and authoritative later studies of the same figures. Their leisurely, impressionistic accounts—sometimes as interesting for what is omitted as for what is emphasized—reveal a good deal about late Victorian assumptions, cultural and social, and about the vicissitudes of literary reputation.

Each volume in the series is introduced by a recognized scholar who was encouraged to write an idiosyncratic appraisal of the biographer and his work. The introductions vary in emphasis and point of view, for the biographies are not of equal quality, nor are the writers memorialized equally appealing. Yet a kind of consensus is discernible in these random assessments: surprise at the insights still to be found in ostensibly unscientific and old-fashioned works; in some instances admiration for the solidity and liveliness of the biographer's prose and quality of mind; respect for the pioneer historians among them who made excellent use of the limited material at their disposal.

The volumes in this American Men and Women of Letters series contain none of the startling "private" and "personal" episodes modern readers have come to expect in biography, but they illuminate what Henry James called the "visitable past." As such, they are of particular value to all students of American cultural and intellectual history.

Cambridge, Massachusetts
Spring, 1980

INTRODUCTION TO THE CHELSEA HOUSE EDITION
R.W.B. Lewis

The Facts in the Case of Mr. Poe

> Mr. L——l was so kind as to accede to my desire that he would take notes of all that occurred; and it is from his memoranda that what I now have to relate is, for the most part, either condensed or copied *verbatim.*
> —"The Facts in the Case of M. Valdemar"

ONE OF THE important recurring games in American literary history has been that of revising the received human image of Edgar Allan Poe. Something about Poe's personality and the spasmodic circumstances of his short life (1809-1849), especially when linked with the wayward quality of his tales and poems, has periodically convinced literary scholars that he has never hitherto been understood. Over a number of decades, the revisionary process has become standardized. It begins by positing as fundamentally false the image perpetrated by earlier biographers. More often than not, this image partakes of a romantic legend wherein Poe rather resembles the haunted figures that stalk through his most horrific tales—feverishly brilliant, tormented, doomed, sexually askew almost beyond mortal comprehension, betimes a murderer and a necrophiliac. Then, as against that version, there is brought into view the "real" Poe, a person whom the ascertainable facts disclose to have been quite humanly recognizable. This Poe is a man among men, even a social being, who shifted about between Richmond and Philadelphia and New York, and who suffered terribly from poverty, illness and an intolerance for alcohol; who nonetheless produced fiction, poetry and criticism at an incredible rate—some of it, at least, among the wonders of our literature—and performed with striking success as magazine editor; who married his thirteen-year-old cousin Virginia Clemm and late in his life courted a dizzying series of widow-women of uncertain years; and who died, somewhat mysteriously, in Baltimore at the age of forty.

Such, in essence, was the biographical procedure of Arthur Hobson Quinn, whose life of Poe in 1941 did indeed set the record straight in many valuable particulars; of Edward Wagenknecht, the title of whose *Edgar Allan Poe: The Man Behind the Legend* in 1963 announced the familiar intention; and, among several others, of Robert W. Beyer, in an ambitious forthcoming study. Such also was precisely the procedure, almost a century ago, of George Edward Woodberry in his *Edgar Allan Poe* of 1885.

George Woodberry, in 1885, was a thirty-year-old aspiring scholar and poet; a few years later he would become Professor of Comparative Literature at Columbia, and in the course of time he would compile an impressive *oeuvre* of critical biographies, literary essays and poems. He was a gentleman-scholar of the old school—not a bad school, seen in retrospect; and if its graduates displayed a sort of cultivated and well-mannered shrewdness rather than any genuine drive of insight, they possessed an utter integrity of scholarship. This was why Woodberry was so shocked by his findings: everyone had *lied* about Poe, he had come to believe; all the witnesses disputed and quarreled with each other. The moment his *Poe* was in print, Woodberry fled to Europe to recuperate amid the old Mediterranean humanities. Writing a friend from Capri and referring to John Ingram, whose life of Poe had appeared in 1880, Woodberry remarked a bit dazedly: "Ingram did an extraordinary amount of lying about Poe, and I still wonder at it." In the preface to his own book, after listing his sources, Woodberry summarized: "The statements of facts in these sources are extraordinarily conflicting, doubtful, and contested; and in view of this, as well as of the spirit of rancor excited in any discussion of Poe's character, the author has made this, as far as was possible, a documented biography."

One of the worst of the liars Woodberry had to contend with was Rufus N. Griswold, the former Baptist minister and failed poet who somehow managed to become Poe's literary executor, and who, in that capacity, exhibited a positive genius in the defamation of Poe's character and behavior. Griswold accomplished this masterpiece of blackguarding, in his edition of Poe's works, by wholesale lying and invention, by groundless assertions, and in particular by the systematic forgery of Poe's letters. It was a performance rooted, it seems, in a psychopathic hatred of Poe (no one has really explained it); and although Griswold was quickly denounced, and Poe defended, by the more knowing and well-disposed, Poe's enduring reputation in many quarters was that of a drunkard, debauchee, drug addict and madman. George Woodberry, however, showed a sturdy reluctance to be taken in. He was unaware of the extent of Griswold's fraudulence

—it would not be fully revealed until Arthur Hobson Quinn's meticulous exposé in 1941— but he regarded Griswold's rancorous statements as typical of the argument over Poe's character that occurred at the time. "An unsupported statement by Griswold regarding Poe is liable to suspicion," he tells us mildly and typically; Woodberry's Poe is anything but the libertine lunatic depicted by Griswold.

But the first liar Woodberry was faced with was, of course, Poe himself. Woodberry seems not to have come upon the yarns Poe took to spreading about his life during the late 1820s, tales of adventuring and dueling in Europe (in no other respect does William Faulkner so resemble his Southern literary ancestor as in this business of creative autobiography). But he spotted enough wilful misstatements by Poe to lead him, early on, to advance the customary formula: "It may as well be confessed at once that any unsupported assertion by Poe regarding himself is to be received with great caution."

Woodberry does not pause to meditate on Poe's habit of falsification, or to observe any connection between it and certain characteristic tactics in Poe's fiction. He informs us, sifting the evidence, that Edgar Poe was born on January 19, 1809; that for a period, after his adoption, he was called Edgar Allan; that when he enlisted in the United States Army in 1828, he gave his name as Edgar A. Perry and his birthdate as 1806; and that when he entered West Point in 1830, he changed his birthdate to 1811, having said publicly not long before that he was not yet twenty. Despite all that, Woodberry gives no sign of being struck by Poe's evasiveness, in his fiction, about names and dates—by the narrator of "Berenice" flatly refusing to tell us his family name; the narrator of "Ligeia" saying that he can no longer remember when he first met the Lady Ligeia and that he never did get to know her last name; and even more suggestively, by the narrator of "William Wilson" confiding that his real name is not William Wilson but something quite like it (as Edgar A. Perry, one thinks, is like Edgar A. Poe) and that his birthdate, like that of his double and namesake at the English school, is January 19, 1813.

If Woodberry fails to remark on these recurrences, it is partly because he resolutely refuses at any moment to read from the life to the writing. In this, to be sure, he would have been warmly applauded by W. H. Auden and no few others, since Woodberry's time, who regard all biographical interpretation as impertinent and risky; and it is to be admitted that Woodberry's noninterventionist policy allows the reader to have all the fun of tracing the connections. At the same time, Woodberry appears blind to those many occasions when Poe sought slyly to fob off as a true story, thoroughly vouched for, some palpable and incredible fiction—as in "The Facts in the Case of M. Valdemar," which purports to tell how a dying man's body was kept alive for seven months by a mesmeric spell and instantly decomposed when the spell was lifted; and for which the narrator claims a documentary veracity almost identical to that claimed by George Woodberry for his biography of Poe.

Even so, working his way through this network of historical and literary fibs and misrepresentations, Woodberry came astonishingly close to establishing all the significant facts in the case of Edgar Allan Poe. His biographical report has of course been corrected in a host of minor details; new facts have been uncovered (for instance that Poe, making his way to Boston on a coal barge in 1827, briefly assumed the name of Henri le Rennet); we know a good deal more now about Poe's erudition, both actual and spurious, and several persons of importance in Poe's life have been more fully identified—most notably, Mrs. Charles Richmond, to whom Woodberry refers simply and discreetly as "Annie." But the basic story is all here, and it does not differ very much from the one laboriously arrived at by later generations of scholars.

Woodberry, moreover, may be said in a certain perspective to have had an advantage over those later generations. In his far-off age of innocence, he did not have to struggle through the miasma of the Freudian interpretation of Poe that grew thickest with Marie Bonaparte's study (1933, and still damnably fascinating). And so, for example, Woodberry is able to remark accurately that nothing whatever is known about Poe's father, the young actor David Poe, after the summer of 1810—without indulging in speculation as to whether David Poe "rejected" his wife and children and what the effect of such "rejection" might have been upon the infant Edgar.

To move to the very end of the story (or "the end of the play," as Woodberry appropriately calls it), Woodberry passes on the rumor that Poe's death in Baltimore, in October 1849, was brought on by his having been dragged about the city in a sick and intoxicated state and forced to vote in a succession of polling places. But, says Woodberry, "the basis of this tradition is now lost." The "tradition" caught hold and for a long time provided the concluding episode in the Poe legend. The most recent scholarship, peeling away the speculation about Poe's father and the alleged melodrama of Poe's death, has been content to leave these and other matters almost exactly where Woodberry left them.

Woodberry obviously lost patience with Poe the man before he completed his work—"really," he told his correspondent from Capri, "it became a very unwelcome task before I was at the end"—and his final summing-up is moralistic and scolding. Still, his biographical account holds firm. And indeed, the truly telling change regarding Poe in the past decades has not been a major clarification of his life but a radical reassessment of his imaginative intentions and his literary achievement.

As to the latter, Woodberry is extremely sound within the limits of a cultivated impressionism. He is eloquent in describing the *effect* of Poe's tales and poems (notice his remarks about "Ligeia" and "Ulalume"), something that would have gratified Poe, who said that a particular effect was what he invariably aimed at in his writing. On the whole, Woodberry discriminates acutely (to our modern judgment) between the best, the second best and the trifling in Poe's work—his most striking lapse being his failure to appreciate "The Purloined Letter." Woodberry, in 1885, could hardly have foreseen Poe's contribution to the immense future of the English-language detective story—the first Sherlock Holmes tale, *A Study in Scarlet* (in which Holmes refers to Poe's Dupin as "a very inferior fellow"), did not appear until 1887; but taken by itself, "The Purloined Letter," with its tantalizing echoes and secret quotations, might have stirred Woodberry's curiosity more than it did.

As an instance of Woodberry's critical common sense, we can cite his treatment of the story, put forward by John Ingram, of the composition of "The Bells," and the alleged part in it of Mrs. Mary Louise Shew, a friend of the Poe family in the latter 1840s. Claiming to draw on Mrs. Shew's diary, Ingram had written that Poe arrived at the lady's home one day, tired, dispirited, totally lacking in inspiration. Through the open windows there came the sound of church bells; and when Poe declared that he was not in the mood for bells, Mrs. Shew thrust a piece of paper in his hands. Woodberry's paraphrase continues:

Mrs. Shew then wrote, "The Bells, by E.A. Poe," and added "The little silver bells;" on the poet's finishing the stanza thus suggested, she again wrote, "The heavy iron bells," and this idea also Poe elaborated, and then copying off the two stanzas, headed it, "By Mrs. M.L. Shew," and called it her poem.

This preposterous account of how a great poem gets written is received courteously by Woodberry, but he suggests that the origins of "The Bells" were far more plausibly to be found in Poe's lifelong fascination with bell-ringing and in his careful reading (documented by Woodberry) of a book by Chateaubriand that spoke of the emotions aroused by varieties of bell sounds.*

But common sense, as we have gradually learned, is not the most trustworthy guide to Poe's imaginative landscape. Richard Wilbur in a series of essays (the most accessible being his full-scale introduction to the Poe section in the anthology *Major Writers of America*, 1966) and Daniel Hoffman in *Poe Poe Poe Poe Poe Poe Poe* (1972) have argued convincingly, if some-

---

* What might be called the Ingram theory of creativity has been exemplified in our time by a scene in the film *Night and Day*. Cole Porter (played by Cary Grant) is seated at the piano in his Foreign Legion uniform, waiting for inspiration. From outside, he hears the sound of drums, and the first line of a song immediately presents itself: "Like the beat beat beat of the tom-toms." He hears a clock ticking in the room, and the second line arises: "Like the tick tick tock of the stately clock ..." Raindrops are espied on the window: "Like the drip drip drop of the raindrops;" and then Porter, hands moving swiftly and confidently over the keyboard, is in full swing into the chorus of "Night and Day."

what differently, that the characteristic action of Poe's best tales is nothing external or "realistic" but rather an allegorical dream-journey. Within the dream, one part of the narrator's psyche goes desperately in search of that other part of himself from which he has been disjoined in some actual or metaphorical childhood. Thus the narrator of "Ligeia" is separated from the maternal and godlike Ligeia at the instant of her death; the narrator of the more complex "Fall of the House of Usher" had been Roderick Usher's closest boyhood friend before their ways parted; and even William Wilson, contemplating his double at the English school, has the strong belief of "having been acquainted with the being who stood before me, at some epoch very long ago—some point of the past infinitely remote."

The dream-journey towards reunion may be beset by horror, loss of reason, premature burial and even murder—but these (the argument runs) are necessary phases in the escape from the fallen earthbound state, the imprisoning world of prosaic fact and banal morality. The climactic re-encounter, however terrifying in any normal viewpoint, may accordingly be a kind of triumph within Poe's unique vision. Speaking of the moment in which Madeline Usher "in her violent and now final death-agonies, bore [her brother Roderick] to the floor a corpse," Wilbur contends that: "grisly as their death-embrace may seem, it actually symbolizes the momentary reunion of a divided soul; and . . . the final restoration and purification of that soul in the life to come."

Wilbur's thesis is the following:

> The typical Poe story is, in its action, an allegory of dream-experience; it occurs within the mind of the poet; the characters are not distinct personalities, but principles or faculties of the poet's divided nature; the steps of the action correspond to the successive states of a mind moving into sleep; and the end of the action is the end of a dream. Sometimes, as in "William Wilson," the narrative will have a strong admixture of realism and of credible psychology; else as in "The Fall of the House of Usher," there will be no such admixture, and the one available coherence will be allegorical.

Daniel Hoffman, deploying his own vocabulary, would essentially agree; and the rest of us can find our own terms of interpretation. But that Poe's stories variously enact the effort of a psyche to regain a lost primal harmony seems to me incontestable. The thesis serves to explain, as nothing else does, Poe's contempt (referred to earlier) for factual truth, and his imaginative involvement with criminality and violence—the psyche, en route to transcendent beauty, must as it were conceive itself to be blasting through and beyond the dullness of the true, as humanly understood, and the drabness of the good. Poe's most interesting poems—including "The Raven," "Ulalume" and "The City in the Sea"—can be freshly grasped by means of the thesis; and his most elaborate hoaxes, especially when they describe spectacular journeys, can be seen as huge parodies of the persistent intention—products of the same imagination in its season of jocosity.

There are definite hints that George Woodberry would not have been altogether shocked by this reading of Poe. He says about the Lady Ligeia, after all, and in clear pre-Wilburian terms, that she "has still no human quality. ... She is, in fact, the maiden of Poe's dream, the Eidolon he served, the air-woven divinity in which he believed; for he had the true myth-making faculty, the power to make his senses aver what his imagination perceived." But Woodberry's New England temperament would scarcely have approved the correlative impulse to violate truth and outrage morality in the course of the visionary enterprise. It was, apparently, a lingering sense of something equivocal, something ethically flawed, in Poe's achievement that led Woodberry, in his final verdict, to withhold his highest critical accolade. Faced with the present-day reading of Poe, Woodberry might have reconsidered that verdict, though it is doubtful. There is not much else, in all fairness, that he should have felt called on to reconsider.

New Haven, Connecticut
June, 1980

AUTHOR'S PREFACE
TO THE
1885 EDITION

———•———

THE principal printed sources for a narrative of Poe's life are the following, of which the first three were inspired by himself and published before his death: I., Griswold's sketch, in "The Poets and Poetry of America," 1842; II., Hirst's sketch, in the Philadelphia "Saturday Museum," 1843; III., Lowell's sketch, in "Graham's Magazine," 1845; IV., Griswold's "Memoir," founded on the documents put into his hands as Poe's executor and prefixed to the third volume of the original edition of Poe's "Works," 1850, but now suppressed; V., Mrs. Whitman's "Edgar Poe and his Critics," 1860; VI., Didier's "Life," prefixed to an edition of Poe's "Poems," 1876; VII., Gill's "Life," 1877; VIII., Stoddard's "Life," prefixed to a volume of selections from the "Works," 1880, and now included in the latest complete edition (A. C. Armstrong & Son, 1884, 6 vols.); IX., Ingram's "Life" (London), 1880. These authorities, each of which contains original matter peculiar to itself, and numerous personal reminiscences of Poe in periodicals and newspapers, have been used in the preparation of the present biography. The statements of fact in these sources are extraordinarily conflicting, doubtful, and contested; and in view of this, as well as of the spirit of rancor excited in any discussion of Poe's character, the author has made this, so far as was possible, a documentary biography, has verified all facts positively stated at first hand, and has felt obliged to assign the authority followed, in any questionable assertions, in foot notes. This method, which seemed the only practicable one if truth was to be arrived at, has involved a more direct obligation to previous works than would otherwise have been the case; but the author in this matter has been treated with marked courtesy, and he takes pleasure in thanking Mr. Eugene L. Didier and W. Fearing Gill, Esq., for voluntarily offering to him the use of their material, and Messrs. A. C. Armstrong & Son, the owners of the copyright of the Griswold and Stoddard memoirs, for permission to extract the passages found in the text. To Mr. Gill he is indebted also for the use of the incomplete MS. "Life" by T. C. Clarke, once Poe's partner. To Mr. Ingram's work the present biography is under obligation, as the foot notes exhibit, especially for extracts (the briefest possible) from Poe's correspondence with women. The letters designated "Poe to ——," and accredited to Ingram's "Life" where they had been previously printed, were placed at the author's disposal by their owner; and for this favor, as well as for a copy of the *Addenda* to "Eureka," he desires to express his thanks.

Notwithstanding the amount of printed matter regarding Poe, his life has not been exhaustively treated. The larger portion of the following pages consists of wholly new information, or of old statements so radically corrected as to become new. In preparing this the author has been indebted to the assistance of very many persons, of whom he can thank by name only a few, but he trusts that the lack of any public acknowledgment will not be misconstrued as neglect. Not to enter upon minor matters and the incessant corrections of detail made by the present volume, the account of Poe's parentage and marriage is for the first time given according to the facts, from original investigation. The discovery of the papers that settle Poe's history during the years concerning which nothing whatever has hitherto been definitely known, was due to the consideration of Robert Lincoln, Secretary of War, and the kindness of Adjutant-General R. C. Drum. The MSS. and other material collected by the late Judge Neilson Poe, and hitherto unpublished, are of great value, particularly the papers that give the only contemporary account of Poe's death, and the Snodgrass correspondence, which affords interesting details of Poe's years in Philadelphia. The correspondence of Poe with Mr. James Russell Lowell, the most interesting of all from a literary point of view, throws much light into obscure portions of Poe's mature life, as well as upon his mind and character, and the correspondence between Mr. C. F. Briggs and Mr. Lowell is the most direct and the only authoritative piece of evidence regarding Poe's affairs during his connection with the "Broadway Journal." Letters of Poe, MSS. and other original material bearing upon his life have also been furnished by Messrs. Ferdinand T. Dreer, Thomas H. Ellis, W. J. McClellan, T. B. Aldrich, Allan B. Magruder, Douglass Sherley, William Nelson, Mrs. Susan A. Weiss, William E. Foster, John Parker, J. N. Ireland, F. O. C. Darley, and Arthur Mazyck.

EDGAR ALLAN POE.

CHAPTER I.

PARENTAGE.

EDGAR ALLAN POE was born at Boston, January 19, 1809. His parents were regular members of the company then playing at the Federal Street Theatre. His father, who was about thirty years of age, had been known in his youth at Baltimore as the son of the ardent Revolutionary patriot, David Poe, whose name he bore, and as, ostensibly, a student of law. His friends, however, thought of him rather as a clever amateur actor and a boon companion of the Thespian Club; and after he had emigrated to Georgia, where one of his father's brothers had settled, they may have found nothing out of keeping with his affable, impulsive, and unreflecting character in the report that he had left the brown law books ranged on the shelves of his uncle's brother-in-law and gone upon the stage. Old General Poe, as the citizens called him in recognition of his Revolutionary services, was not a man to condone such an offense in his eldest born. He was in his sixtieth year, with at least three younger children to provide for, and he let the runaway shift for himself, — a situation tediously familiar, in after years, to the young actor, who was most successful on the boards in that part of the "Wild Gallant" which he had first essayed in real life; but his father was by no means the worldly-minded, dry-hearted miser of the playwrights.

General Poe, indeed, left a memory full of virtue. Every action of his life bespeaks a strong and decisive man, from the time he first comes into public notice as "one David Poe, a wheelwright," leader of the mob that ousted Robert Christie, the Royal Sheriff, from the city, and afterward attacked the Tory editor, William Goddard, the slanderer of Washington. He had a natural right to a rude and resolute strength, since by a not improbable tradition he traced his descent through his father, John Poe, who had emigrated about 1745 from the north of Ireland and settled in Pennsylvania, to one of Cromwell's officers who had received grants of Irish land, while on his mother's side he is said to have been nephew to John MacBride, who fought under Nelson at Copenhagen, and rose to be an Admiral of the Blue. In his Revolutionary post of Assistant Quartermaster-General for Baltimore, he was a prompt and effective official, whose patriotism was genuine and deep-seated, since he advanced money from his scanty private funds, for which, be it added, no repayment was made, except long afterwards in the form of a pension to his widow. His country's injustice, however, did not lessen his devotion. In 1814, when he was in his seventy-second year, the old spirit blazed out again in his active service as a volunteer in the battle of North Point, against his old enemies, the British. An honest, vigorous, sensible man, capable of worldly sacrifice, — so much he was; and if the ties of natural affection seem to have been in his heart neither strong nor tender, even toward his orphaned grandchildren, it must be remembered that he was not prosperous, and they were well cared for by their adoptive parents. The last record concerning him is that Lafayette, on his parting visit to this country, went to his grave and kissed the sod above him exclaiming, " Ici repose un cœur noble ! "

On the maternal side, the record of Edgar Poe's lineage belongs to the fleeting memories of the stage, and is both briefer and more obscure. The few facts that remain in regard to his mother and grandmother have been practically ignored by our books of theatrical annals, and are to be found only in contemporary newspapers. The "Independent Chronicle and the Universal Advertiser," published at Boston, in its issue of February 11, 1796, announced that Mrs. Arnold, an English actress from the Theatre Royal, Covent Garden, would make her first appearance in America at the Federal

Street Theatre, on February 12. If the success of her first night was an earnest of her future fortune, she must have received a considerable share of applause, as is seen by the following characteristic notice: —

"We have had the pleasure of a complete fruition in the anticipation of the satisfaction a Boston audience would receive from the dramatic abilities of Mrs. Arnold. The theatre never shook, with such bursts of applause, as on her first appearance, on Friday evening last. Not a heart but was sensible of her merits; not a tongue but vibrated in her praise; not a hand but moved in approbation. Nor did these expressions of satisfaction die with the evening, her merits have since been the pleasing theme of every conversation." [1]

Mrs. Arnold, whose forte seems to have been in vocal music, sang often, and also acted in comic operas, burlettas, and romantic plays, until the close of the season, May 16. On June 1 she gave a vocal concert, at which her daughter, Elizabeth, made her first appearance and sang some popular songs adapted to her youth. The fascination of the mother was not confined to the stage. She had now captivated — "Nobody Coming to Marry Me" was one of her piquant ditties — the impressionable heart of one Mr. Tubbs, a player on the pianoforte; and after their speedy union the bridegroom set up a theatre at Portland, Me. A very little theatre it must have been, hardly more than a

[1] *Massachusetts Mercury*, February 16, 1796.

family affair, since it was recruited from the amateurs of the town, and had for its chief attractions only Tubbs's piano, his wife's voice, and the precocity of his step-daughter, — "the beautiful Miss Arnold, whose powers as an actress command admiration."[1] One winter's experience of the theatrical enthusiasm of Maine proved enough, and when spring came the three were engaged as members of the troupe made up by Manager Solee from the Boston and Charleston comedians to play in the latter city. On their way South they stopped at New York, where two performances were given at the John Street Theatre in August, but the company was soon afterwards scattered by the fatal yellow fever of that year. During the autumn the family went South, and on the opening of the Charleston theatre, in November, made their debut. They performed the whole winter, but Miss Arnold in only slight parts, — a child, a nymph, a Cupid; and at the close of the season, in April, the name of Poe's grandmother Tubbs and her obscure consort, the piano-forte player, disappeared from history, while young Miss Arnold returned to the North and joined the Philadelphia company. With her new associates she acted the next four seasons (1798–1802), during their winter engagements in the city, their summer ventures at Southwark, and on their excursions to Washington and elsewhere; her rôles were usually unimportant, but she enjoyed

[1] *The Eastern Herald and Gazette of Maine*, December 12, 1796.

benefits and was apparently under the protection of Mr. Usher and Mrs. Snowden. On March 14, 1800, Mr. C. D. Hopkins, a young man, made a reputation on his very first appearance as "Tony Lumpkin," and became a popular member of the company, with which he continued to play, except during occasional absences at the South. In 1802, after the season had closed with the engagement of Mr. Green, of the Virginia company, Miss Arnold played at Baltimore, and there received a benefit, June 4. Possibly it was on this occasion that the charms of the *petite* and arch beauty inflamed the heart of young Poe; but if it were so the spark must quickly have grown dim and cold, for within two months she was married to Mr. Hopkins, who had been acting during the spring at Norfolk. Early in August the pair were delighting the people of Alexandria, and they were long to hold good rank among the Virginia players, as may still be read in old files of Petersburg, Norfolk, and Richmond papers.

In the fall of 1804 a new member was added to the company in the person of Mr. David Poe. This youth of twenty-five summers[1] had left his uncle's

[1] The age of both David Poe and Miss Arnold has been reckoned (Ingram, i. 3) as if they were born in 1787. The youthfulness of the lovers, however, disappears with the other romantic features of their mythical elopement. The mention of Miss Arnold at Boston and Portland in 1796 can hardly be thought to apply to a child of nine years, and her rôles the next summer in New York (the play-bill ascribes one of these, "Agnes," in "The

at Augusta, and made "his second appearance on any stage" at Charleston, December 5, 1803; but he had previously performed at the same place, December 1, without any special announcement. He had continued uninterruptedly in the same company until the close of the season in the spring, a diffident, easily abashed actor, although in his own rôle as "Harry Thunder" in "Wild Oats." He was not, as has hitherto been asserted, drawn to the South and tempted before the footlights by any inamorata except the Comic Muse; nor is it likely that his uncle, who died the following September, withdrew him, as the tradition avers, from the fascination of the theatre after he had entered on his career. In November, at all events, the new actor, for whom particular favor was asked as being American born, was playing in the Virginia company at Petersburg, and with it he continued as it moved from place to place through its wide circuit, until, early in September, 1805, it opened the season at Mr. Green's new theatre in Washington. Mr. Green was particularly unfortunate in this venture, and not the least of his losses was that of the popular comedian, as he is styled, Mr. Hopkins, who died, after a brief

Mountaineers," to "Mrs. Arnold," but presumably by a misprint, as the name of "Mrs. Tubbs" is in the same list) could not have been filled by a person so young. The character of her life and the notices of her acting make it exceedingly improbable that she was much, if at all, younger than her husband. He was born "certainly not later than 1780." — John P. Poe, Esq., to the author, June 19, 1883.

illness, on October 26. The company, and his widow among the rest, performed until Christmas, and then went southward again. Within a month Mr. Poe, with some pecuniary aid from a friend (for these actors were always poor), married Mrs. Hopkins, and early in February they were already playing at Richmond. They remained in Virginia until May, when they started North; and after acting at Philadelphia in June and July, and at the new Vauxhall Gardens, New York, from the middle of July until late in August, they arrived at Boston by October, and were welcomed by Mrs. Poe's old friends, the Ushers.

Here they had their permanent home for the three following years. From the contemporary criticisms [1] it is easy to form a clear and complete idea of the personal appearance and histrionic talent of the poet's father and mother. David Poe was a man of prepossessing figure, suitable for the juvenile and gallant parts, the Henrys and Charles Sedleys, which he habitually took; his voice was full and manly, but untrained, deficient in modulation and in power, his utterance distinct but mechanical, his gesture either too stiff or too flaccid. He was sometimes praised, but more often censured, or even made fun of, for his lack of dignity and his

[1] These are contained in the various journals of all the cities in which the Poes acted, and more particularly in a few periodicals of elegant literature, — *The Polyanthos, The Emerald, The Theatrical Censor and Critical Miscellany, The Rambler's Magazine and Theatrical Register*, and *The New Englander*.

dependence on the prompter. His range was narrow, his manner always remained amateurish, and after repeated trials he sank at last, it is said, into insignificance. But his wife, who had been born and trained to the stage, rose above mediocrity, although she apparently never equaled her mother in popularity or in merit. She was fragile in figure (Ariel was one of her rôles), and her voice, when she sang, lacked richness and volume. She began her Boston engagement with light impersonations, and soon won upon the public by her archness and roguery in the comic and her sweetness in the romantic plays. Mr. Buckingham, the somewhat exacting critic of "The Polyanthos," pronounced the hoyden to be her forte, but others were more indulgent to her serious representations. In the course of time she became the leading female performer; when Cooper and Fennell were enjoying their greatest triumphs, she was the Cordelia, Ophelia, or Blanche of the drama, and when the youthful prodigy, John Howard Payne, first came on the Boston boards in 1809, she still maintained her position, playing Palmyra to his Zaphna, Sigismunda to his Tancred, and the like parts. An impression of the regard in which she was held, and of her own theatrical labors, can, perhaps, best be got from the following favorable notice, which, moreover, throws a suggestive light on the worldly condition of the lesser players of that time: —

"If industry can claim from the public either favor or support the talents of Mrs. Poe will not pass unrewarded. — She has supported and maintained a course of characters more numerous and arduous than can be paralleled on our boards during any one season. Often she has been obliged to perform three characters on the same evening, and she has always been perfect in the text, and has well comprehended the intention of her author.

"In addition to her industry, however, Mrs. Poe has claims for other favors from the respectability of her talents. Her Romps and Sentimental characters, have an individuality which has marked them peculiarly her own. But she has succeeded often in the tender personations of tragedy; her conceptions are always marked with good sense and natural ability. We are confident to hope therefore that the Bostonians will not suffer her merits to be so slighted that poverty and distress are to result from her benefit night; as has been the case with other performers."[1]

This appeal was ineffective, since the Poes advertised a second benefit, in conjunction with the Ushers, to indemnify them, as they state in their personal card to the public (in which they "hope for that sanction, influence, and liberal support which has ever yet distinguished a Boston audience"), for what they term "the great failure and severe losses sustained by their former attempts."[2] A friendly effort was made by one "Senex" to increase Mrs. Poe's reputation by

[1] *Boston Gazette*, March 21, 1808.
[2] *Ibid.*, April 18, 1808.

praise of her moral qualities and domestic virtues, and she was supported by the good will of some ladies in society; but there was clearly a party against her among the critics, to which she must finally have succumbed, even if she had been more successfully defended by the characteristic arguments to which, as Mr. Buckingham relates, her husband resorted by calling upon that gentleman with the purpose of caning him for his impertinence. From such incidents and from the general tone of criticism the natural conclusion is that Mrs. Poe was an interesting rather than a brilliant actress, more deserving than fortunate, and indebted for her moderate share of favor rather to her painstaking care than to native talents.

She played very often during these years; frequently she sang, and sometimes she danced a Polish minuet, — the feminine counterpart to her husband's hornpipes, reels, and strathspeys. There are but two marked breaks in her appearances: one in the early months of 1807, when her son William may have been born; the other in the same months of 1809, when she suffered her second confinement. The child, born January 19,[1] was named

[1] This is the date recorded by Poe on matriculating at the University of Virginia in 1826. The argument by which Mr. R. H. Stoddard seeks to discredit it, on the ground that Mrs. Poe acted through January, rests on a too cursory examination of the evidence. During that month Mrs. Poe appeared only as a peasant in a pantomime, apparently three times, and was so advertised to appear January 20. Mr. Stoddard, assuming that she

Edgar. The mother went again upon the stage February 10, and played until the end of the season almost incessantly. The family then left Boston, never to return, but not without grateful feelings toward the city, at least on Mrs. Poe's part, since on the back of a painting from her own hand she charged her son to "love Boston, the place of his birth, and where his mother found her best and most sympathetic friends."[1]

Early in September the Poes had become members of the New York company, in which they remained until the following July, still engaged in acting the romantic and sentimental drama and light comedy of the period. They made little impression. At the close of the season they left New York, and within six weeks Mrs. Poe had joined her old friends of Mr. Green's Virginia company, and was announced at Richmond, but there is no further mention of her husband: whether he was

did appear on that evening, puts the date of birth forward one month; but the matter is settled by several notices, of which the following is one: —

"We congratulate the frequenters of the Theatre on the recovery of Mrs. Poe from her recent confinement. This charming little Actress will make her re-appearance To-morrow Evening, etc." *Boston Gazette*, February 9, 1809.

The suggested date, *February* 19, is further inadmissible because Mrs. Poe played in important rôles five times between the 10th and 24th of that month. The date upon Poe's monument, January 20, apparently derived from Judge Neilson Poe, of Baltimore, has no extant authority whatever to support it.

[1] Ingram, i. 6.

already dead, or lived on in a lingering consumption, is uncertain. Mrs. Poe continued to play in the field of her early triumphs, and from the warm commendation she received it would seem that her charms and beauty had suffered no loss of power over the audiences of the Southern circuit. A year later, after having given birth to her third child, Rosalie, she fell into a rapid decline. At the opening of the Richmond season, in August, 1811, she was still an active member of the troupe, nor did she cease to appear until after her benefit night, early in October. The family, which was in the utmost destitution, immediately became the object of the charity of the Richmond ladies. The players, too, advertised a second night for her benefit, "in consequence of the serious and long-continued indisposition of Mrs. Poe, and in compliance with the advice and solicitation of many of the most respectable families,"[1] and on the morning of that day the following card appeared: —

TO THE HUMANE.

"On this night Mrs. Poe, lingering on the bed of disease and surrounded by her children, asks your assistance; and *asks it perhaps for the last time.*"[2]

A few days later, December 8, she died. A few kind words in a Richmond paper, a single line in one at Boston, was all that marked the close of a

[1] *The Virginia Patriot,* November 29, 1811.
[2] *The Enquirer,* November 29, 1811

career which, though honorable, must have been full of labor, anxiety, and poverty. The tinsel crown, the gauze and the flash of the paste jewels, the robes and the red shoes, went into the chest of faded things. Harlequin must seek a new Columbine before the footlights flare up again ; and there, left over from the comedy, were three children, the eldest five years old, all helpless and in want. Possibly the actors might have afforded them some protection, but the disastrous conflagration of the theatre on Christmas night prevented. That fatal calamity, which threw the city into mourning and turned the play-house into a church, deeply stirred the community, and in the charity immediately extended to all the sufferers these orphans were not neglected. Mrs. Allan, a young wife of twenty-five years, and her friend, Mrs. MacKenzie, who were attracted by the younger children, took, one Edgar, the other Rosalie, into their homes; William, the eldest, was cared for by his father's friends at Baltimore.

CHAPTER II.

EDUCATION.

Mr. John Allan, who now with great reluctance gave his family name to the orphan of the poor actors, had emigrated from Ayrshire, and, as a member of the firm, Ellis & Allan, had already at the age of thirty-one acquired position and fortune in the Virginia tobacco trade. He had been married for some time, but was still childless; and although in admitting a stranger's offspring to his family he had at first merely yielded to his wife's urgent entreaties, the black-eyed, curly-haired boy naturally soon became a pet in the empty home, especially as his precocity and beauty blended with the charm of his young affection to minister to the pride as well as touch the heart of the foster-father. At the age of six he could read, draw, and dance; of more showy accomplishments (the long, narrow Virginia table, cleared for dessert, being his stage), his trick before company was to pledge their healths, and his talent was to declaim, for each of which he had, perhaps by inheritance, an equal aptitude. He received the rudiments of knowledge in a private school at Richmond, and spent the three summers following his mother's death at the White Sulphur Springs, then the fashionable Southern resort; in both places tradition still affords glimpses of him, — a prettily-dressed boy riding his pony or running with his dogs, indulged in public as a general favorite, and fondled at home as an only child. About June 17, 1815,[1] Mr. Allan sailed for England, with his wife, her sister, and Edgar, apparently for a long stay, since he disposed of some of his household goods and effects by auction sale before leaving. He provided an Olive Branch, a Murray's Reader, and two Murray's Spelling Books for Edgar's entertainment during the voyage, and shortly after his arrival placed the child, then six years old, at the Manor House School, Stoke Newington, a suburb of London.

His residence there seems to have left deep marks of remembrance upon his mind, nor is it unlikely that the delight in the ancient, which afterwards characterized him, sprang partly from this early familiarity with a memorable past not yet vanished from the eye and hand. The main village, which has since been lost in the overflow of the metropolis, then consisted of a long elm-embowered street of the Tudor time, following the track of a Roman road; near the old Green, by deeply-shaded walks, that still bear the names of Henry and Elizabeth,

[1] Colonel Thomas H. Ellis, to the author, May 28, 1884. These statements regarding Mr. Allan's absence are based on the books of the firm, Ellis & Allan, in Colonel Ellis's possession.

stood the houses of Anne Boleyn's ill-fated lover, Earl Percy, and of her daughter's fortunate courtier, the favorite Leicester; to the west ran the green lanes, over hazy inland fields, and to the east the more modern street of Queen Anne and early Georgian architecture, where behind its formal box-bordered parterre rose the white Manor House School, old and irregular, sloping in the rear to the high brick wall, with its ponderous spiked and iron-studded gates, which inclosed the playground. In the seclusion of these grounds Poe spent his school-days from his seventh to his twelfth year; there in the long, narrow, low school-room, oak-ceiled, gothic-windowed, with its irregular, black, jackknife-hewed desks and the sacred corner-boxes for master and ushers (in one of them once sat the murderer, Eugene Aram), he conned his Latin and mispronounced his French; in the bedroom beyond the many tortuous passages and perplexing little stairways, he first felt the wakening of the conscience, whose self-echoing whispers he afterwards heightened into the voice and ghostly terror of the Spanish *Hombre Embozado;* in that wide, graveled, treeless, and benchless playground he trained his muscles in the sports, and when on Saturday afternoon the mighty gate swung open he and his mates filed out to walk beneath the gigantic and gnarled trees, amid which once lived Shakespeare's friend, Essex, or to gaze with a boy's eyes of wonder at the thick walls, deep windows and doors, massive with locks and bars, behind which Robinson Crusoe was written; and on Sunday, after the holiday ramble, he would obey the summons of the hollow-toned church bell, sounding from its fretted tower, and witness from the scholars' remote gallery pew that miraculous weekly transformation in the pulpit, — "This reverend man, with countenance so demurely benign, with robes so glossy and so clerically flowing, with wig so minutely powdered, so rigid and so vast, — could this be he who, of late, with sour visage and in snuffy habiliments, administered, ferule in hand, the Draconian Laws of the academy? Oh, gigantic paradox!"[1]

It seems a monotonous existence; but, touched by the spirit and the flush of boyhood, it was really a full one, the life of keen sensation, of personal rivalries and party strife, the first battle and the first prize. "*Oh, le bon temps,*" Poe cries, "*que ce siècle de fer!*" and, indeed, he must have passed many a lonely hour, too, under that meagre and rigid régime of inferior English school-mastery; and though he learned to run and leap, construe Latin and speak French, and during some portion of the time regularly visited the Allans in London, yet, remembering that these five years are the ones in which home ties are drawn closest about the hearts of most American boys, and the lessons of concession learned by them, a too curious mind might discover in this

[1] *Works*, iii. 419.

stretch of the boy's life the first workings of the sinister influence which afterwards struck so impassably the circle of isolation about the man. Dr. Bransby, however, the parson-teacher, remarked nothing in Edgar Allan, as he was called, except that he was clever, but spoilt by " an extravagant amount of pocket money."[1] The village, indeed, was said by Beaumont and Fletcher to be a place " where ale and cakes are plenty ; " but the boy's wildest excesses were probably in the same raspberry tarts and ginger beer on which at the Grey Friars a year or two later Clive Newcome dissipated his pocketful of sovereigns. Poe, no doubt, took the fun, the homesickness, and the good things as other boys did ; and when, in the June of 1820, he left behind him the old trees and ruinous houses, the mist and fragrance and mould of the drowsy English parish, and returned to Richmond, he was not much different from his mates, except that he made his first trials at verse and kept the manuscripts.

He arrived home with the Allans on August 2, and at once renewed his studies in the English and Classical School of Joseph H. Clarke, who is described as a fiery, pedantic, pompous Irishman from Trinity College, Dublin. Here he read the ordinary classical authors of the old preparatory curriculum, continued his French, and capped Latin verses, a pastime of which he is reported to have been fond. He was lacking in diligence and accuracy, but was

[1] *The Athenæum*, No. 2660, p. 497, October 19, 1878.

quick and brilliant, and when it came the turn of his set to be at the top of the school he had but one rival in scholarship. In athletic exercises, the other half of youthful life, he was especially active, being aided in this, perhaps, by the training of the Manor House playground; slight in figure at first, but robust and tough, he was a swift runner and far leaper, and he possessed, together with some skill in boxing, the English school-boy's readiness to use it; in particular he was a fine, bold swimmer, and as, since Byron, poets seem to have a prescriptive right to the mention of their aquatic feats, be it once more recorded that in his fifteenth year Poe swam in the James River from Ludlam's wharf to Warwick Bar, six miles, against a very strong tide and in a hot June sun, and afterwards walked back to the city with little apparent fatigue. He evidently cut a considerable figure in the school; he was its champion in the simple tournaments of those days, prominent in its debating society, and known as a versifier in both a gallant and a satiric vein, — no slight distinction in the eyes of the fellows who listened to the English ode in which, on the retirement of Master Clarke to give place to Master William Burke, in the fall of 1823, he addressed the outgoing principal.

But neither his facile scholarship, nor his aptness in quoting Latin hexameters and stringing English rhymes, nor his fame in the sports made him the favorite of the school. His aristocratic mates, it is

EDUCATION. 21

said by one of themselves, remembered that he was sprung from the poor actors, and were averse to his leadership. Poe, too, partly it may be because he was aware of the reason for this slight but cutting ostracism, helped it by a defiant and irritable spirit that sometimes broke through the restraint of his well-bred manners. One who was counted nearer to him than the rest describes him as "self-willed, capricious, inclined to be imperious, and though of generous impulses not steadily kind, or even amiable."[1] The indulgence to which he had been accustomed at home with its resulting lawlessness of nature, and his marked ability with its attendant intellectual pride, contributed somewhat to form this temper; but he was always reserved, a quality especially liable to misconstruction by boys, and in his youth as in later life he never formed the habit — he may not have had the power — of making intimate friends. No one, it would seem, ever knew him. He had his chums in his own and his fags in the younger set, and he showed them his poems just as he quoted Horace, in search of a certain sort of recognition; he was sensible of affection, too, and capable of warm attachment, as in his friendship for young Sully, the artist's nephew, who was a refined but difficult boy; amid all such associations, however, he lived most to himself. He was a dreamer, too, and in the light of his insubstantial visions, as well as through ruder experience, he felt his solita-

[1] Ingram, i. 24.

riness. The sense of social wrong, the brooding disposition, the imaginative temperament, the wayward will, the excitable, impatient, imperious nature — these lines of character were coming out, fainter or stronger, in the moody, self-conscious boy, and he found himself alone and left to his own will. His foster-father was liberal in a worldly way, his foster-mother considerate, forgiving, and faithful, but in spirit as in blood he was of a different strain from them; his kindred were unknown to him, his teachers were the merest pedagogues, his companions cast in another mould. It is not meant that all usual attention was not given to him. He was not neglected, nor were his surroundings unpleasant. Mr. Allan, although he had not yet settled in a house of his own, belonged to the most cultivated and agreeable society that Virginia knew in the days of her old-fashioned and justly famed courtesy and hospitality, and a childhood spent in association with such gentlemen as Edgar constantly and familiarly met could not fail to be both pleasant and of the highest utility in forming both manner and character. A boy, however, is little sensible of the value of such surroundings, and in the unfolding of his heart Poe may, amid all such mere kindliness, have missed what to a child of genius was of far more consequence, — responsive sympathy, and the secret understanding that springs from love. He was, however it happened, a lonely boy.

Under these circumstances there is no inherent

unlikelihood in the story that rests only on his own words, that one day, in the home of a much younger schoolmate, when his friend's mother, lovely, gentle, and gracious, spoke to him with some unusual tenderness, the tones thrilled him with a new sensation, and kindled within him, in his own phrase, the first purely ideal love of his soul. To this lady, Jane Stith Stanard, he became strongly attached, as a lonely boy of fourteen, whose affections were beginning to wander from an unsympathetic home, naturally would; but she was his confidante and friend for only a short time. She died April 28, 1824, at the early age of thirty-one years; and for a long while he haunted her grave by night, brooding on the mystery of the dead, and there in the sigh of the dry grasses and the louder moan of autumn winds his young heart caught the first faint notes of that pæan of passionate regret and self-sprung terror which afterward, struck on his lyre, became the *Io Triomphe* of despair. The fascination of this lady did not cease with her life, but grew with his years; the direct experience of death in her loss was the ground on which his imagination long worked, and determined the early bent of his mind toward a sombre supernaturalism. One need not try to disentangle the bare facts from this, as it seems, almost legendary anecdote;[1] however much its romantic element may have been heightened,

[1] *Edgar Poe and his Critics*, by Sarah Helen Whitman. New York: Rudd & Carleton, 1860: p. 49.

still, through all the unconscious transformations of time and genius, the individuality of Poe is plainly discernible in two of its marked traits, — his tendency to idealize a woman's memory, and the kinship of his emotional beliefs with superstition.

Poe left Master Burke's in March, 1825, and spent the remainder of the year in preparing himself, with the aid of private instruction, for the University of Virginia, then in its first session. In his not too scanty leisure hours he nursed his first flame, in the ordinary way of mortal love, by his devotions to a neighbor's daughter, younger than himself, Miss Sarah Elmira Royster; but, her father diligently intercepting all letters, this romance ended on the young lady's part in an early marriage, and on Poe's in some reproachful stanzas *à la* Byron, wherein the rejected suitor seeks to immortalize the fair one's infidelity. The inamorata's reminiscences of her lover, too, are prettily conventional: he was, she says,[1] beautiful, sad, and silent, but as she adds that he was fond of music and clever at his sketching, particularly of herself, he evidently, like undistinguished youths, found humble means to overcome the difficulties of conversation. The most fondly recollected hours of this year, however (the last in which he lived under the same roof with Mr. Allan), must have been spent in the pleasant and spacious home which Mr. Allan purchased in this summer for his set-

[1] *Appletons' Journal*, N. S., iv. 429 (May, 1878).

tled abode. From its high southward windows he would look down on the green islands that stud the foaming rapids of the James, and see across the winding river the village of Manchester and the wooded fields beyond, bathed in the warm afternoon; or, stepping out between the shutters upon the adjoining wide-roofed balcony with its sanded floor, where stood the fine London telescope that perhaps, gave to his childish mind its bent toward astronomy, would look at the stars, or more idly would watch the moonlight falling on the myrtles and jessamines, the box and the fig-trees, the grapevines and raspberry bushes planted by the former Andalusian owner in the quiet garden close, which, now wild and desolate, keeps no fragrance save the romance of his memory. To that fair prospect, the landscape of his innocent years, he was unconsciously bidding farewell.

On February 14, 1826, he wrote his name, and the place and date of his birth, in the matriculation book of the University of Virginia, and entered the schools of ancient and modern languages. He was now seventeen years old, somewhat short in stature, thick-set, compact, bow-legged, with the rapid and jerky gait of an English boy; his natural shyness had become a fixed reserve; his face, clustered about by dark, curly hair, wore usually a grave and melancholy expression, the look that comes rather from the habit of reverie than any actual sadness, but his features would kindle with lively animation when, as frequently happened, he grew warm in his cause. He divided his time, after the custom of undergraduates, between the recitation room, the punch bowl, the card table, athletic sports, and pedestrianism. He was a member of the classes in Latin and Greek, French, Spanish, and Italian, and attended them regularly; but being facile rather than studious, he did not acquire a critical knowledge of these languages. Outside he moved in a jolly set. At first he had roomed with a chum, one Miles George, of Richmond, on the lawn, to adopt the local description, but after a quarrel and pugilistic duel in correct form between them (the combatants shook hands at the end of it) Poe settled in No. 13 West Range, decorated the walls with charcoal sketches out of Byron, and there gathered the fellows to enjoy peach and honey, as the delectable old-time Southern punch was called, and to play at loo or seven-up. Both in drinking and in card-playing Poe acted capriciously, and either was or affected to be the creature of impulse.

"Poe's passion for strong drink," writes one of his intimate college mates, "was as marked and as peculiar as that for cards. It was not the *taste* of the beverage that influenced him; without a sip or smack of the mouth he would seize a full glass, without water or sugar, and send it home at a single gulp. This frequently used him up; but if not, he rarely returned to the charge."[1]

[1] Thomas Goode Tucker to Douglass Sherley, Esq., April 5, 1880. MS. The substance of this and other letters from Mr

If the full glass was one of peach and honey, or merely of the peach brandy unmixed, Poe's susceptibility to such a draught, it should be remarked, by no means indicates a weak head, particularly in a youth of seventeen; but this fashion of drinking *en barbare* (as Baudelaire styles it) he kept up through life. Not intoxication, however, but gambling, was then his vice; and for this, too, as was to be expected from his excitable temperament, he was ill adapted, or else luck ran strong against him, since he ended the year with heavy debts of honor. By his recklessness in card-playing he is said to have lost caste in the aristocratic cliques. Whatever his private history may have been, he did not come under the notice of the Faculty, which is stated to have been at that time unusually watchful and strict; but as the administration of the University was somewhat peculiar, owing to the theories of its founder, Jefferson, an anecdote of the time will make the facts clearer.

It seems that the Faculty desired to check gambling, which had reached a great height, and as in Jefferson's judgment as much of the discipline as possible should be left to the civil authorities, arrangements were made to observe, indict, and try the principal offenders. One morning the county sheriff and his posse appeared at the doorway of a

Tucker was embodied by Mr. Sherley in an article in the *Virginia University Magazine*, 1880. Cf. "Edgar A. Poe and his College Companions," *New Orleans Times-Democrat*, May 18, 1884.

lecture room where the students, already warned, were answering roll-call; a glance was enough for suspicion, and a shadow of suspicion for flight, as they made good their escape by windows and doors, and, eluding pursuit by striking into an unfrequented by-path for a wooded knoll on the skirts of the Ragged Mountains, safe among the hills they enjoyed their favorite diversion unmolested, until at the end of a three days' vacation they were allowed to respond to the roll-call in peace.

Under such rules of government as this story implies, freedom from censure by the Faculty is not convincing proof of a blameless life; but there is no reason to suppose that Poe's habits, judged by the standard of morals that obtained where he was, gave occasion for much unfavorable remark, or were widely different from the habits of those members of his own set who became the pious judge and the acceptable Episcopalian clergyman. He plunged into debt as did others whose extravagance at the tradesmen's shops and the hotels led to the enactment of a statute that declared all debts beyond the reasonable wants of a student null and void. But amid the dissipations of his private life, he found leisure to cultivate his own genius, and would gather his friends about him to listen to some extravaganza of his invention, read in declamatory tones, or to some poem he had made during his long solitary rambles in the Ragged Mountains. He still had no confidential friends. "No one knew

EDUCATION. 29

him," is the unanimous testimony of his classmates; but they all describe him consistently in terms that show he was a spirited youth, who led a self-absorbed life, frequently of high intensity, but was easily diverted into the commonplace pleasures of a fashionable set, and probably entered on them with the more recklessness because of his habitual reserve. While Poe was still at the University, however, Mr. Allan thought it best to inquire into the state of his affairs personally, and went up to Charlottesville, where he paid all of his debts that he thought just; but, not being a father to take his boy's luck without wincing, he refused to honor losses at play, which amounted to about twenty-five hundred dollars.[1] At the close of the session, December 15, 1826, Poe came home with the highest honors in Latin and French; but this did not mollify his guardian, who, instead of allowing him to return, placed him in his own counting-room. From this confinement Poe soon broke, and went out to seek his fortune in the world.

[1] *Edgar Allan Poe.* A letter by Colonel Thomas H. Ellis to the editor of the *Richmond Standard*, April 22, 1881.

CHAPTER III.

WANDERINGS.

POE made his way at once towards Boston, and there in the spring tried to make a good start in the world by publishing his youthful verses. He persuaded Calvin F. S. Thomas, a poor youth of nineteen, who had just set up a shop at 70 Washington Street, to undertake the job, and in due course he saw the first and unacknowledged heir of his invention in the shape of a small, thin book, mean in appearance and meagre in contents, entitled " Tamerlane and other Poems." [1] This volume, the only venture of Thomas in the book-trade, was published about midsummer; its receipt was advertised by the leading magazines,[2] and two years

[1] *Tamerlane and other Poems.* By a Bostonian. Boston: Calvin F. S. Thomas . . . Printer. 1827, pp. 40. The volume contained, besides preface and notes, *Tamerlane* and nine fugitive pieces: 1. *To —— ——* (" I saw thee on the bridal day "); 2. *Dreams;* 3. *Visit of the Dead;* 4. *Evening Star;* 5. *Imitation;* 6. No title (" In youth have I known one with whom the earth "); 7. No title (" A wilder'd being from my birth "); 8. No title (" The happiest day — the happiest hour "); 9. *The Lake.* Of these *Tamerlane* and the first, third, and ninth of the short poems are included, in revised versions, in Poe's works. *Vide* Mr. Richard Herne Shepherd's reprint, London, 1884.

[2] *The United States Review and Literary Gazette,* ii. 399 (Aug. 1827); *The North American Review,* xxv. 471 (Oct. 1827).

later, although the edition was small and obscure, it was still sufficiently known to find mention in the first comprehensive work on American Poetry.[1]

It passed into circulation such as is indicated by these contemporary notices, and in view of that fact Poe's statement that it was suppressed for private reasons counts for little. It may as well be confessed at once that any unsupported assertion by Poe regarding himself is to be received with great caution. In this case, as will presently be seen, his circumstances give no plausibility to his story.

There is, perhaps, more color of truth in the claim put forth in his boyishly affected preface that this volume was written in 1821-22. As that was the time when his mind would naturally rapidly unfold, and as the statement agrees with the tradition of a manuscript volume shown to Master Clarke by Mr. Allan, in order to obtain the former's advice respecting its publication, it is probable that some of the poems at least were then drafted; but from the passages that reveal the depressing influence of his own home and imply his experience of love and death, as well as from what is recorded of his habits at the University, it is clear that they were re-written, and really represent his genius at the stage it was in when they were printed. The precocity of the verses is

[1] *Specimens of American Poetry*, by Samuel Kettell. Boston: S. G. Goodrich & Co., 1829: iii. p. 405.

marked, but it is a full-grown youth, not a child of thirteen, who has been bitten by the Byronic malady; and, indeed, striking as they are, their relief is mainly due to the light flashed back on them from Poe's perfect work.

"Tamerlane" in its first form shows more poetic susceptibility, if less literary power, than in its present one. In the story itself there is little difference between the two versions. In both the great conqueror relates to a conventional friar how, in his boyhood, among the mountains of Taglay, he had loved a maiden, and stirred alike by his ambition for her and for himself had one day determined to go away and seek the empire which the prescience of genius assured him would be his. In pursuit of this plan, he says, without giving any hint of his departure or its purpose, he left her asleep in a matted bower; and naturally enough when, after the fulfillment of his hopes, he returned to seat her on "the throne of half the world," he found his destined bride had died in consequence of his desertion. *Hinc illæ lachrymæ.*

Neither in this tale, nor in the nine fugitive pieces of a personal character which followed it, was there anything to command public attention, especially as the style and spirit were distinctively imitative, the constructions involved, the meaning dark, and the measure as lame as the old Tartar himself is fabled to have been. The interest of the volume now lies partly in its plainly autobiographical passages, such as those which describe how conscious genius takes its own impulse for the unerring divine instinct, or express the poet's naive and slightly bitter resentment on finding himself not a prophet in his own household; and partly in the subtler self-revelation afforded by the reflection of passing poetic moods, which it may be remarked are surer signs of promise than poetic ideas, because, although they may as easily become conventional, they cannot be so successfully appropriated from others by patience and art, nor can their language ever ring true except *numine præsenti* by the very breath of the indwelling Apollo. Slow, confined, and stammering as is their expression in these earliest poems, they show that, however affected by the artificiality and turgidity, the false sentiment, the low motive, and the sensational accessories of the Byronic model, the young poet turned naturally to his own experience, and could write from his heart.

In particular, two characteristics come out as primary in Poe's nature. He was one of the proudest of men, and from many expressions here it is plain that he cultivated pride, even in boyhood. He thought it the distinctive manly quality. He declares with emphasis that every nobly endowed soul, conscious of its power, will ever

"Find *Pride* the ruler of its will."

Byron had sown the evil seed, but it had fallen in

very favorable soil. This personal trait, however, needs only to be glanced at in passing. The second characteristic belongs rather to his temperament, and affected his art more directly. The sight of beauty did not affect his æsthetic sense so much as it aroused his dreaming faculty. He looks out on the world as a vague and undefined delight; he notes only the broad and general features of the landscape; he does not see any object in detail; his imagination so predominates over his perceptive powers, he is so much more poet than artist, that he loses the beautiful in the suggestions, the reveries, the feelings, it awakens, and this emotion is the value he found in beauty throughout his life. The mood was a part of his ordinary experience. Sometimes he describes it : —

> "In spring of life have ye ne'er dwelt
> Some object of delight upon,
> With steadfast eye, till ye have felt
> The earth reel — and the vision gone ?"

Sometimes he expresses it (and in the lines is heard the first whisper of "Ligeia") : —

> " 'T was the chilly wind
> Came o'er me in the night, and left behind
> Its image on my spirit."

This exaltation is continually the object of his regrets and of his longings; he ascribes to it a symbolic spiritual meaning, and even a moral power, as being something

> "given
> In beauty by our God, to those alone

> Who otherwise would fall from life and Heaven
> Drawn by their heart's passion " —

This value, whether true or false, which he gave to such emotional moods, is the significant thing in his poetic life, and shows that the dreaming faculty was a primary element in his genius. Sometimes, it is true, the real scene remains prominent in his mind, but even then, although it does not fade away into mere emotion, it is not unchanged; it ceases to be natural, and is removed into the preternatural. In two of these early poems — "The Lake" and "Visit of the Dead" — is this the case, and it is noticeable that Poe retained both among his works, as if he perceived that of all in this collection they alone have his peculiar touch. In the latter, especially, the treatment of landscape is wholly his own; crude as its expression is, it affords the first glimpse of that new tract of Acheron, as it were, which he revealed "out of space, out of time:" —

> " And the stars shall look not down
> From their thrones, in the dark heaven,
> With light like Hope to mortals given,
> But their red orbs, without beam,
> To thy withering heart shall seem
> As a burning, and a fever
> Which would cling to thee forever.
> But 't will leave thee, as each star
> In the morning light afar
> Will fly thee " —

Such imaginings — the vision of the throned stars with averted faces, the identifying of the outer fascination of an ill-omened nature with the mortal fever within, the dissolving of the spell as the red orbs flee far in the streaming eastern light — might well portend in poetry a genius as original as was Blake's in art.

The abundant alloy in the substance of the work, however, and the rudeness of its execution justly condemned the volume to speedy oblivion. It brought neither fame to the poet nor money to the printer, and shortly after its publication the disappearance of Poe, which had already occurred, was followed by the removal of Thomas to New York. Neither in his stay in that city nor during his later life in Buffalo, N. Y., and Springfield, Mo., did Thomas, who lived until 1876, ever mention, either to his own family or, so far as is known, to his friends or associates, that his first venture in the book-trade was Poe's verses. In view of this fact,[1] in connection with the general publication of reminiscences by all who were ever well acquainted with Poe, and the special interest of this obscure portion of his life, it may be safely inferred that Thomas never identified the first author he knew with the famous poet who wrote "The Raven." The obvious conclusion is that Poe lived in Boston under an assumed name.

Whether this were so or not, a few months had sufficed to exhaust Poe's resources, and he now found himself, a youth of eighteen, poor and friend-

[1] Mrs. Martha (Thomas) Booth to the author, June 14, 1884.

less in the city of his birth, and without means of self-support. In this extremity he took the readiest way out of his difficulties, and on May 26 enlisted at Boston in the army of the United States as a private soldier, under the name of Edgar A. Perry.[1] He stated that he was born at Boston and was by occupation a clerk; and although minors were then accepted into the service, he gave his age as twenty-two years. He had, says the record, gray eyes, brown hair, and a fair complexion, and was five feet eight inches in height. He was at once assigned to Battery H, of the First Artillery, then serving in the harbor at Fort Independence; on October 31, the battery was ordered to Fort Moultrie, Charleston, S. C., and exactly one year later was again transferred to Fortress Monroe, Va. The character of Poe's life during this period can now be but imperfectly made out, since the officers under whom he served are dead; but from papers presently to be given, it appears that he discharged his duties as company clerk and assistant in the commissariat department so as to win the good will of his superiors, and was in all respects a faithful and efficient soldier. On January 1, 1829, he was appointed Sergeant-Major, a promotion which, by the invariable custom of the army, was made only for merit.

[1] These statements are based on the papers relating to Edgar A. Perry, or Poe, now on file in the War Department, of which certified copies were sent to the author.

At some time after reaching Fortress Monroe he is said to have made his situation known to Mr. Allan. It is not unlikely that his officers, becoming acquainted with his ability and education, and being interested in his character, urged his endeavoring to enter West Point (the only way by which he could rise in the service), and advised his applying to his foster-father for aid. How Mr. Allan received this news cannot, unfortunately, be determined; but as he apparently did not move in the matter until after the mortal illness of his wife, there is ground for the inference that he recalled the wanderer in compliance with her dying request. At all events, it seems to have been some days after Mrs. Allan's death, which occurred February 28, 1829, that Poe returned to Richmond on leave of absence granted by his colonel on Mr. Allan's application. The result of his visit is told in the following letter, which betrays a surprising inaccuracy in some of its details: —

FORTRESS MONROE, *March* 30*th*, '29.

GENERAL:

I request your permission to discharge from the service Edgar A. Perry, at present the Sergeant-Major of the 1st Reg't of Artillery, on his procuring a substitute.

The said Perry is one of a family of orphans whose unfortunate parents were the victims of the conflagration of the Richmond theatre in 1809. The subject of this letter was taken under the protection of a Mr. Allen, a gentleman of wealth and respectability, of that city, who, as I understand, adopted his protégé as his son and heir; with the intention of giving him a liberal education, he had placed him at the University of Virginia from which, after considerable progress in his studies, in a moment of youthful indiscretion he absconded, and was not heard from by his Patron for several years; in the mean time, he became reduced to the necessity of enlisting into the service and accordingly entered as a soldier in my Regiment, at Fort Independence in 1827. — Since the arrival of his company at this place, he has made his situation known to his Patron at whose request, the young man has been permitted to visit him;[1] the result is, an entire reconciliation on the part of Mr. Allen, who reinstates him into his family and favor, and who in a letter I have received from him requests that his son may be discharged on procuring a substitute; an experienced soldier and approved sergeant is ready to take the place of Perry so soon as his discharge can be obtained. The good of the service, therefore cannot be materially injured by the discharge.

I have the honor to be,
With great respect, your obedient servant,
JAS. HOUSE,
Col. 1st Art'y.

To the General Commanding the
E. Dept. U. S. A., New York.

The official reply to this application was an order, dated April 4, in accordance with which Poe was discharged, by substitute, April 15. Before leaving his post he obtained the following letters from his officers, which show conclusively

[1] There is no record of this furlough.

that he had already formed the plan of entering West Point, and indicate that this entered into the understanding on which Mr. Allan took him into favor: —

FORTRESS MONROE, VA., *20th Apl.* 1829.

Edgar Poe, late Serg't-Major in the 1st Art'y, served under my command in H. company 1st Reg't of Artillery, from June 1827 to January 1829, during which time his conduct was unexceptionable. He at once performed the duties of company clerk and assistant in the Subsistent Department, both of which duties were promptly and faithfully done. His habits are good and intirely free from drinking.

J. HOWARD,
Lieut. 1st Artillery.

In addition to the above, I have to say that Edgar Poe[1] was appointed Sergeant-Major of the 1st Art'y: on the 1st of Jan'y, 1829, and up to this date, has been exemplary in his deportment, prompt and faithful in the discharge of his duties — and is highly worthy of confidence.

H. W. GRISWOLD,
Bt. Capt. and Adjt. 1st Art'y.

I have known and had an opportunity of observing the conduct of the above mentioned Serg't-Maj'. Poe some three months during which his deportment has been highly praiseworthy and deserving of confidence. His education is of a very high order and he appears to be free from bad habits, in fact the testimony of Lt. Howard and Adjt. Griswold is full to that point. Un-

[1] Originally written *Perry*, but changed to read *Poe*.

derstanding he is, thro' his friends, an applicant for cadet's warrant, I unhesitatingly recommend him as promising to aquit himself of the obligations of that station studiously and faithfully.

W. J. WORTH,
Lt. Col. Comd'g Fortress Monroe.

With these credentials in his pocket, the discharged Sergeant-Major, aged twenty, went to Richmond, where no time was lost in attempting to place him at West Point. At Mr. Allan's request, Andrew Stevenson, the Speaker of the House, and Major John Campbell, under date of May 6, also wrote letters of recommendation, not of any interest now; and a week later James P. Preston, the father of one of Poe's closer school friends and representative of the district in Congress, lent his influence in these terms: —

RICHMOND, VA., *May 13th*, 1829.

SIR:

Some of the friends of young Mr. Edgar Poe have solicited me to address a letter to you in his favor believing that it may be useful to him in his application to the Government for military service. I know Mr. Poe and am acquainted with the fact of his having been born under circumstances of great adversity. I also know from his own productions and other undoubted proofs that he is a young gentleman of genius and taleants. I believe he is destined to be distinguished, since he has already gained reputation for taleants and attainments at the University of Virginia. I think him possessed of feeling and character peculiarly intitling him to public patronage. I am entirely satisfied that the salutary system of military discipline will soon develope his honorable feelings, and elevated spirit, and prove him worthy of confidence. I would not write in his recommendation if I did not believe that he would remunerate the Government at some future day, by his services and taleants, for whatever may be done for him.

I have the honor to be

Very respectfully your obt. serv't,

JAMES P. PRESTON.

MAJOR JOHN EATON, Sec'y of War, Washington.

Of more interest than all these, however, is Mr. Allan's own communication: —

RICHMOND, *May 6th*, 1829.

D*r* SIR:

The youth who presents this, is the same alluded to by Lt. Howard, Capt. Griswold Colo. Worth, our representative and the speaker, the Hon'ble Andrew Stevenson, and my friend Major Jno. Campbell.

He left me in consequence of some gambling at the University at Charlottesville, because (I presume) I refused to sanction a rule that the shopkeepers and others had adopted there, making Debts of Honour of all indiscretions. I have much pleasure in asserting that he stood his examination at the close of the year with great credit to himself. His history is short. He is the grandson of Quartermaster General Poe, of Maryland, whose widow as I understand still receives a pension for the services or disabilities of her husband. Frankly Sir, do I declare that he is no relation to me whatever; that I have many [in] whom I have taken an active interest to promote theirs; with no other feeling than that, every man is my care, if he be in distress. For myself I ask nothing, but I do request your kindness to aid this youth in the promotion of his future prospects. And it will afford me great pleasure to reciprocate any kindness you can show him. Pardon my frankness; but I address a soldier.

    Your ob'd't se'v't,   JOHN ALLAN.

THE HON'BLE JOHN H. EATON,
 Sec'y of War, Washington City.

The coldness of feeling with which Mr. Allan here classes the boy he had brought up almost from infancy with the objects of his general charity might lead one to believe that possibly he did not intend to make Poe his heir, but on the contrary thought to be honorably rid of the burden of further patronage by having paid a sum of money for a substitute in the army, and helping to open a career for his protégé in his self-chosen profession. Such a letter must have been galling to Poe's pride. He presented it with the others to the Secretary of War in person.

On this journey to Washington he made the closer acquaintance of his blood relations in Baltimore, where, pending his appointment as a cadet, he now determined to publish his second volume of poems, the fruit of his leisure in the army. He also entered into some obscure relations with William Gwynn, Esq., then editor of the "Federal Gazette and Baltimore Daily Advertiser," and showed him the manuscript of "Al Aaraaf," which was declared to be "indicative of a tendency to anything but the business of matter-of-fact life."[1] For his introduction the poet was probably indebted to Neilson Poe, his cousin at the third remove, who was employed in Gwynn's office; and possibly, as has been stated, it was at the suggestion of Neilson's father, George Poe, that he also sought the critical advice of John Neal, who had resided in Baltimore some few years before, and was now editing the "Yankee" at Boston. In the correspondence columns of that periodical, in its issue for September, 1829, the following appeared:—

"If E. A. P. of Baltimore —whose lines about *Heaven*, though he professes to regard them as altogether superior to anything in the whole range of American poetry, save two or three trifles referred to, are, though nonsense, rather exquisite nonsense — would but do himself justice, might [sic] make a beautiful and perhaps a magnificent poem. There is a good deal here to justify such a hope.

> Dim vales and shadowy floods
> And cloudy-looking woods,
> Whose forms we can't discover,
> For the tears that — drip all over.
> . . . .
> The moonlight . . .
> . . . . . falls
> Over hamlets, over halls,
> Wherever they may be,
> O'er the strange woods, o'er the sea —

[1] *Works*, i. cl.

> O'er spirits on the wing,
> O'er every drowsy thing —
> And buries them up quite
> In a labyrinth of light,
> And then how deep! — *Oh deep!*
> *Is the passion of their sleep!*

He should have signed it Bah! We have no room for others."[1]

The tone of this indicates that Poe was not backed by any strong personal friend of the critic. He received the doubtful satire with good grace, however, and replied in a letter printed in the December issue, and prefaced by these editorial remarks: —

"The following passages are from the manuscript works of a young author, about to be published in Baltimore. He is entirely a stranger to us, but with all their faults, if the remainder of 'Al Aaraaf' and 'Tamerlane' are as good as the body of the extracts here given — to say nothing of the more extraordinary parts, he will deserve to stand high — very high — in the estimation of the shining brotherhood. Whether he *will* do so however, must depend, not so much upon his worth now in mere poetry, as upon his worth hereafter in something yet loftier and more generous — we allude to the stronger properties of the mind, to the magnanimous determination that enables a youth to endure the present, whatever the present may be, in the hope, or rather in the belief, the fixed, unwavering belief, that in the future he will find his reward."

[1] *The Yankee and Boston Literary Gazette*, iii. 168 (new series).

The poet's letter follows: —

"I am young — not yet twenty — *am* a poet — if deep worship of all beauty can make me one — and wish to be so in the more common meaning of the word. I would give the world to embody one half the ideas afloat in my imagination. (By the way, do you remember — or did you ever read the exclamation of Shelley about Shakespeare? — 'What a number of ideas must have been afloat before such an author could arise!') I appeal to you as a man that loves the same beauty which I adore — the beauty of the natural blue sky and the sunshiny earth — there can be no tie more strong than that of brother for brother — it is not so much that they love one another, as that they both love the same parent — their affections are always running in the same direction — the same channel — and cannot help mingling. I am, and have been from my childhood, an idler. It cannot therefore be said that

> "'I left a calling for this idle trade,
> A duty broke — a father disobeyed'—

for I have no father — nor mother.

"I am about to publish a volume of 'Poems,' the greater part written before I was fifteen. Speaking about 'Heaven' the editor of the 'Yankee' says, 'He might write a beautiful, if not a magnificent poem'— (the very first words of encouragement I ever remember to have heard). I am very certain that as yet I have not written *either* — but that I *can*, I will take oath — if they will give me time.

"The poems to be published are 'Al Aaraaf'— 'Tamerlane' — one about four, and the other about

WANDERINGS. 47

three hundred lines, with smaller pieces. 'Al Aaraaf' has some good poetry, and much extravagance, which I have not had time to throw away.

"'Al Aaraaf' is a tale of another world — the star discovered by Tycho Brahe, which appeared and disappeared so suddenly — or rather, it is no tale at all. I will insert an extract about the palace of its presiding Deity, in which you will see that I have supposed many of the lost sculptures of our world to have flown (in spirit) to the star 'Al Aaraaf' — a delicate place more suited to their divinity: —

'Uprear'd upon such height arose a pile,' etc."

After Poe's quotations from this poem and "Tamerlane," and from the verses now known in a revised form as "A Dream within a Dream," the editor concludes: —

"Having allowed our youthful writer to be heard in his own behalf, — what more can we do for the lovers of genuine poetry? Nothing. They who are judges will not need more; and they who are not — why waste words upon them? We shall not."[1]

The volume[2] which gave rise to this correspond-

[1] *The Yankee and Boston Literary Gazette*, vi. 295-298 (new series).

[2] *Al Aaraaf, Tamerlane, and Minor Poems*, by Edgar A. Poe. Baltimore: Hatch & Dunning, 1829: pp. 71. This volume begins with an unentitled sonnet, the first draft of *To Science*, continues with *Al Aaraaf* and *Tamerlane*, both nearly as now printed, and concludes with a *Preface*, now known, revised, as *Romance*, and nine miscellaneous poems: 1. *To* —— ("Should my early life seem"), forty lines, now printed, revised, as *A Dream within a*

ence was published at the close of the year. It was a thin book, but respectably printed, with a profusion of extra leaves bearing mottoes from English and Spanish poets, and with liberal margins. "Al Aaraaf," the leading poem, is generally regarded as incomprehensible. Its obscurity is largely due to Poe's attempting, not only to tell à story, but also to express in an allegoric form some truth which he had arrived at amid the uneventful leisure of the barracks. In the rapid growth of his intelligence, beauty, which had been merely a source of emotion, became an object of thought, — an idea as well as an inspiration. It was the first of the great moulding ideas of life that he apprehended. Naturally his juvenile fancy at once personified it as a maiden, Nesace, and, seeking a realm for her to preside over, found it in Al Aaraaf, — not the narrow wall between heaven and hell which in Moslem mythology is the place of the dead who are neither good nor bad, but the burning star observed by Tycho Brahe, which the poet imagines to be the abode of those spirits, angelic or human,

Dream; 2. *To* —— ("I saw thee on thy bridal day"); 3. *To* —— ("The bowers whereat, in dreams, I see"); 4. *To the River* ——; 5. *The Lake. To* ——; 6. *Spirits of the Dead;* 7. *A Dream;* 8. *To M* —— ("I heed not that my earthly lot"), twenty lines, now printed, revised, as *To* ——; 9. *Fairyland,* the lines entitled *Heaven* in *The Yankee.* Of these *Tamerlane,* of which the former edition is said to have been "suppressed," is wholly rewritten, and the second, fifth, sixth, and seventh of the miscellaneous poems are from the 1827 edition, but revised.

who choose, instead of that tranquillity which makes the highest bliss, the sharper delights of love, wine, and pleasing melancholy, at the price of annihilation in the moment of their extremest joy. At this point the allegory becomes cumbrous, and the handling of it more awkward, because Poe tries to imitate Milton and Moore at the same time. By the use of incongruous poetic machinery, however, he contrives to say that beauty is the direct revelation of the divine to mankind, and the protection of the soul against sin. The action of the maiden in whom beauty is personified begins with a prayer descriptive of the Deity, who in answer directs her, through the music of the spheres, to leave the confines of our earth and guide her wandering star to other worlds, which she should guard against the contagion of evil, —

"Lest the stars totter in the guilt of man."

In obedience to this mandate she chants an incantation in which she calls upon her subjects, and especially her handmaid Ligeia, the personified harmony of nature, to attend her. At this point the allegory terminates, and the story begins. It now appears that among the inhabitants of Al Aaraaf are two, Angelo and Ianthe, who cannot hear the summons because of their mutual passion, and so in reminiscences of the past and dreams of the future, unmindful, the lovers

"whiled away
The night that waned and waned and brought no day."

Here, with singular abruptness, the poem concludes.

Of course, as serious work it was a failure. After "Queen Mab," "Heaven and Earth," or even "The Loves of the Angels," it was pardonable only in a boy. The obscure allegory, the absence of any structural relation between it and the brief romance, the discordant influence of other poets who had broken Byron's ascendency over Poe's mind, and finally the style itself, with its long and ill-timed parentheses, its inconsequential pursuit of image into image and thought into thought, until all consistency in the meaning is lost, and other analogous defects of youthful composition, combine their separate elements of confusion to make the poem seemingly unintelligible. In fact, it seems as if Poe had stopped without completing his original conception; as if he found his constructive power too weak, and broke off without trying to unify or clarify his work. Nevertheless, it shows a gain of both mental and literary power; it has, too, a lively fancy, a flowing metre, and occasionally a fine line, that place it above "Tamerlane" as a product of crude genius. In particular, the characteristics of Poe, the attempt to seize the impalpable, to fix the evanescent, to perceive the supersensual, are strongly marked, and although the management is in general as much Moore's as that of "Tamerlane" is Byron's, and there is nothing original in its substance except the symbolization of the per-

WANDERINGS. 51

vasive music of nature in Ligeia, it proved that the author had a poetic faculty, and, if he could break from his masters and learn the clear use of words, was well starred. Poe's experience in this effort was probably one premise of the conclusion which, helped by Coleridge's dictum, he soon made, and held firmly ever after, — that a long poem is a contradiction in terms, and hence impossible.

The remainder of this pamphlet-like volume is, biographically, of little consequence. "Tamerlane," wholly rewritten, has gained in rhetorical effectiveness, though it has lost in spontaneity, and in its present form is as clever and uninteresting an imitation of Byron as was ever printed. In some of the personal pieces, too, in which Poe takes the traditional attitude of the Pilgrim toward his past bliss and present desolation, Byron's influence continues strong. The ruling genius of the hour, however, was plainly Moore, who in his poems supplied a model to be imitated, and in his prefaces and notes information to be either worked up into verse, or transferred bodily to the foot of the new pages. In the annotations to "Al Aaraaf," it must be noticed, Poe began the evil practice, which he continued through life, of making a specious show of learning by mentioning obscure names and quoting learned authorities at second hand. Among the sources used by him, besides Moore's notes, Chateaubriand's "Itinéraire de Paris à Jérusalem" is of most interest, since that author afforded suggestions for later work. On a line of the last page he himself comments with a sort of bravado: "Plagiarism — see the works of Thomas Moore — passim;" but, curiously enough, this occurs in the only one of the new poems which bears the mark of his originality. It is "Fairyland," the sketch of the mist lighted by the moon, — the broad, pallid glamour descending at midnight on the vaporing earth, drowsing all things into deep slumber beneath its elfish light, and at noon soaring like a yellow albatross in far-off skies. There is a unique character in this imagery that makes it linger in the memory when the crudities of its expression are forgotten.

On the issue of this volume Poe returned to Richmond, where, on the second evening after his arrival, he met a companion of his school-days, to whom he told some of his adventures, and gave *carte blanche* for copies of his poems at the booksellers, to be distributed among his former friends. While "Al Aaraaf" was puzzling those to whom it came as a kind of Christmas gift, and was struggling against the private merriment of the young wits of Baltimore and the public gibes of the literary oracle of that city, "The Minerva and Emerald," edited by John H. Hewitt and Rufus Dawes, on the latter of whom full vengeance was wreaked long afterwards, Poe waited for his commission probably with some anxiety, as he reached and passed the age of twenty-one, the legal limit within which he could be appointed. Mr. Allan, too, may have felt some sympathetic uneasiness, inasmuch as he was preparing to take a new and youthful wife, who might not find Edgar's presence in the house desirable. Poe's attainment of his majority was not regarded as an insuperable obstacle. It was as easy to grow two years younger now as it had been to grow four years older when he enlisted, and he had already made up his mind to this rejuvenation some months before, when he wrote to John Neal that he was "not yet twenty." Relying on this fiction, he solicited the influence of Powhatan Ellis, a younger brother of Mr. Allan's partner, and then United States Senator from Mississippi, who wrote to Secretary Eaton, March 13, recommending him not from any personal acquaintance, but on information[1] from others. This letter received immediate attention. Poe was forthwith appointed a cadet, and on March 31 Mr. Allan gave his formal consent as guardian to his ward's binding himself to serve the United States for five years. The die being cast, Mr. Allan furnished Poe with whatever was necessary, and he probably thought, as he turned to the enjoyment of his wedded bliss, that

[1] This may have been furnished by Judge Marshall and General Scott, whose wife was a cousin of Mr. Allan's *fiancée*, but of their interference, first alleged by Hirst (*Edgar A. Poe*, Philadelphia *Saturday Museum*, 1843) and repeated by later biographers (Mr. Stoddard adds the name of John Randolph), there is no record. Hirst's sketch, it may be remarked here, though resting primarily on Poe's authority, is full of errors.

his duty by the child he had adopted was finally done. Poe, after a second visit at Baltimore, during which he called on Mr. N. C. Brooks,[1] a young littérateur, and got a poem accepted by him for a forthcoming annual, went on to West Point, where he soon forgot all about the promised contribution.

He entered the Military Academy on July 1, 1830, and settled at No. 28, South Barracks. His age is recorded as being then nineteen years and five months, but to the cadets he seemed older, and it was jokingly reported among them, much to Poe's annoyance, that " he had procured a cadet's appointment for his son, and the boy having died the father had substituted himself in his place." [2] His room-mate, who tells this anecdote, recalls his expression as weary, worn, and discontented, and his conversation on literary topics as without exception carping and censorious. The three occupants of the room, it is added, gave it a bad reputation; and Poe, in particular, besides joining his two fellows in the consumption of brandy, totally neglected his studies. The features of this sketch, notwithstanding its being drawn by one of the actors, are too grim. On others of his classmates he left a more agreeable impression. One of them, Allan B. Magruder, Esq., writes of him as a fel-

[1] Dr. N. C. Brooks to the author, June 3, 1884. All subsequent statements regarding the relations of Poe and Brooks are made on the same authority.

[2] Harper's *New Monthly Magazine*, xxxv. 754 (Nov. 1867).

low " of kindly spirit and simple style," and continues his brief reminiscences as follows : —

" He was very shy and reserved in his intercourse with his fellow-cadets — his associates being confined almost exclusively to Virginians. He was an accomplished French scholar, and had a wonderful aptitude for mathematics, so that he had no difficulty in preparing his recitations in his class and in obtaining the highest marks in these departments. He was a devourer of books, but his great fault was his neglect of and apparent contempt for military duties. His wayward and capricious temper made him at times utterly oblivious or indifferent to the ordinary routine of roll-call, drills, and guard duties. These habits subjected him often to arrest and punishment, and effectually prevented his learning or discharging the duties of a soldier." [1]

This account is supported by the official records, which show that at the examination at the end of the half-year Poe stood third in French and seventeenth in mathematics, in a class of eighty-seven members; he was not in arrest, however, before January, and whether he incurred minor academic censure for neglect of his military duties cannot be determined, as the books were destroyed by fire in 1838. His life at West Point, so far from being the long-continued college prank that it has been represented, did not differ from his course at the University, except that his predominant literary taste, which found expression only in talk about the poets and pasquin-

[1] Allan B. Magruder, Esq., to the author April 23, 1884.

ades on the academy officials, isolated him among his associates, while the custom of the place and his own lack of means forbade the excessive gambling in which he had formerly indulged. He was the intellectual, self-absorbed, exclusive young fellow that he had been, but older, and consequently more discontented and unsettled. As before, he bore his share in the school-boy follies of his mates, and his greater neglect of routine duty may be ascribed in part to its increased irksomeness to him after his year of freedom from such restraints.

After the first six months had passed he made up his mind to leave the service. Whether he was merely tired of the profession he had voluntarily chosen, or felt that the recent marriage of Mr. Allan, which took place at New York, October 5, cut off his expectation of an inheritance, and threw him on his own resources, or whether he was convinced that literature was his unavoidable career, makes little difference. Mr. Allan, as was to be expected, refused to sanction his alleged resignation, and consequently he had to employ indirect means to accomplish his purpose.[1] On January 5, 1831, a court-martial was convened at West Point, to try offenders against discipline, and after a short sitting adjourned until January 28. For the two

[1] This statement, which has no authority except Hirst, must have been originally derived from Poe. It is probably correct, although accompanied by the evident misrepresentation, repeated in all the biographies, that the reason why Poe determined to leave was the birth of an heir to Mr. Allan.

weeks preceding this adjourned meeting Poe neglected practically all his duties as a cadet, and was consequently cited to appear before the court and answer to two charges of two specifications each, to the effect that he had absented himself from certain parades, roll-calls, guard duty, and academical duties, and in the course of this remissness had twice directly disobeyed the orders of the officer of the day. He pleaded guilty to all, except one specification, and as it was the one alleging the most patent of his offenses — his absence from parade, roll-call, and guard duty — he thus shut the gates of mercy on himself. The court found him guilty, and passed a sentence of dismissal, which, however, in order that his pay might suffice to meet his debts to the academy, they recommended should not take effect until March 6; on February 8, 1831, the Secretary of War approved the proceedings of the court, and ordered the sentence to be executed in accordance with the recommendation. On the morning of March 7, consequently, Poe found himself as free as he had been in Boston, four years before, when he first entered the service, and apparently as penniless, since only twelve cents remained to his credit.

Funds for his journey to New York may have been provided from the subscriptions of the cadets (seventy-five cents, which the superintendent allowed to be deducted from their pay),[1] of which

[1] Allan B. Magruder, Esq., to the author, July 1, 1884.

a part only was advanced, for a volume of his poems which he proposed to publish in that city. Mr. Elam Bliss, a reputable publisher, who is said to have come to West Point on the business, undertook the job presumably on the strength of the subscription. The book, which was entitled simply "Poems,"[1] purported to be a second edition of the Baltimore volume, from which it differed in many of its readings, and materially by the omission of six short poems and the addition of the first forms of "To Helen," "The Sleeper," "Lenore," "The Valley of Unrest," "The City in the Sea," and "Israfel." In the expansion of the earlier poems and of "Fairyland" in particular, Poe approached very near to the inane, but in the half dozen new ones, inferior as they are to the revised

[1] *Poems.* By Edgar A. Poe. Second edition. New York. Published by Elam Bliss, 1831: pp. 124. This volume is dedicated to the United States Corps of Cadets, and opens with a preparatory letter to Mr. ——, dated West Point, 1831, and addressed "Dear B—— ;" it contains : 1. *Introduction*, 66 lines, an expansion of *Preface* in the 1829 edition ; 2. *To Helen;* 3. *Israfel*, 44 lines; 4. *The Doomed City*, 58 lines, the first version of *The City in the Sea;* 5. *Fairyland*, 64 lines, an expansion of the poem of the same name in the 1829 edition ; 6. *Irene*, 74 lines, the first version of *The Sleeper;* 7. *A Pæan,* 44 lines, the first version of *Lenore;* 8. *The Valley Nis*, 46 lines, the first version of *The Valley of Unrest* ; 9. *Al Aaraaf,* slightly revised, and introduced as in the 1829 edition by "*To Science;*" 10. *Tamerlane*, again considerably revised, particularly by the insertion of *The Lake* in a new form, and of lines from *To* —— ("Should my early life seem "), from the 1829 edition. Each poem has a bastard title, and the volume is further pieced out by mottoes, to each of which a page is given.

versions now known, his genius first became manifest both in the character of his poetic motives and in the fascination of some perfect lines. The first three are based on his own experience, and are essentially personal, — an imaginative amplification of the lines of the "Introduction:" —

> "I could not love except where Death
> Was mingling his with Beauty's breath, —
> Or Hymen, Time, and Destiny
> Were stalking between her and me."

Of these, however, "To Helen," which has been overpraised, owes much of its finish to the slight changes since made in it. "Irene," although impressive in conception and original in handling, is far too rude to be regarded as more than a poem of some promise, and the "Pæan" is happily forgotten. The remaining three, which are developed from slight Oriental suggestions, are of a different kind. In these for the first time the strangeness and distance and mystical power of Poe's imaginations are so given as to be henceforth identified with his genius. Two are landscape effects. In one, far down in the east, the Valley of Unrest discloses its tremulous trees beneath the ceaseless flow of swift-motioned clouds, — a glow of deep color; and in the other, as far in the west, gleams the weird diablerie of that strange city lying all alone in its glare and gloom, shadowed in those black waves: —

> "Around by lifting winds forgot
> Resignedly beneath the sky
> The melancholy waters lie."

The melodious monotone, the justness of touch in lines like these, are as artistic as the idea is poetic. But fine as is the substance of these two poems and excellent as is the execution at its best, neither rises to the rank of "Israfel," in which rings out the lyric burst, the first pure song of the poet, the notes most clear and liquid and soaring of all he ever sang, that waken and tremble in the first inspiration not less magnetically because narrower in compass and lower in flight than in the cadences of the perfected song.

As his genius had developed, Poe had formed a theory of poetry, which he expressed, so far as he had made it out to himself, in the prefatory "Letter to Mr. ———." In this, after some thin logic to the effect that pleasure instead of utility is the end of all rational human activity, and consequently of poetry, he subjects Wordsworth's theories and practice to a very supercilious criticism, and asserts that poetry should be pursued as "a passion," not as "a study," since "learning has little to do with the imagination — intellect with the passions — or age with poetry;" at the end he sums up his creed in an article which shows the strong influence of Coleridge's criticism, as follows: —

"A poem in my opinion, is opposed to a work of science by having, for its *immediate* object, pleasure, not truth; to romance, by having for its object an *indefinite* instead of a definite pleasure, being a poem only so far as this object is attained; romance presenting perceptible images with definite, poetry with indefinite, sensations, to which end music is an *essential*, since the comprehension of sweet sound is our most indefinite conception. Music, when combined with a pleasurable idea, is poetry; music without the idea is simply music; the idea without the music is prose from its very definiteness."

These crude generalizations, together with the incidental remarks that no one enjoys long poems, and that delicacy is the poet's peculiar kingdom, are the fundamental ideas out of which he afterward slowly developed and finally perfected his poetic theory; to the canons thus laid down he submitted his own practice the more easily because they were consonant with his own genius.

For the present neither his statement of the poetic ideal nor his attempted illustration of it interested the world. The only notice his poetry received was from the laughter of the cadets, who were disappointed because the little green volume of dingy paper had not turned out to be a book of local squibs. He himself went South, but whether he returned to Mr. Allan's house must be regarded as doubtful. He had not been a regular inmate of that home since he left it for the University, a boy of seventeen, over five years before; and in the mean time a Miss Paterson, aged thirty, had come to take the place of his foster-mother, and his own successor in the shape of a lineal heir was at hand. Poe remained but a short time, if at all, at Richmond. His own characteristic description of the rupture with the family was that, led by a chivalric feeling, he "deliberately threw away a large fortune rather than endure a trivial wrong;"[1] but this statement is worth nothing as evidence. Mr. Allan plainly regarded him as ungrateful, reckless, and untrustworthy; and Poe's conduct toward him, to say the least, had been that of a son who, since he wished his own will, ought to make his own way.

[1] Poe to Mrs. Whitman, October 18, 1848. Ingram, ii. 171.

CHAPTER IV.

AT THE SOUTH.

POE determined to settle at Baltimore, probably because he had a grateful remembrance of the kindness of his relatives there during his visits two years before, and because he had no prospects elsewhere nor money to seek them. He at once asked employment of his former acquaintance, William Gwynn, the editor, who apparently had some cause to distrust him, and it is noticeable that the form of his application shows that he still kept ostensibly on some terms with Mr. Allan: —

May 6th, 1831.

MR. W. GWYNN.

DEAR SIR, — I am almost ashamed to ask any favour at your hands after my foolish conduct upon a former occasion — but I trust to your good nature.

I am very anxious to remain and settle myself in Baltimore as Mr. Allan has married again and I no longer look upon Richmond as my place of residence.

This wish of mine has also met with his approbation. I wish to request your influence in obtaining some situation or employment in this city. Salary would be a minor consideration, but I do not wish to be idle.

Perhaps (since I understand Neilson has left you)

you might be so kind as to employ me in your office in some capacity.

If so I will use every exertion to deserve your confidence. Very respectfully yr. ob. st.,

Edgar A. Poe.

I would have waited upon you personally but am confined to my room with a severe sprain in my knee.[1]

Mr. Gwynn seems not to have exercised the Christian grace of forgiveness. Within a few weeks Poe turned to another Baltimore acquaintance, Mr. N. C. Brooks, who had recently opened a school at Reisterstown, not far from the city, and offered himself as an assistant; but of this, too, nothing came. To a man of Poe's talents and poverty there was left only a literary career.

Baltimore was not the most promising field for a young and friendless poet to seek his fortune in. Less than four years before, Pinkney, who had resided there since childhood, had died at the age of twenty-five from the effects of poverty and discouragement suffered just as his genius was breaking forth. At the present time there were two literary sets in the city, of which Kennedy and his friends of the club constituted one, and a half dozen obscure young men — Arthur, Carpenter, MacJilton, Brooks, Hewitt, and Dawes, whose names were current in the literature of the day and will occur in this narrative — made up the other; but to the former Poe was a stranger, and to the latter

[1] Poe to Gwynn, MS.

he was only slightly known. In the course of the first eighteen months of his life at Baltimore, where he was always understood to have resided at this time, he bought his experience of anonymous and unappreciated authorship dearly. He now turned to prose to gain his living. Bulwer and Disraeli, the popular writers of the time, gave direction to his genius, both in subject and style. Under their influence he wrote at least six tales, but he had found no publisher for them when, in 1833, in the summer, the Baltimore "Saturday Visiter," a weekly literary paper recently started by Mr. Lambert A. Wilmer, a young journalist, sought public attention in a way not unusual among contemporary periodicals of its class by offering two prizes: one of one hundred dollars for the best tale in prose, the other of fifty dollars for the best short poem, which should be presented within a fixed time. On learning this Poe determined to send in the tales which he was so fortunately supplied with, and the better to secure his success to send in all of them.

The judges of this literary contest were Dr. James H. Miller, J. H. B. Latrobe, Esq., and John P. Kennedy, Esq., who had published a year before his pleasant sketches entitled "Swallow Barn." When these gentlemen met, according to the narrative [1] of Mr. Latrobe, — which, although clearly very inaccurate in detail, seems substantially true, — nearly all the manuscripts were examined

[1] *Works,* cxlvii–clii.

more and more cursorily before a certain small quarto-bound book was noticed; Mr. Latrobe on taking it up found it entitled "Tales of the Folio Club," and written very neatly in Roman characters, and on reading it to his associates the stories proved so agreeable a diversion over the wine and cigars that the first prize was immediately awarded to its author. Among the poems, too, one entitled "The Coliseum" was regarded the best, but being in the same hand as the successful tales was ruled out, and the second prize awarded to Hewitt, the reviewer of Poe's "Al Aaraaf" four years before. On October 12 these decisions were announced in the "Saturday Visiter;" one of the tales, "A MS. Found in a Bottle," was published as the prize story, and the name of its author given as Edgar Allan Poe.

To that young man, whose fortunes were then at their lowest ebb, the hard cash, as well as the encouragement and the flattering card of the judges, advising the author to print all his tales in a book, must have been very welcome. The low state to which he had become reduced is briefly and pointedly shown in a passage in Kennedy's diary: —

"It is many years ago, I think, perhaps as early as 1833 or '34, that I found him in Baltimore in a state of starvation. I gave him clothing, free access to my table and the use of a horse for exercise whenever he chose; in fact brought him up from the very verge of despair." [1]

[1] *Life of John Pendleton Kennedy.* By Henry T. Tuckerman. New York: G. P. Putnam's Sons, 1871 : p. 376.

AT THE SOUTH. 67

It is further illustrated by the following self-explanatory note from Poe to that kind-hearted gentleman, who all his life was seeking out and advancing merit: —

"Your invitation to dinner has wounded me to the quick. I cannot come for reasons of the most humiliating nature — my personal appearance. You may imagine my mortification in making this disclosure to you, but it is necessary." [1]

And if further proof be needed (for the facts have been denied), it is furnished by a letter of Poe's years afterwards, in which he says, "Mr. Kennedy has been, at all times, a true friend to me — he was the first true friend I ever had — I am indebted to him for *life itself*." [2] Poe also made the acquaintance of Dr. Miller, with whom he afterwards had some correspondence, and of Mr. Latrobe, who describes [3] him as below the middle stature, erect in carriage, self-possessed in manner, and grave in countenance until he became animated in conversation, when his face lighted up and his manner became demonstrative.

[1] *Life of John Pendleton Kennedy*, p. 375.
[2] Poe to F. W. Thomas. Stoddard, xcv.
[3] Mr. Latrobe states that this visit was made on the Monday following the award, but he is clearly in error or has confused two visits, since he makes Poe mention the *Southern Literary Messenger*, which did not appear until nine months later, and *Hans Pfaall*, which by Poe's own statement was suggested to him by reading a book published a year afterward.

For the following six months Poe employed his time in contributing to the "Saturday Visiter," of which no file is now known, and upon such hack work as Mr. Kennedy could procure for him, none of which has been traced; but he attracted no further public notice. He lived from the summer of 1833, at least, if not earlier, in a very retired way with his father's widowed sister, Mrs. Clemm, who, with her single surviving child, Virginia, seems to have settled in Baltimore in the spring, after a long absence from the city; and whatever he earned went into the small common stock of the family. Mr. Wilmer, the editor of the "Saturday Visiter," was a constant companion. Nearly every day they walked out together in the suburbs, and sometimes took Virginia, a child of eleven, with them. Poe was then neatly, though inexpensively, clad (Hewitt, his successful rival, says he wore "Byron collars and a black stock, and looked the poet all over"), and in his features there was a delicacy which was perhaps the pallor of his Southern complexion; his companion, who was of a coarse fibre, mistook his refinement for effeminacy, but perceived that he was possessed of quick sympathies and an affectionate disposition. During an unbroken intimacy of some months, Wilmer saw no sign of bad habits in his friend, except on one occasion when Poe set out some Jamaica rum at his lodgings and drank moderately with his guest; and on another when Mrs. Clemm scolded the young man for coming home intoxicated the night before from a tavern supper, but as if it were a rare occurrence. These recollections,[1] however, cover only a comparatively short period. Wilmer was soon crowded out of his editorship by Hewitt, and left Baltimore on foot and in want, to follow journalism in other quarters. A cousin, Miss Herring, on whom Poe used to call, says he would write poems in her album and read to her; but his attentions were discouraged by her father on account both of the relationship and of Poe's use of liquor. These visits began as early as 1831, and continued until her marriage in 1834. It would appear, too, from her account that he went at times to Philadelphia and other places.[2]

On March 27, 1834, Mr. Allan died of the dropsy. Shortly before this event Poe called at his house, and being told by Mrs. Allan, who did not recognize him, that the physicians had forbidden her husband to see any one he thrust her aside and walked rapidly to Mr. Allan's chamber; on his entrance Mr. Allan raised the cane which he used to walk with, and, threatening to strike him if he came within his reach, ordered him out, a command that Poe at once obeyed.[3] This was the so-called

[1] *Recollections of Edgar A. Poe.* By L. A. Wilmer, *Baltimore Daily Commercial*, May 23, 1866.

[2] Miss A. F. Poe to the author, September 13, 1884.

[3] *Edgar Allan Poe.* A letter by Colonel Thomas H. Ellis to the Richmond *Standard*, April 22, 1881. Mr. Ellis had the very best means of judging the truth in this matter.

violent scene in which the two parted. Mr. Allan left three children; his will cut off any lingering hopes of inheritance Poe may have indulged in, and threw him irretrievably on his own resources. About this time he gathered his tales together and sent them to a Philadelphia house. He probably employed the summer upon the tragedy "Politian," and the autumn upon "Hans Pfaall." He also projected a new literary magazine, to be edited at Baltimore by himself and Wilmer, to whom he sent a prospectus;[1] and after the new year opened, upon Kennedy's recommendation, he sent some tales to the "Southern Literary Messenger," still in the first struggles of its existence. Mr. T. W. White, the editor, was attracted by his new contributor's talents, and in March published one of the stories, "Berenice," with a very flattering notice; at the same time he addressed a letter of inquiry to Mr. Kennedy, which elicited the following response: —

"BALTIMORE, *April* 13, 1835.

"DEAR SIR: Poe did right in referring to me. He is very clever with his pen — classical and scholar-like. He wants experience and direction, but I have no doubt he can be made very useful to you. And, poor fellow! he is *very* poor. I told him to write something for every number of your magazine, and that you might find it to your advantage to give him some permanent

---

[1] *Our Press Gang; or, A Complete Exposition of the Corruptions and Crimes of the American Newspapers.* By Lambert A. Wilmer (ex-editor). Philadelphia: J. T. Lloyd, 1859: p. 36.

employ. He has a volume of very bizarre tales in the hands of ——, in Philadelphia, who for a year past has been promising to publish them. This young fellow is highly imaginative, and a little given to the *terrific*. He is at work upon a tragedy, but I have turned him to drudging upon whatever may make money, and I have no doubt you and he will find your account in each other." [1]

"Berenice" was followed in successive numbers by other tales and some criticism. On the 30th of May he wrote to Mr. White, thanking him for his kindness: —

"In regard to my critique of Mr. Kennedy's novel I seriously feel ashamed of what I have written. I fully intended to give the work a thorough review, and examine it in detail. Ill health alone prevented me from doing so. At the time I made the hasty sketch I sent you, I was so ill as to be hardly able to see the paper on which I wrote, and I finished it in a state of complete exhaustion. I have not, therefore, done anything like justice to the book, and I am vexed about the matter, for Mr. Kennedy has proved himself a kind friend to me, in every respect, and I am sincerely grateful to him for many acts of generosity and attention. You ask me if I am perfectly satisfied with your course. I reply that I am — entirely. My poor services are not worth what you give me for them." [1]

A month later, in reply to some advances made by Mr. White, he again wrote: —

[1] Griswold, xxix.

"You ask me if I would be willing to come on to Richmond if you should have occasion for my services during the coming winter. I reply that nothing would give me greater pleasure. I have been desirous for some time past of paying a visit to Richmond, and would be glad of any reasonable excuse for so doing. Indeed I am anxious to settle myself in that city, and if, by any chance, you hear of a situation likely to suit me, I would gladly accept it, were the salary even the merest trifle. I should, indeed, feel myself greatly indebted to you if through your means I could accomplish this object. What you say in the conclusion of your letter, in relation to the supervision of proof-sheets, gives me reason to hope that possibly you might find something for me to do in your office. If so, I should be very glad — for at present only a very small portion of my time is employed." [1]

In the first of these letters is the earliest mention of ill-health in Poe; but from this time he frequently complains of nervous exhaustion, which can be ascribed only to the reaction of drugs and stimulants on a weakened system. Neither at college, nor in the army, nor at West Point, is there any proof that he showed any dangerous or even injurious taste for liquor; the evidence goes rather to indicate that he was free from the vice of intoxication. Now, however, when he emerges from his obscurity, he seems to have already fixed upon himself the habits of indulgence, which, although less strong in their hold and less violent in their ef-

[1] Griswold, xxix.

fects than they afterwards became, were gradually accustoming him to surrender at longer or shorter intervals to a temptation which, once yielded to, rendered him irrational and irresponsible for days, and left him prostrated. At some time between his abandonment by Mr. Allan and his literary adoption by Mr. Kennedy, the weakest spot in his nature had been found. During this period Poe was very poor; he was solitary, proud, and despairing. That a nervous system extraordinarily sensitive should have been permanently weakened by such bodily privation and mental strain is not unlikely; that a youth of twenty three or four years, possibly with an hereditary taint in his blood, should indulge in such a vice admits no wonder; and that under the circumstances his frame retained an unusual susceptibility to such influences, even after better days had come, offers nothing strange to ordinary experience. His excesses, however, seem to have been infrequent, and he was now trying to overcome his temptation. In Mr. Kennedy, to whom he apparently confided all his troubles, he had a kind and invigorating friend, and in Mrs. Clemm he had found more motherhood and in her daughter more tender affection than he had ever known. He had no choice but to go to Richmond, but he seems to have felt that separation from these friends would cast him back into that state of loneliness and despondency out of which they had helped him to rise. Virginia was greatly attached to him, and Mrs.

Clemm had no one else to look to for support. Under the circumstances it was not so unnatural as it was unwise that, before leaving for Richmond, Poe proposed to keep the family united by marrying his cousin, and the engagement was approved by her mother.

In midsummer, with this understanding, Poe left Baltimore apparently without regret, for he owed little gratitude to that city, nor did he ever return to it to live, although there he was destined to die and be buried. He went directly to Richmond, to the home and associates of his childhood; nor did he doubt that, in spite of the changes in his lot, life there would be pleasant to him; he may have thought that his literary position would compensate for his loss of social pretension and the consideration that attaches to wealth, or even that his old acquaintance would be advantageous to him. However this turned out, he entered at once on his duties as an assistant, although he was not nominally an editor until November, at a salary of ten dollars a week. It was not high pay, but the position he held was a good opening and well adapted to his talents. He had on hand nine tales besides those which had already been published ("A MS. Found in a Bottle," "Berenice," "Morella," "Lionizing," "Hans Pfaall," "The Visionary," and "Bon-Bon"), and he expected to print the whole sixteen in the fall at Philadelphia. He had been highly praised by Paulding, Tucker, Kennedy, and others who were the literary autocrats of their day. The Southern press welcomed him loudly. His fortunes, however regarded, were in bright contrast to his immediate past; but not long after his arrival all this was made as naught, because an obstruction arose in the course of true love.

The engagement between Edgar and his cousin Virginia had come to the ears of his relative, Neilson Poe, who, himself a third cousin to both, had recently married her half-sister, also his third cousin; and, led by his wife, who thought Virginia too young to marry (as indeed she was, having been born August 15, 1822,[1] and consequently hardly turned of thirteen years), he offered to take her into his family and care for her until she should be eighteen, when, if she desired to marry Edgar, she would be free to do so. The communication of this news to Poe had an extraordinary effect upon him, and seems to have cast him into the deepest dejection. He wrote to Mrs. Clemm, August 29, imploring her not to consent to separate him from Virginia, and appealing to her pity for himself in such terms that his sincerity cannot be questioned. Some days later, evidently under the same influence, he wrote to Mr. Kennedy as follows: —

RICHMOND, *Sept.* 11, 1835.

DEAR SIR, — I received a letter yesterday from Dr. Miller, in which he tells me you are in town. I hasten,

[1] The Records of St. Paul's Parish, Baltimore. The date August 13 has some authority by family tradition.

therefore, to write you, and express by letter what I have always found it impossible to express orally — my deep sense of gratitude for your frequent and ineffectual assistance and kindness. Through your influence Mr. White has been induced to employ me in assisting him with the editorial duties of his Magazine at a salary of five hundred and twenty dollars per annum. The situation is agreeable to me for many reasons, — but alas! it appears to me that nothing can now give me pleasure or the slightest gratification. Excuse me, my dear sir, if in this letter you find much incoherency. My feelings at this moment are pitiable, indeed. I am suffering under a depression of spirits, such as I have never felt before. I have struggled in vain against the influence of this melancholy; *you will believe* me, when I say that I am still miserable in spite of the great improvement in my circumstances. I say you will believe me, and for this simple reason, that a man who is writing for *effect* does not write *thus*. My heart is open before you — if it be worth reading, read it. I am wretched, and know not why. Console me, — for you can. But let it be quickly, or it will be too late. Write me immediately. Convince me that it is worth one's while — that it is at all necessary to live, and you will prove yourself indeed my friend. Persuade me to do what is right. I do mean this. I do not mean that you should consider what I now write you a jest. Oh, pity me! for I feel that my words are incoherent; but I will recover myself. You will not fail to see that I am suffering under a depression of spirits which will ruin me should it be long continued. Write me then, and quickly — urge me to do what is right. Your words will have more weight with me than the words of others, for you were my friend when no one else was. Fail not, as you value your peace of mind hereafter. E. A. POE.[1]

To this painful letter, exhibiting an unmanned spirit, Mr. Kennedy replied: —

"I am sorry to see you in such plight as your letter shows you in. It is strange that just at this time, when everybody is praising you, and when fortune is beginning to smile upon your hitherto wretched circumstances, you should be invaded by these blue devils. It belongs, however, to your age and temper to be thus buffeted — but be assured, it only wants a little resolution to master the adversary forever. You will doubtless do well henceforth in literature, and add to your *comforts*, as well as to your reputation, which it gives me great pleasure to assure you is everywhere rising in popular esteem."[2]

Probably before receiving this letter Poe left Richmond and arrived at Baltimore to plead his suit in person, since on September 22 he took out a license in that city for the marriage.[3] It has been said, on the authority of Mrs. Clemm's conversation taken down in short-hand, that the ceremony was performed by the Rev. John Johns, at Old Christ Church, and that the next day Poe returned to his duties.[4] If this was actually the case

[1] *The Life of John Pendleton Kennedy*, pp. 375, 376.

[2] Griswold, xxix, xxx.

[3] Marriage Records of Baltimore City.

[4] Didier, p. 58. The date of marriage is given as September 2. As Mr. Didier knew nothing of the record of the marriage license granted September 22, the error is of a kind to support rather

the matter was kept very private. There is now no complete legal proof of the marriage; but this is not conclusive against its having taken place, as the marriage records of Old Christ Church were badly kept and are very defective. It is certain, however, that Poe so far succeeded in his entreaties that the proposal of Neilson Poe was rejected, and Mrs. Clemm and her daughter removed to Richmond within a few weeks, where the three continued to live together. There they planned to start a boarding-house, and with this in view Poe sent the following letter to George Poe in Alabama: —

RICHMOND, *Jan.* 12, 1836.

DEAR SIR, — I take the liberty of addressing you in behalf of a mutual relation, Mrs. William Clemm, late of Baltimore — and at her earnest solicitation.

You are aware that for many years she has been suffering privations and difficulties of no ordinary kind. I know that you have assisted her at a former period, and she has occasionally received aid from her cousins, William and Robert Poe, of Augusta. What little has been heretofore in my own power I have also done.

Having lately established myself in Richmond, and undertaken the editorship of the Southern Literary Messenger, and my circumstances having thus become better than formerly, I have ventured to offer my aunt a home.

than to discredit the marriage. The license was the last issued on that day, and it fails to prove the marriage only because there is no return of the minister officiating; but such a return was not obligatory, and there are several other entries in the records that are similarly incomplete.

She is now therefore in Richmond, with her daughter Virginia, and is, for the present boarding at the house of a Mrs. Yarrington. My salary is only at present about $800 per ann., and the charge per week for our board, (Mrs. Clemm's, her daughter's, and my own,) is $9. I am thus particular in stating my precise situation that you may be the better enabled to judge in regard to the propriety of granting the request which I am now about to make for Mrs. Clemm.

It is ascertained that if Mrs. C. could obtain the means of opening, herself, a boarding-house in this city, she could support herself and daughter comfortably with something to spare. But a small capital would be necessary for an undertaking of this nature, and many of the widows of our first people are engaged in it, and find it profitable. I am willing to advance, for my own part, $100, and I believe that Wm. & R. Poe will advance $100. If then you would so far aid her in her design as to loan her yourself $100 she will have sufficient to commence with. I will be responsible for the repayment of the sum, in a year from this date, if you can make it convenient to comply with her request.

I beg you, my dear Sir, to take this subject into consideration. I feel deeply for the distresses of Mrs. Clemm, and I am sure *you* will feel interested in relieving them.

[Signature cut off.]

P. S. I am the son of David Poe, Jr. Mrs. C.'s brother.[1]

George Poe sent the money, but the history of the plan belongs to a later period.

[1] Poe to George Poe, MS.

From the first Poe had entered upon his work with vigor, and he soon took entire charge of the magazine. Besides fulfilling the manifold and distracting duties incident to mere editorship he contributed tales, poems, and reviews, signed and unsigned, as well as compendious articles, which although unclaimed are clearly from his hand. A considerable portion of this matter had been written before he came to Richmond, but the entire mass is so large as to prove that he was a not less diligent than facile author. Much of his work was of slight importance then, and now posterity is interested in little more of it than a few poems and the seven new tales, "Loss of Breath," "King Pest," "Shadow," "Metzengerstein," "Duc de L'Omelette," " Epimanes," and " A Tale of Jerusalem," which he added to the seven already issued.

These fourteen, presumably all but two of the "Tales of the Folio Club," which the Philadelphia house had so long held under consideration, stand in a group by themselves as the first fruits of Poe's genius. In conception and execution they afford types of his later works in both the arabesque and grotesque manner, as he afterwards happily named the two extremes of his style, and without requiring too close a scrutiny they illustrate the development of his mind and art. Only five of them are purely imaginative, and of these "Berenice" is the most varied and comprehensive; in it Poe's hero first comes upon the stage, a man struck with some secret disease, given to the use of drugs and to musing over old books in an antiquated and gloomy chamber, and reserved for a horrible experience. In it, too, are such themes of evil fascination for his mind as the epileptic patient and the premature burial; such marks of his handling as the cousinship of the principal actors, the description of morbid physical changes, the minute analysis of sensations, the half-superstitious reference to metempsychosis, and the vivid analysis of the effects of drugs; and such traits of literary style as the absence of conversation, the theatrically elaborated scene of the action, the speed of the narrative with its sudden and yet carefully prepared catastrophe. " Berenice " reveals a mind at once analytical and constructive, in which the imagination is the dominant faculty and a taste for sensuous effects, melodramatic incidents, and fantastic suggestions is the most shaping influence. Defective as the tale is in refinement — Poe never but once indulged again in a *dénoûment* of such mere physical horror — it exhibits, in however crude a form, the capacity to conceive startling imaginative effects and to select the right means to bring them about directly, forcibly, and without observation; in a word, artistic power. In the Venetian story of " The Visionary," now known as "The Assignation," there is more of splendid coloring, of the purely spectacular and decorative element; in the Hungarian myth of " Metzengerstein " there is a more violent and raw superstition; in "Morella"—the history of the revolting victory of that aspiring will, by which the dying mother's spirit, passing into her new-born babe, retained in that childish frame the full intelligence and ripe passions of womanhood — there is a solemn and breathless dread beneath the coming of a vague but sure terror: and these several traits individualize the three tales, but in none of them is there the finely wrought complexity of "Berenice." All yield, however, in comparison with the fifth and last of the early arabesque series, the parable called "Shadow," which, within its narrow limits of a page or two, is at once the most noble and most artistic expression of Poe's imagination during the first period of his career, and furthermore is alone distinguished by the even flow and delicacy of transition that belong to his best prose style. The elements in this rhapsody of gloom are simple and massive, the accessories in perfect keeping; the fine monotone of stifled and expectant emotion in the breasts of the Greek revelers in the lighted, sepulchral, plague-isolated hall is just sustained at its initial pitch until the one thrilling, solitary change arises in the emergence of the shadow from the black draperies of the chamber, and its motionless relief under the gloom of the seven iron lamps, against the burnished, brazen door, opposite to the feet of the young and shrouded Zoilus — as it were the semblance of a man, but "the shadow neither of man, nor of God, nor of any familiar thing," — the vague, formless One that was not indifferent to the low-voiced question of Oinos, but spoke and told its dwelling-place and its appellation; "and then did we, the seven, start from our seats in horror, and stand trembling, and shuddering, and aghast, for the tones in the voice of the shadow were not the tones of any one being, but of a multitude of beings, and, varying in their cadences from syllable to syllable, fell duskily upon our ears in the well-remembered and familiar accents of many thousand departed friends."

Perhaps the "MS. Found in a Bottle," reprinted as from Miss Eliza Leslie's annual, "The Gift," full as it is of fantasy and magnificent scenic effects of ocean views, should be placed among the tales of pure imagination; it stands slightly apart from them only because it has some relationship with those stories, partly of adventure, partly of science, which Poe built rather out of his acquired knowledge than his dreams. Of this class "Hans Pfaall," the narrative of a voyage to the moon, is the first complete type. The idea of such a passage from the earth to its nearest neighbor in space was not novel, nor was the astronomical information involved by any means abstruse, being furnished in fact by Herschel's popular treatise, then first published in America; but Poe claimed that the design of making a fiction plausible by the use of scientific facts and principles was original, and he certainly worked it out with great patience and skill, and even a high degree of scientific consistency. It is not without obligation to an obscure *deus ex machina*, a providence unknown to physics, which overruled the balloonist's fate; but, with all its whimsicalities, it exhibits for the first time the keenness and lucidity of Poe's intelligence as distinguished from his imagination, and proves that he then possessed a considerable power of applied thought. It is noteworthy, too, as the earliest of those attempts to gull the public, for which he afterwards became notorious. At the time it was less successful in this respect than the celebrated "Moon-Hoax" of Mr. Locke, published a few weeks later in the "New York Sun," which made fools of many highly intelligent citizens and caused Poe some chagrin, as he showed in his later comments upon it, because so many more people were taken in by it than by "Hans Pfaall," while he had put himself to so much more pains than Mr. Locke to seem truthful; certainly if verisimilitude were the gauge of the crowd's folly in credulity, he deserved better luck than his rival.

The remainder of the tales Poe would have called grotesque. Unfortunately he was not so plentifully gifted with humor as with either imagination or intelligence, and consequently his fame would suffer less by the omission than by the retention of these lucubrations. Some of them are the merest extravaganzas, such as the "Duc de L'Omelette," in which the devil poses as a gambler who can lose, or

"Bon-Bon," in which he plays his part as a cannibal of human souls. Some are satirical, and among them is to be reckoned one of his weakest productions, "Loss of Breath, A Tale *à la* Blackwood," which in its first form, with its expanded narrative of the hanging and the burial alive, was more perceptibly aimed at the inane jargon (as it was then thought) of German metaphysics. In all of them, too, Poe is less original than in his other tales; he shows more plainly the traces of his reading. "King Pest" is very closely modeled on Vivian Grey's adventure in the castle of the Grand Duke of Johannisberger (the cabinet of the Prince of Little Lilliput in the same novel contains the double of the Saracen's horse in Metzengerstein's tapestry); and "Lionizing," a sketch which was repeatedly and elaborately corrected in later years, apart from its Shandean touch, copies in style and conception "Too Beautiful for Anything" in Bulwer's "The Ambitious Student in Ill Health, and other Papers," apparently a favorite book of Poe's. "Epimanes" and "A Tale of Jerusalem," the flattest of the series, need hardly be mentioned. The humor in all, where it exists in any degree, is too hollow, too mocking and sardonic, to be agreeable; there is no laughter in it. The fact is that just as Poe desired to be considered precocious he had also the weakness of wishing to be thought a universal genius. The grotesque tales are the spectral progeny of this illusion.

But it was as a critic, not as an imaginative or humorous author, that Poe made the editorial hit that placed the new Southern monthly at once beside the "Knickerbocker" and the "New Englander" as a national magazine. While at Baltimore he had contributed a few perfunctory book notices, but only when he was publicly known as editor did he, to use the expression of a contemporary, "fall in with his broad-axe." Late in the fall of 1835 there appeared the loudly-announced, much-bepuffed "Norman Leslie," one of the popular novels of its day; it was ambitious, crude, and foolish, but its pretentiousness seems the particular quality which led Poe to single it out for an example. In the issue for December, therefore, he subjected it to such scrutiny as had never been known in our country before, and he did his task so trenchantly and convincingly, with such spirit and effect, that the public were widely interested; they bought, read, and looked for more. The Southern press with one voice cried on havoc; they were only too glad to find in their own country a youth with the boldness to rouse and the skill to worry Knickerbocker game, for the young author, Theodore S. Fay, was a pet of the metropolitan littérateurs and an associate editor of the "New York Mirror," then the best literary weekly of the country. Even if Poe had not been applauded to the echo, he was not of a nature to hesitate in following up a predetermined line of policy; but he soon found a stand making against him. There was some show at first of closing the New York columns, with gentleman-like contempt, to any remonstrance against the insult; but at length the "Mirror," after several insidious attacks, made one openly, to wit: —

" ☞ Those who have read the notices of American books in a certain 'southern' monthly which is striving to gain notoriety by the loudness of its abuse, may find amusement in the sketch, in another page, entitled 'The Successful Novel.' The Southern Literary Messenger knows ☞ *by experience* ✍ what it is to write a successless novel. ✍ " [1]

The sketch referred to was a clever squib in the style of Poe's "Lionizing," and while satirizing his attention to the minutiæ of style and his readiness to cry plagiarism somewhat in a jackdaw manner, as if the word were his whole stock in trade, insinuated further that the Harpers had rejected Poe's longer, as the "Mirror" itself had his shorter, effusions. In this charge there was little, if any, truth; and to the point Poe replied with a flat denial: he "never in his life wrote or published, or attempted to publish, a novel either successful or *successless*," [2] — a statement which must be understood as relegating into nonentity the alleged early work of Poe, "An Artist at Home and Abroad."

[1] *New York Mirror*, April 9, 1836.
[2] *Southern Literary Messenger*, ii. 327 (April, 1836).

This trivial incident drew from Poe a statement of the spirit in which he believed himself to be undertaking the reform of criticism, and the grounds of his action: —

"There was a time, it is true, when we cringed to foreign opinion — let us even say when we paid a most servile deference to British critical dicta. That an American book could, by any possibility, be worthy perusal, was an idea by no means extensively prevalent in the land; and if we were induced to read at all the productions of our native writers, it was only after repeated assurances from England that such productions were not altogether contemptible . . . Not so, however, with our present follies. We are becoming boisterous and arrogant in the pride of a too speedily assumed literary freedom. We throw off with the most presumptuous and unmeaning hauteur, *all* deference whatever to foreign opinion — we forget, in the puerile inflation of vanity, that *the world* is the true theatre of the biblical histrio — we get up a hue and cry about the necessity of encouraging native writers of merit — we blindly fancy that we can accomplish this by indiscriminate puffing of good, bad, and indifferent, without taking the trouble to consider that what we choose to denominate encouragement is thus, by its general application, precisely the reverse. In a word, so far from being ashamed of the many disgraceful literary failures to which our own inordinate vanities and misapplied patriotism have lately given birth, and so far from deeply lamenting that these daily puerilities are of home manufacture, we adhere pertinaciously to our original blindly conceived idea, and thus often find ourselves involved in the gross paradox of liking a stupid book the better, because, sure enough, its stupidity is American."[1]

These views were by no means novel or unshared. The periodical press was frequently weighted or padded with essays, reports of lectures, or editorial remarks, endeavoring to explain the feebleness of American criticism, and deprecating it. A writer in the "Knickerbocker" itself ascribes many causes, not confined, perhaps, to that period, such as the interests of publishers, the social relations of editors, the wish to encourage the young, the fear of being esteemed unpatriotic, and the like. What distinguished Poe was the audacity with which he took the unenvied post, and the vigor with which he struck. Undoubtedly his worldly fortunes were affected by the enmities he thus made. The New Yorkers never forgave him. Colonel Stone, of the "Commercial Advertiser," and W. Gaylord Clarke, of the "Philadelphia Gazette," denounced him, and in the house of his friends the "Newbern Spectator" was an envious foe. But the presumptuous young critic did not therefore withdraw his hand; and though at a time when Gifford and Wilson handed down the traditions of critical style he did not write with the urbanity that now obtains, though he was not choice in his phrase nor delicate in his ridicule, all of his adverse decisions but one (that on "Sartor Resartus") have been

[1] *Southern Literary Messenger*, ii. 326 (April, 1836).

sustained. Moreover, the severity, what is called the venom and heartlessness, of these critiques has been much exaggerated; there were in all but four like that upon "Norman Leslie," and these were milder than the first, a fact very creditable to Poe when one recollects how loudly he was urged "to hang, draw, and Quarterly," and how aptly such a literary temper fell in with the proud self-confidence of his nature. His end was justice, if his manner was not courtesy.

In fact, his reputation as a critic would now suffer rather for the mercy he showed than for the vengeance he took. With what hesitancy he suggests that Mrs. Sigourney might profitably forget Mrs. Hemans; with what consideration he hints a fault in Mrs. Ellet, or just notices a blemish in Miss Gould; with what respect he treats Mellen and Gallagher! And if he asserts that Drake had an analogical rather than a creative mind, and insinuates that Halleck's laurel was touched with an artificial green, — these were the names that a lesser man would have let pass unchallenged. The whole mass of this criticism — but a small portion of which deals with imaginative work — is particularly characterized by a minuteness of treatment which springs from a keen, artistic sensibility, and by that constant regard to the originality of the writer which is so frequently an element in the jealousy of genius. One wearies in reading it now; but one gains thereby the better impression of Poe's patience and of the alertness and compass of his mental curiosity. Here and there, too, one sees signs of his growth, as when he praises with enthusiasm Godwin and Coleridge, Bulwer, Disraeli, and Scott; or one finds the marks of his peculiar individuality, the early bent of his mind, as when he mentions the love of analytical beauty in this author, and whispers to the next the secret of verisimilitude by obscuring the improbability of the general in the naturalness and accuracy of the particular. In especial some progress is made in his poetic theory, but this must be treated by itself.

He had reprinted without a signature his "Letter to B——" from the 1831 edition of his poems, with the editorial remark that " of course we shall not be called upon to indorse all the writer's opinions." To the somewhat bald conclusions there advanced, that poetry should aim at pleasure, and be brief, indefinite, and musical, he now had something to add in a peculiar dialect of German metaphysics and phrenology, then the fashion. The most significant passage is one in which, after identifying " the Faculty of Ideality " with the " Sentiment of Poesy," he goes on as follows: —

"This sentiment is the sense of the beautiful, of the sublime, and of the mystical. Thence spring immediately admiration of the fair flowers, the fairer forests, the bright valleys and rivers and mountains of the Earth — and love of the gleaming stars and other burning glories of Heaven — and, mingled up inextricably with this love and this admiration of Heaven and of Earth, the unconquerable desire — *to know*. Poesy is the sentiment of Intellectual Happiness here, and the Hope of a higher Intellectual Happiness hereafter. Imagination is its soul. With the *passions* of mankind, — although it may modify them greatly — although it may exalt, or inflame, or purify, or control them — it would require little ingenuity to prove that it has no inevitable, and indeed no necessary co-existence. . . . We do not hesitate to say that a man highly endowed with the powers of Causality — that is to say, a man of metaphysical acumen — will, even with a very deficient share of Ideality, compose a finer poem (if we test it, as we should, by its measure of exciting the Poetic Sentiment) than one who, without such metaphysical acumen, shall be gifted, in the most extraordinary degree, with the faculty of Ideality. For a poem is not the Poetic faculty, but *the means* of exciting it in mankind." [1]

Poe's meaning may not be entirely plain at first sight, built up as it is out of obscure Coleridgian elements, which he derived mainly from the "Biographia Literaria." In the plainest words, Poe conceived that beauty, whether natural or imaginary, whether springing from the creative act of God or the creative thought of man, affects the mind as a glimpse of the infinite, and thus excites instantaneous pleasure, and furthermore, by intimating a fuller delight beyond, stimulates men to endeavor to penetrate deeper into the mystery that encom-

[1] *Southern Literary Messenger,* ii. 328 (April, 1836).

passes them. Beauty is thus a revelation of infinite truth, seized only by the imagination. Poetry consequently, according to Poe's view at this time, makes its highest appeal to the intellect instead of the passions, and requires imagination rather than sympathetic power in both its makers and its readers.

The remainder of his proposition amounts only to saying that one who is able to analyze the elements which give rise to his own experience of the vision that poetry brings, and thus to discern how such moods are caused, can by forethought so select and combine these elements as to arouse the same state in others, whereas one who is merely susceptible to such experience might not be capable of reproducing it with certainty: the latter has the poetic temperament, the former has in addition the analytical power which is necessary to art; one is the creature, the other the master, of his inspiration. All this, which means that "The Ancient Mariner" had been written by Coleridge, is a good illustration of the rationalizing by which Poe was accustomed to feed his own vanity indirectly. Did he not possess "analytical power"? Was he not distinguished by "metaphysical acumen"? And through all, too, most noticeable is his constant parroting of Coleridge, who was, taken all in all, the guiding genius of Poe's entire intellectual life.

Of more consequence than either Poe's mysticism or his metaphysical acumen, however, was the lesson he learned from Schlegel, and now adduced in support of his pet canon, that poems should be brief. "In pieces of less extent," he writes, "the pleasure is *unique*, in the proper acceptation of that term — the understanding is employed, without difficulty, in the contemplation of the picture *as a whole* — and thus its effect will depend, in a very great degree, upon the perfection of its finish, upon the nice adaptation of its constituent parts, and especially upon what is rightly termed by Schlegel, the *unity or totality of interest.*"[1] This is the first expression of Poe's intellectual sense of poetic form, the quality in which his early verse was most defective and his latest most eminent.

The new poems which were published in the "Messenger," out of his compositions since 1831, were the five scenes from that academical drama, "Politian," the "Hymn" in "Morella," "To Mary," "To ——" in "The Visionary," "To Eliza," "To Zante," and the "Bridal Ballad."[2] These offer no occasion for remark in this place, except that the latter contained the following stanza, which, per-

[1] *Southern Literary Messenger*, ii. 113 (January, 1836).

[2] Of these *To Mary, To ——, To Eliza,* and the *Bridal Ballad* are now known in revised versions, and the first three are entitled respectively *To F——, To One in Paradise,* and to *To F——s S. O——d.* An earlier version of *To One in Paradise,* from some unknown source, is quoted from *The Athenæum* by Curwen in his *Sorrow and Song. To Zante* was suggested by a passage in Châteaubriand's *Itinéraire de Paris à Jérusalem,* already mentioned.

haps, marks the nadir of Poe's descent into the prosaic, tasteless, and absurd: —

> "And thus they said I plighted
> An irrevocable vow,
> And my friends are all delighted
> That I his love have requited,
> And my mind is much benighted
> If I am not happy now."

It is hardly necessary to add that the maturer judgment of the poet canceled these lines, nor would it be useful to revive their memory were it not to give, by a striking example, an impression once for all of the real worthlessness of much of Poe's early work. Of his old poems he reprinted in the "Messenger," in forms more or less revised, "Irene," "A Pæan," "The Valley Nis," "To Helen," "To Science," "Israfel," "The City of Sin," from the New York volume, and "The Coliseum," a fragment of "Politian," from the Baltimore "Saturday Visiter."

The paucity of Poe's poetic productions while editing the "Messenger" may be laid partly to his lack of leisure. Indeed, he never wrote poetry except in seasons of solitary musing. Now he was largely employed in the correspondence and routine business of the office, or in simply furnishing copy, or attracting public interest by attention to the topics of the hour. The most noted article of this transitory nature was that in which he demonstrated that Maelzel's Chess Player must be operated by human agency, and solved the methods used. The paper was well reasoned, and shows that its author had a quick and observant eye, but it has been vastly overrated, as any one may convince himself by comparing it minutely with Sir David Brewster's "Letters on Natural Magic," to which it stands confessedly obliged, and from which it is partly paraphrased. Another article, "Pinakidia," being selections from Poe's commonplace book, is worth a moment's detention for the light it incidentally throws on his habits as a scholar. In prefacing the clippings (which by an obvious but very unfortunate misprint, never as yet corrected in any edition of his works, are declared to be original instead of *not* original), he says that in foreign magazines extracts of this sort are usually taken "by wholesale from such works as the 'Bibliothèque des Memorabilia Literaria,' the 'Recueil des Bon (sic) Pensées,' the 'Lettres Édifiantes et Curieuses,' the 'Literary Memoirs' of Sallengré, the 'Mélanges Litéraires' of Suard and André, or the 'Pièces Intéressantes et Peu Connues' of La Place."[1] These titles must have been taken down at hap-hazard, for a thorough search of bibliographies fails to reveal the existence of the first two, and the others, apart from their bad French, are incorrectly given. The earmark in this masquerade of borrowed learning is seen in the "'Mélanges Litéraires' of Suard and André," — a title evidently noted from the recent translation of

[1] *Works*, ii. 507.

"Schlegel's Lectures on the Drama" (which furnished some extracts to the body of the article), for there alone it occurs, the translator having erred in rendering "Suard und Andre" (andere), that is, Suard and others; Poe innocently followed him, and so tripped. The satirical young editor goes on to say that "Disraeli's 'Curiosities of Literature,' 'Literary Character,' and 'Calamities of Authors' have of late years proved exceedingly convenient to some little American pilferers in this line, but are now becoming too generally known;" and forthwith he takes from this same convenient repertory several fine bits, including nearly all the alleged plagiarisms of the poets.[1] Similar examples of the disingenuousness of Poe, the flimsiness of his pretended scholarship, and his readiness to appropriate from others by easy paraphrase occur throughout his career.

In Poe's private life during the eighteen months of his residence at Richmond the principal event was his public marriage to his cousin. On May 16,

[1] A more curious instance of Poe's mode of dealing with authorities is his note on *Israfel*, which originally read, "And the angel Israfel, who has the sweetest voice of all God's creatures: *Koran.*" The passage referred to is not in the Koran, but in Sale's *Preliminary Discourse* (iv. 71). Poe derived it from the notes to Moore's *Lalla Rookh*, where it is correctly attributed to Sale. At a later time he interpolated the entire phrase, "whose heartstrings are a lute" (the idea on which his poem is founded), which is neither in Moore, Sale, nor the Koran; and with this highly original emendation, the note now stands in his *Works* as an extract from the Koran.

1836, having secured one Thomas W. Cleland as his surety, he gave a marriage bond as the law required; and Cleland was further obliging enough to take oath before the deputy clerk, Charles Howard, " that Virginia E. Clemm is of the full age of twenty-one years, and a resident of the said city."[1] The ceremony was performed on the evening of the same day at the boarding-house of the family, by the Rev. Amasa Converse, a Presbyterian minister, then editor of the "Southern Religious Telegraph."[2] Mrs. Clemm, whom the minister remembered as "being polished, dignified, and agreeable in her bearing," was present, and gave her consent freely; the bride, too, had a pleasing manner, but seemed to him very young.[3] Virginia was in fact slightly under fourteen. Poe was twenty-seven.

At this time it was expected that Mrs. Clemm, who had not abandoned her plan of starting a boarding-house, would rent a house recently purchased by Mr. White, and would board himself and family as well as the newly-married pair. The arrangement had been made, and Poe had expended all his money and incurred a debt of two hundred dollars in buying furniture before it was discovered that the house was barely large enough for one family, and the scheme was abandoned. In his

[1] Hustings Court Records, Richmond, Va.
[2] *Southern Religious Telegraph*, May 20, 1836; *Richmond Enquirer*, May 20, 1836.
[3] Mrs. F. B. Converse to the author, May 20, 1884.

consequent financial embarrassment, Poe wrote to Kennedy on June 7, and asked a loan of one hundred dollars for six months in order to meet a note for the same amount due in three months (perhaps the money advanced by George Poe in February), which he declared was his only debt. His salary, he said, was fifteen dollars a week, and after November was to be twenty; and added, "Our *Messenger* is thriving beyond all expectation, and I myself have every prospect of success."[1] Kennedy probably acceded to this request; but however that was, the little family took up their abode together, and were temporarily, at least, well provided for.

Poe might now justly regard his future as bright. The "Messenger" had so prospered under his management that it was an assured success, and was likely to afford him a constantly increasing income. His reputation was steadily growing; the veteran Paulding declared him the best of the young and perhaps of the old writers; the Southern press was vociferous in its praises, and Poe, whose virtue was never modesty, took good care that these acclaims should not die away unechoed, as his advertising columns still show. He was settled in life; his salary was seven hundred and eighty dollars, and was to be a thousand and forty; he was actively planning for future work, and plainly contemplated a long residence in the city; and yet in a few months he was again a wanderer. The first number of the

[1] Poe to Kennedy, Ingram, i. 140.

magazine for 1837 announced that, "Mr. Poe's attention being called in another direction, he will decline, with the present number, the editorial duties of the 'Messenger;'" and on a later page Mr. White added that the resignation had taken effect January 3, but would not prevent Poe's contributing articles from time to time. In this number, nearly one third of the matter, about thirty-five octavo pages, was by Poe, but up to this date he had published no original tale since the previous April, and no poem since August; of criticism, however, there was usually no lack. It is more significant that the October issue was delayed by the illness of both editor and publisher, and the November issue by a press of business, while in the latter there is a very marked shrinking of the space devoted to reviews. Some light is thrown upon the matter by the following undated letter: —

MY DEAR EDGAR: I cannot address you in such language as this occasion and my feelings demand: I must be content to speak to you in my plain way. That you are sincere in all your promises I firmly believe. But when you once again tread these streets, I have my fears that your resolutions will fail and that you will again drink till your senses are lost. If you rely on your strength you are gone. Unless you look to your Maker for help you will not be safe. How much I regretted parting from you is known to Him only and myself. I had become attached to you; I am still; and I would willingly say return, did not a knowledge of your past life make me dread a speedy renewal of our separation. If you would make yourself contented with quarters in my house, or with any other private family, where liquor is not used, I should think there was some hope for you. But if you go to a tavern or to any place where it is used at table, you are not safe. You have fine talents, Edgar, and you ought to have them respected, as well as yourself. Learn to respect yourself, and you will soon find that you are respected. Separate yourself from the bottle, and from bottle companions, forever. Tell me if you can and will do so. If you again become an assistant in my office, it must be understood that all engagements on my part cease the moment you get drunk. I am your true friend.   T. W. W.[1]

The circumstance to which this note refers evidently belongs to an early period in Poe's editorship and was antecedent to his marriage. It has been suggested that the direct cause of Poe's resignation was Mr. White's declining to allow him higher wages or a share in the profits of the magazine; but both the demand and the refusal are mere suppositions. It is possible that his head was turned by his rapid and brilliant success, and he was the less solicitous to retain his post, particularly if, as has been asserted,[2] he had received an invitation from Dr. Francis L. Hawks, a North Carolina divine settled in New York city, to contribute to the newly projected "New York Review." But when it is recollected that Mr. White was Poe's attached

[1] Griswold, xxx.   [2] Hirst.

friend, and must have required on business grounds very strong reasons to make him part with the editor who had proved his capacity by making the "Messenger" the good investment it was, to a candid mind it seems more probable that the extraordinary effects of Poe's fits of intoxication, however infrequent, the irregularity they caused at the time and the exhaustion they left behind, furnished the real ground for Mr. White's determination to let his protégé go. Mr. Kennedy, who should have known the facts, writes in reference to this incident of Poe's life, "He was irregular, eccentric, and querulous, and soon gave up his place."[1] Poe himself afterwards confessed, as will be seen, that at Richmond he gave way at long intervals to temptation, and after each excess was invariably confined to his bed for some days. The only contemporary reference by him to this matter occurs in a business letter, in which, although it was written six days after his resignation went into effect, he accepts an article from a West Point classmate without any hint that he had ceased to be the editor of the magazine, except that he begs pardon for delay because of "ill health and a weight of various and harassing business."[2] These facts all go to support the view that Mr. White, after exercising forbearance for a while, at last refused to yield to Poe's penitence, and insisted on a separation, which, however,

[1] *Life of John Pendleton Kennedy*, p. 376.
[2] Poe to Allan B. Magruder, January 9, 1837. MS.

was not suddenly or violently effected. The two parted friends, and Mr. White continued throughout life to speak of Poe with great kindness and warm feeling. When the matter was settled Poe wrote to his old friend Wilmer, who was starving in Baltimore, that if he would come to Richmond the position would be given to him.[1] This Wilmer was unable to do, and it fell to the lot of some other editor to wonder why Poe, who soon left the city, furnished no more installments of his serial narrative, "Arthur Gordon Pym," which had just been begun in the "Messenger."

[1] *Our Press Gang,* p. 40.

CHAPTER V.

IN PHILADELPHIA.

On leaving Richmond Poe made his way with his family by slow stages through Baltimore and Philadelphia to New York, where he took up his residence at 113½ Carmine Street. If he had gone there with the expectation of obtaining literary employment from the editor of the "New York Review," he was soon undeceived. The first number of that magazine had appeared in March, but the financial panic that then swept over the country made the enterprise more difficult and hazardous, and the second issue was delayed until October. In this was a notice by Poe of Stephens' "Travels in Arabia Petræa," prepared at an earlier time and now rewritten. The article, which was attributed to Secretary Cass, is a skillful compilation, by open extract and secret paraphrase, from the book under review and Keith's lately published work on Prophecy; it is written in a very orthodox vein, but its main point is a criticism of that doctor's interpretation of a few verses in Isaiah and Ezekiel respecting Idumæa, and turns on a rendering from the Hebrew about which Poe could have had no original knowledge. Of this passage, probably the most learned in appearance that he ever wrote, Poe was proud, and he reprinted it at every favorable opportunity throughout his life. The scholarship, whoever furnished it, was sound, and in later editions of Keith the objectional paragraphs are omitted. So far as is known Poe did not again contribute to the theological quarterly.

He gave his attention during this winter principally to the "Narrative of Arthur Gordon Pym,"[1] which was announced by the Harpers in May, 1838, and was published at the end of July. Tales of the sea, under the influence of Cooper and Marryatt, were then at the height of their popularity, and many grew up and withered in a day. In selecting his subject, however, Poe was not merely adopting the literary fashion, but with the business adroitness of the born magazinist he was trading on the momentary curiosity of the public, which was highly interested in Antarctic explorations in con-

[1] *The Narrative of Arthur Gordon Pym, of Nantucket:* comprising the Details of a Mutiny and Atrocious Butchery on board the American Brig Grampus, on her Way to the South Seas — with an Account of the Recapture of the Vessel by the Survivors; their Shipwreck, and subsequent Horrible Sufferings from Famine; their Deliverance by means of the British Schooner Jane Gray; the brief Cruise of this latter Vessel in the Antarctic Ocean; her Capture, and the Massacre of her Crew among a Group of Islands in the 84th parallel of Southern latitude; together with the incredible Adventures and Discoveries still further South, to which that distressing Calamity gave rise. 12mo, pp. 198. New York: Harper & Brothers, 1838.

sequence of the expedition then fitting out under the auspices of the government. Poe, who was acquainted with the chief projector, J. N. Reynolds, had found some attraction in the scheme from the first. He had reviewed the Congressional report on the matter and twice written editorially about it while still editor of the "Messenger." In this way his attention was originally drawn to the subject, and in course of time the new book of travels was published, apparently on the recommendation of Mr. Paulding.[1]

The narrative is circumstantial and might well seem plausible to the unreflecting and credulous, although there are a few tell-tale slips, as where in the fifth chapter Augustus, who died on the voyage, is said to have revealed some matters to Arthur only in later years. Its credibility, however, is not so strange, nor the realistic art so ingenious, as might be thought, since portions of it are either suggested from other lately printed books, such as Irving's "Astoria," or directly compiled (the detailed account of the South Seas is taken almost textually from Morell's "Voyages"[2]) by the easy process of close paraphrase. What is peculiar to the book is its accumulation of blood-curdling incidents. All the horrors of the deep are brought in

[1] Hirst.

[2] *Narrative of Four Voyages to the South Seas and Pacific,* 1822–1831. By Benjamin Morell. New York, 1832. Pp. 183 *et seq.*

and huddled up together; the entombment of Arthur in the hold, where he suffers everything possible to his situation, from starvation to an attack by a mad dog, the butchery of the mutineers, the sickening riot, the desperate fight between the two factions on board, poison, shipwreck, cannibalism among friends, make the staple of the first part of Pym's adventures; some portions, such as the disguise of Pym as a putrescent corpse, the ship of carrion men with the feeding gull, or the details of Augustus's death, are so revoltingly horrible, so merely physically disgusting, that one can hardly understand how even Poe could endure to suggest or develop them. Death in every fearful form is the constant theme; even after the ship reaches the Southern regions the author diversifies his geographical and botanical extracts only by the apprehension of living inhumation, or the analysis of the sensation of falling down a precipice, or wholesale murder. Poe's touch is noticeable here and there throughout, it is true, but he does not show the distinctive subtlety, force, and fire of his genius until the very end, and then only in a way to discredit the plausibility he had previously aimed at. When the finely imagined isle of Tsalal comes in view, the real tale in its original part begins, and from that point the keeping and gradation of the narrative is exquisite, while a wonderful interest is afforded by the slight intimation and gradual revelation of the white country to the South. The caverns of the hieroglyphs are suggested by the Sinaitic written mountains; but after the voyagers leave the island and are drawn on toward the pole, the startling scenery, by which expectation is raised to the highest pitch without loss of vagueness, forms one of his most original and powerful landscapes.

The volume was noticed by the press, but had little success in this country, and the author, of course, derived no profit from its reprint by Putnam in England, where the country public are said to have been hoaxed by it. The only income of the family at this time seems to have been derived from Mrs. Clemm's keeping boarders, one of whom, Mr. William Gowans, a bookseller, declares that for the eight months or more during which he lived with the family he never saw Poe otherwise than sober, courteous, and gentlemanly.[1] Mrs. Clemm's earnings seem to have been no more than sufficient, since Poe, when in the summer he decided to remove to Philadelphia, was forced to borrow money.

Thither he went in midsummer, but apparently not without encouragement, since in a letter of September 4, to his old acquaintance, Brooks, he declines to write an article upon Irving on the ground that he has "two engagements which it would be ruinous to neglect." [2] This correspondence was probably begun by Poe on hearing that

[1] *Gowans' Sale Catalogue*, No. 28, 1870, p. 11.
[2] Poe to Brooks, Didier, p. 65.

Brooks had bought Fairfield's review, "The North American Quarterly Magazine" of Baltimore, and was to continue it as a monthly under the name of the "American Museum of Literature and the Arts." To these he had already contributed "Ligeia," composed probably in the past summer, which appeared in the first number, in September, and was followed by the satirical extravaganza "The Signora Psyche Zenobia — The Scythe of Time" ("How to write a Blackwood Article" and "A Predicament") in December, two pages of "Literary Small Talk" in January, as much more in February, and the poem "The Haunted Palace" in April; in the fall he had also sent for the "Baltimore Book," an annual edited by Carpenter and Arthur, "Siope" ("Silence"), a fine piece of imaginative prose which was saved from the waste basket by the intercession of Brooks. For these he received very little pay, — not more than five or ten dollars an article, if anything at all.

The mention which Poe made of engagements at Philadelphia refers probably to his text-book of Conchology, upon which he was employed during the winter. This volume[1] has given rise to so

[1] *The Conchologist's First Book: or, a System of Testaceous Malacology*, arranged expressly for the use of schools, in which the animals, according to Cuvier, are given with the shells, a great number of new species added, and the whole brought up, as accurately as possible, to the present condition of the science. By Edgar A. Poe. With illustrations of two hundred and fifteen shells, presenting a correct type of each genus. Philadelphia: published

much discussion that it must receive more notice than it would otherwise deserve. It was charged in his lifetime that the work was a simple reprint of an English book, Captain Thomas Brown's "Conchology," which Poe had the effrontery to copyright in this country as his own. He indignantly denied the accusation, and said: —

"I wrote the Preface and Introduction, and translated from Cuvier the accounts of the animals, &c. *All school-books are necessarily made in a similar way.*"[1]

What Poe's understanding was of the manner in which authors of school-books use their authorities may be seen from his own words: —

"It is the practice of quacks to paraphrase page after page, rearranging the order of paragraphs, making a slight alteration in point of fact here and there, but preserving the spirit of the whole, its information, erudition, etc., etc., while everything is so completely *rewritten* as to leave no room for a direct charge of plagiarism; and this is considered and lauded as originality. Now, he who, in availing himself of the labors of his predecessors (and it is clear that all scholars *must* avail themselves of such labors) — he who shall copy *verbatim* the passages to be desired, without attempt at palming off their spirit as original with himself, is certainly no plagiarist, even if he fail to make *direct* acknowledgment of indebted-

for the author, by Haswell, Barrington & Haswell, and for sale by the principal booksellers in the United States. 1839. 12mo, pp. 156.

[1] Poe to ———, Ingram, i. 168.

ness, — is unquestionably *less* of the plagiarist than the disingenuous and contemptible quack who wriggles himself, as above explained, into a reputation for originality, a reputation quite out of place in a case of this kind — the public, of course, never caring a straw whether he be original or not."[1]

In this passage Poe wrote from experience; for in the parts of the "Conchologist's First Book" which he claims as his own both methods are pursued. The first is illustrated by the "Introduction," (pp. 3-8), which is a close paraphrase from Brown's[2] volume, the thoughts being identical in both, their sequence similar, and the authorities quoted the same. The second is illustrated by the plates, which are copied from Brown, and by the "Explanation of the Parts of Shells" (pp. 9-20), which is *verbatim* from the same source, and the "classification," which is reprinted from "Wyatt's Conchology,"[3] a large and expensive volume published the preceding year, to which Poe acknowledges his obligations in his preface. In the body of the work,

[1] *Works*, ii. 46.

[2] *The Conchologist's Text-Book.* Embracing the arrangements of Lamarck and Linnæus, with a glossary of technical terms. By Captain Thomas Brown, Fellow, etc., etc. Illustrated by 19 engravings on steel. Fourth edition. Glasgow: Archibald Fullarton & Co. 1837.

[3] *A Manual of Conchology according to the System laid down by Lamarck, with the Late Improvements of De Blainville. Exemplified and arranged for the Use of Students.* By Thomas Wyatt, M. A. Illustrated by 36 plates, etc., etc. New York: Harper & Brothers. 1838.

the order, the nomenclature, and the descriptions of the shells are a paraphrase of Wyatt, at first close, but as the writer grew more deft at the phraseology more free ; and the description of the animals is, as Poe stated, translated from Cuvier. The volume concludes with an original glossary and an index from Wyatt.

These being the facts as they are shown by a direct comparison of all the books involved, there can be no doubt that the real state of the case is given by Professor John G. Anthony, of Harvard College, who received his information from Wyatt. The latter said that as his work of the previous year proved too expensive for the public, and as the Harpers refused to bring it out in a cheaper form, it was determined to publish a new book which should be sufficiently different from the former to escape any suit for the infringement of copyright ; and Poe was selected to father it.[1] This is supported by the fact that Wyatt, who went about lecturing on the subject, carried the volume with him for sale. It was copyrighted in Poe's name, and appeared about April, 1839, when it was favorably noticed by the press.[2] The most that can be said for Poe is that he shared the responsibility with others, unless, indeed, some one should be

[1] Professor John G. Anthony to John Parker, June 22, 1875. MS.

[2] *Saturday Evening Chronicle and Mirror of the Times*, Philadelphia, April 27, 1839.

found with sufficient hardihood to maintain that Poe was ignorant of the true character of the book to which he put his name. He has been credited, too, with a translation and digest of Lemonnier's "Natural History," which was published the same spring under Wyatt's name; but there is no indication that he had any hand in this work except his own statement, in reviewing it, that he spoke "from personal knowledge, and the closest inspection and collation."[1]

While this volume was in preparation Poe had begun to establish some connection with the city press, perhaps by the assistance of Wilmer, who was now pursuing his checkered journalistic career in Philadelphia, and on May 8 he published the grotesque sketch of "The Devil in the Belfry," in the "Saturday Evening Chronicle." In one way and another he made his name known at least locally, and found work to do, however humble and ill paid. One E. Burke Fisher, an old contributor to the "Messenger," who in May of this year had ventured with another sanguine man, Mr. W. Whitney, to start a magazine, "The Literary Examiner and Western Monthly Review," at Pittsburg, then at the extreme confines of the American literary world, made him an offer of four dollars a page for critical reviews; but as Fisher published the single article which he received editorially, and with emendations of his own, it led only to Poe's

[1] *Burton's Gentleman's Magazine*, v. 62 (July, 1839)

declaring that "no greater scamp ever lived," [1] and congratulating himself that the magazine died the next month without circulating its fourth number. He took the insult probably with a more cheerful if not a higher spirit because he had already obtained permanent employment and a fresh opportunity to distinguish himself as an editor.

In July, 1837, William Evans Burton, an English comedian who was ambitious of winning literary as well as histrionic fame in his adopted country, had launched "The Gentleman's Magazine" in the very darkest period of the financial depression, and with singular felicity he had succeeded in his venture. At first this periodical, which he both owned and edited, was characterized by the lightest of stories and the most sluggish of poems; it was padded with clippings, translations, and the usual *et cœtera* of its kind, including the scrappy reviews, made principally by the scissors, that then went under the name of criticism; but Burton devoted himself to developing local talent, and the Philadelphia editors, novelists, and poetasters, male and female, stood by their patron. The fourth volume began, in 1839, with golden promises of better printing, elegant engravings, and contributions from a long list of writers, in which, beside the names of Leigh Hunt, Douglas Jerrold, and James Montgomery, whose wares were presumably stolen, figured the patronymics of thirty-two native au-

[1] Poe to J. E. Snodgrass, July 12, 1841. MS. copy.

thors, for the most part of Philadelphian or Southern extraction, now all alike impartially forgotten. Poe's friends, Wilmer and Brooks, were among them, but he himself was not mentioned. Once indeed, in the previous September, he had come under the notice of the magazine, but only anonymously as the author of " Arthur Gordon Pym," in which capacity he had been flippantly treated. There is no evidence, and not the least likelihood, that he wrote anything for Burton until July, when his name was printed in conjunction with the former's as associate editor of the periodical whose variable title was then " Burton's Gentleman's Magazine and American Monthly Review."

The paucity of Poe's early contributions goes to confirm this view. In the first number he printed nothing of his own except some old poems and a few brief book notices; and at the close of the year the only original work done by him exclusively for " Burton's," besides numerous but entirely perfunctory reviews, consisted of one sonnet, conjecturally his, though never afterwards acknowledged, and three tales, " The Man that was Used Up," "The Fall of the House of Usher," and "The Conversation of Eiros and Charmion." " William Wilson" was reprinted from "The Gift" for 1840, and " Morella " from the " Tales of the Grotesque and Arabesque,".[1] published at the end of the year.

[1] *Tales of the Grotesque and Arabesque.* By Edgar A. Poe. In two volumes. Philadelphia: Lea & Blanchard. 1840. 16mo.

This collection of Poe's stories was in two volumes, and included all those thus far mentioned, and in addition the grotesque "Von Jung" and "Why the Little Frenchman wears his Hand in a Sling," making twenty-five in all. The publishers, Lea & Blanchard, with whom he had previously had some slight correspondence in 1836 in regard to some rejected manuscripts, engaged, September 28, 1839, to print an edition of 750 copies, on condition that Poe should have the copyright and a few copies (afterwards limited to twenty) for distribution among his friends, and they should have the profits. When the volume was nearly ready Poe endeavored to obtain better terms, and in reply received the following letter, which may account for his professed indifference at a later time regarding the fate of the tales: —

November 20, 1839.

EDGAR A. POE, — We have your note of to-day. The copyright of the Tales would be of no value to us; when we undertook their publication, it was solely

The work was copyrighted in 1839, and was dedicated to Colonel William Drayton. Vol. i. (pp. 243) contained a preface and fourteen tales, that is, Morella, Lionizing, William Wilson, The Man that was Used Up, The Fall of the House of Usher, The Duc De L'Omelette, MS. Found in a Bottle, Bon-Bon, Shadow, The Devil in the Belfry, Ligeia, King Pest, The Signora Zenobia (How to write a Blackwood Article), The Scythe of Time (A Predicament). Vol. ii. (pp. 228) contained Epimanes, Siope, Hans Pfaall, A Tale of Jerusalem, Von Jung, Loss of Breath, Metzengerstein, Berenice, Why the Little Frenchman wears his Hand in a Sling, The Conversation of Eiros and Charmion. Appendix.

to oblige you and not with any view to profit, and on this ground it was urged by you. We should not therefore be now called upon or expected to purchase the copyright when we have no expectation of realizing the Capital placed in the volumes. If the offer to publish was now before us we should certainly decline it, and would feel obliged if you knew and would urge some one to relieve us from the publication at cost, or even at a small abatement.[1]

The volumes appeared early in December, and were widely and favorably noticed by the city press and in New York. The sale, however, was not large, and after Poe's own copies were dispatched he broke off intercourse with the firm for some time.

Three of these reprinted stories deserve some further notice. Two of them, "Ligeia" and "The Fall of the House of Usher," mark the highest reach of the romantic element in Poe's genius, and for the first time exhibit his artistic powers in full development and under easy command. He had matured in the six years since he penned his first story (he was now thirty), but his growth had been within singularly well-defined limits; his mind pursued the strong attraction that fascinated him in that haunted borderland upon the verge but not beyond the sphere of credibility, as the magnet obeys the pole; but this absorption of his imagination in the preternatural was not more extraordinary than the monotony of the themes that exercised

[1] Letter-Book of Lea & Blanchard.

it. In plot "Ligeia" is the same as "Morella," and "The Fall of the House of Usher" the same as "Berenice;" in each a single dramatic event had gathered about it in Poe's mind rich accretions of fancy, thought, and suggestiveness, but practically there was no change except in treatment, — in the art by which the effect originally sought was secured more finely, and in an intenser and more elemental form. In all his best work, however, Poe not only told a story, he also developed an idea, and his later renderings of early conceptions are markedly characterized by an increase in this suggested, or, as he designated it, mystic, meaning.

In "Ligeia," which he regarded as his finest tale, he re-wrote "Morella," but for much of its peculiar power he went back to the sources of his youngest inspiration. In "Al Aaraaf" he had framed out of the breath of the night-wind and the idea of the harmony of universal nature a fairy creature, —

"Ligeia, Ligeia, my beautiful one!"

Now by a finer touch he incarnated the motions of the breeze and the musical voices of nature in the form of a woman: but the Lady Ligeia has still no human quality; her aspirations, her thoughts and capabilities, are those of a spirit; the very beam and glitter and silence of her ineffable eyes belong to the visionary world. She is, in fact, the maiden of Poe's dream, the Eidolon he served, the air-woven divinity in which he believed; for he had the true myth-making faculty, the power to make his senses aver what his imagination perceived. In revealing through "Ligeia" the awful might of the soul in the victory of its will over death and in the eternity of its love, Poe worked in the very element of his reverie, in the liberty of a world as as he would have it. Upon this story he lavished all his poetic, inventive, and literary skill, and at last perfected an exquisitely conceived work, and made it, within its own laws, as faultless as humanity can fashion. He did not once lapse into the crude or repulsive; he blended the material elements of the legend, the mere circumstance and decoration of the scene, like married notes of a sensuous accompaniment, and modulated them with minute and delicate care to chime with the weird suggestions of the things above nature, until all unites and vanishes in an impression on the spirit, — in an intimation of the dark possibilities that lie hidden in the eternal secret, adumbrated in the startling event when the raven hair of Ligeia streams down beneath the serpentine flames of the writhing censer, and her eyes open full on her lost lover, as they stand embosomed within the wind-swayed golden hangings whereon the ghastly and sable phantasmagoria keeps up its antic and ceaseless dance. Without striving to unwind the mazes of the spell that confuses the reader into momentary belief in the incredible, one cannot but note the marvelous certainty with which Poe passes from vaguely suggestive and slightly unusual mutations of the senses, and advances by imperceptible gradations to accustom the mind to increasingly strange and complex changes, incessant and seemingly lawless variations, until one is fairly bewildered into accepting the final impossible transformation of the immortal into mortality as merely the final phase of the restless movement in all, and afterwards, on returning to the solid world, can scarcely tell where he overstepped the boundaries of reality.

As in "Ligeia" the idea of change is elaborated, so in "The Fall of the House of Usher" the intellectual theme is fear. For the purposes of this story Poe used again the plot of "Berenice," but so purified and developed in its accidents as to be hardly recognizable. Not a few would rank this tale more high than "Ligeia;" for, if that be more distinguished by ideality, this is more excellent in the second virtue in Poe's scale, unity of design. In artistic construction, it does not come short of absolute perfection. The adaptation of the related parts and their union in the total effect are a triumph of literary craft; the intricate details, as it were mellowing and reflecting one ground tone, have the definiteness and precision of inlaid mosaic, or, like premonitions and echoes of the theme in music, they are so exactly calculated as to secure their end with the certainty of harmonic law itself. The sombre landscape whose hues Poe alone knew the secret of; the subtle yet not overwrought sympathy between the mansion and the race that had reared it; the looks, traits, and pursuits of Usher, its representative; and the at first scarce-felt presence of Madeline, his worn sister, — all is like a narrowing and ever-intensifying force drawing in to some unknown point; and when this is reached, in the bright copper-sheathed vault in which Madeline is entombed, and the mind, after that midnight scene, expands and breathes freer air, a hundred obscure intimations, each slight in itself, startle and enchain it, until, slowly as obscurity takes shape in a glimmer of light, Usher's dread discloses itself in its concrete and fearful fulfillment, and at once, by the brief and sudden stroke of death, house, race, and all sink into the black tarn where its glassy image had so long built a shadowy reality.

Where every syllable tells, it is folly to attempt an analysis of the workmanship. By way of illustration, however, it may be well to remark on the mode in which the mind is prepared for the coming of Madeline, and made almost to share Usher's diseased acuteness of hearing, by the legendary tale, with its powerful and exclusive appeal to the senses; or to observe such a slight touch as the small picture painted by Usher, — the interior of a long rectangular tunnel, deep in the earth, with low, smooth walls, closed and without a torch, yet flooded with intense rays, — so clearly prophetic of Madeline's vault, gleaming with metallic lustre, of which, too, some reminiscence still survives in the mind when the same unnatural luminous exhalation glows from the under-surface of the storm clouds that press upon the turrets of the trembling house before its fall. Never has the impression of total destruction, of absolute and irremediable ruin, been more strongly given; had the mansion remained, it would seem as if the extinction of Usher had been incomplete. Doom rests upon all things within the shadow of those walls; it is felt to be impending; and therefore, Poe, identifying himself with his reader, places the sure seal of truth on the illusion as he exclaims, "From that chamber and from that mansion I fled aghast." The mind is already upon the recoil as it turns to view the accomplished fatality.

These two tales deserve more attention in that they are in Poe's prose what "The Raven" and "Ulalume" are in his poetry, the richest of his imaginative work. On them he expended his spirit. There had been no such art before in America; but, like Hawthorne, he had to wait for any adequate recognition of his genius. His work in this kind was done; it could be left, safe as the diamond.

In "William Wilson" he opened a new vein. It is the first of his studies of the springs of terror in conscience. The idea itself which is developed in the story, the conception of a double dogging one's steps and thwarting one's evil designs, is an old fancy [1] of men that has taken many shapes

[1] It has been suggested (Ingram and Stoddard) that this tale

since Zoroaster saw his phantom in the garden. The psychological element in it is less insisted on than is usual in Poe's finest work, and it consequently lacks the intensity and spiritual power of his later sketches on similar subjects. It has a peculiar interest as containing an autobiographical account of his school-days in England, but in his own life there was little to serve as a basis for other portions of the narrative.

Poe had already formed the habit, which no author ever practiced so flagrantly, of republishing old material slightly if at all revised. With the exception of the fine sonnet entitled "Silence," all his poetic contributions to "Burton's" were of this sort; the 1829 edition of his poems afforded "Spirits of the Dead,"[1] "Fairyland,"[2] and "To the River ——,"[2] and the "Messenger" yielded "To Ianthe in Heaven" and "To ——,"[1] the stanzas originally addressed to Eliza White. At the beginning of the New Year he applied the same con-

---

was from a rare drama by Calderon, *El Embozado* or *El Capotado*, mentioned by Medwin to Irving, and vainly sought for by the latter in Spanish libraries. (*Irving's Life and Letters*, ii. 232; iv. 70-72.) Medwin undoubtedly had the plot from Shelley. The reference is plainly to *El Purgatorio de San Patricio*, a favorite of Shelley's (from which he took a passage of *The Cenci*), in which Un Hombre Embozado is a character. Poe read Medwin's *Shelley;* but it is extremely unlikely that he ever saw the drama in question, nor is there any reason to seek so far for his knowledge of a superstitious idea common to literature.

[1] Unsigned.
[2] Signed "P."

venient aid to the department of criticism, which had hitherto been very feebly conducted, although he had found opportunity to reproach Longfellow for using so crudely, in "Hyperion," material capable of being highly wrought by art, and had praised Fouqué's "Undine" with delightful appreciation. In the January issue Moore's "Alciphron" drew from him one of those partial reviews that seem to invalidate the usefulness of any criticism of contemporaries, and in piecing it out he availed himself of his former remarks on Drake and Marvell in the "Messenger," but openly under the form of self-quotation. In a mediocre notice of Bryant, somewhat later, he again had recourse to the old files, and in other insignificant criticisms he is found airing the bastard Hebrew learning of his article in the "New York Review," and even enumerating once more the storehouses of literary odds and ends, including the mythical memoirs of "Suard and André." The most noticeable article is that review of Longfellow's "Voices of the Night," in which he first urged against the New England poet the charge of plagiarism. He instanced in particular Tennyson's "The Death of the Old Year" as the source of "The Midnight Mass for the Dying Year." This he characterized as belonging "to the most barbarous class of literary robbery; that class in which, while the words of the wronged author are avoided, his most intangible, and therefore his least defensible and least reclaimable property, is purloined." [1] In other ways than such book-reviewing as this Poe's mind was also unprofitably employed. A satirical sketch, "Peter Pendulum, the Business Man," and the first of his articles respecting decoration, "The Philosophy of Furniture," were his only signed contributions, for the mere plate or sporting articles may be neglected.

In each number, however, from January to June appeared an installment of his anonymous work, "The Journal of Julius Rodman, Being an Account of the First Passage across the Rocky Mountains of North America ever achieved by Civilized Man." This narrative is constructed, like that of "Arthur Gordon Pym," so as to win credence by circumstantial detail and an affected air of plainness, and Poe would probably have concluded it similarly with weird marvels of nature. Julius Rodman was the son of an Englishman who had settled in Kentucky. Being left alone by his father's death, he started in his twenty-sixth year professedly on a trapping expedition up the Missouri River, and pushing on for mere adventure crossed the Rocky Mountains in northern regions in 1792, but on returning to Virginia, after three years' absence, never conversed respecting his journey, and took great pains to secrete his diary. Unfortunately, although the characters of the exploring party are much more carefully selected than was the case in

[1] *Burton's Gentleman's Magazine*, vi. 102–103 (February, 1840).

"Arthur Gordon Pym," Poe conducted the travelers only to the head waters of the Missouri. The description of the trip, in which he followed very closely the obvious authorities, such as Sir Alexander Mackenzie, Lewis and Clarke, Pike, and Irving, is enlivened only by an attack on the Sioux, the sight of a beaver dam, and a hand-to-hand conflict with a bear. As before, too, he was led to his subject by the public interest which was now especially directed to the exploration of the West. The work as a whole bears no relation to his genius, except in a single passage which contains a faint suggestion of the Valley of the Many-Colored Grass in "Eleonora."

With the June installment of the "Journal" Poe's contributions to the magazine ceased, and at the same time his engagement with Burton abruptly terminated. There was evidently a serious quarrel between the two editors, but the exact truth regarding it can only be inferred. Poe asserted that Burton had acted dishonorably in advertising prizes for contributions which he never intended to pay, and that this was the ground of his own resignation; Burton, on his side, circulated scandalous reports in regard to Poe's habits and actions, and described these as the cause of the trouble. It will be best to confine attention to the documentary evidence, an important part of which is contained in Poe's letters to Dr. J. E. Snodgrass, of Baltimore, who had been Brooks's associate on the "Museum," and was afterwards known as an early abolitionist in that city. This correspondence, which began in 1839 with a request from Poe that his friend would see that a puff of himself in a St. Louis paper was reprinted and the last numbers of "Burton's" noticed by the Baltimore press, extends over three years, and relates mainly to the minor literary affairs of the two, but incidentally some light is thrown on more important matters, and among them on this disagreement between Poe and Burton. In reply to a question regarding the prizes offered by Burton, Poe writes, December 19, 1839, as follows: —

"Touching the Premiums. The Advertisement respecting them was written by Mr. Burton, and is not I think as explicit as might [be]. I can give you no information about their desig[nation furth]er than is shown in the advertisement itself. The tr[uth is,] I object, *in toto*, to the whole scheme — but merely follow[ed in] Mr. B.'s wake upon such matters of business."[1]

Dr. Snodgrass sent on a contribution, but had difficulty in recovering possession of it. Just after the quarrel, Poe wrote to him again, in answer to what seems to have been a pressing letter, as follows: —

[1] Poe to Snodgrass, December 19, 1839. This, and all subsequent quotations from the Snodgrass correspondence (partly published in the New York *Herald* March 27, 1881) not otherwise credited, is from a very careful MS. copy of the originals, made some years since by Dr. William Hand Browne of Baltimore, who annotates on this passage, "MS. burnt and broken. Restorations in brackets."

"Touching your Essay, Burton not only *lies*, but deliberately and wilfully lies; for the last time but one that I saw him I called his attention to the MS. which was then at the top of a pile of other MSS. sent for premiums, in a drawer of the office desk. The last day I was in the office I saw the Essay in the same position, and am perfectly sure it is there still. You know it is a peculiar looking MS. and I could not mistake it. In saying it was not in his possession his sole design was to vex you, and through you myself. Were I in your place I would take some summary method of dealing with the scoundrel, whose infamous line of conduct in regard to this whole Premium scheme merits, and shall receive exposure. I am firmly convinced that it was never his intention to pay one dollar of the money offered; and indeed his plain intimations to that effect, made to me personally and directly, were the immediate reason of my cutting the connexion so abruptly as I did. If you could, in any way, spare the time to come on to Philadelphia, I think I could put you in the way of detecting this villain in his rascality. I would go down with you to the office, open the drawer in his presence, and take the MS. from beneath his very nose. I think this would be a good deed done, and would act as a caution to such literary swindlers in future. What think you of this plan? Will you come on? Write immediately — in reply." [1]

In support of Burton's charge of Poe's habits of drinking at this time, nothing has been brought forward except an undated letter from himself to Poe: —

[1] Poe to Snodgrass, June 17, 1840. MS. copy.

IN PHILADELPHIA. 129

"I am sorry you have thought it necessary to send me such a letter. Your troubles have given a morbid tone to your feelings which it is your duty to discourage. I myself have been as severely handled by the world as you can possibly have been, but my sufferings have not tinged my mind with melancholy, nor jaundiced my views of society. You must rouse your energies, and if care assail you, conquer it. I will gladly overlook the past. I hope you will as easily fulfill your pledges for the future. We shall agree very well, though I cannot permit the magazine to be made a vehicle for that sort of severity which you think 'so successful with the mob.' I am truly much less anxious about making a monthly 'sensation' than I am upon the point of fairness. You must, my dear sir, get rid of your avowed ill-feelings toward your brother authors. You see I speak plainly; I cannot do otherwise upon such a subject. You say the people love havoc. I think they love justice. I think you yourself would not have written the article on Dawes, in a more healthy state of mind. I am not trammelled by any vulgar consideration of expediency; I would rather lose money than by such undue severity wound the feelings of a kind-hearted and honorable man. And I am satisfied that Dawes has something of the true fire in him. I regretted your word-catching spirit. But I wander from my design. I accept your proposition to recommence your interrupted avocations upon the *Maga*. Let us meet as if we had not exchanged letters. Use more exercise, write when feelings prompt, and be assured of my friendship. You will soon regain a healthy activity of mind, and laugh at your past vagaries."[1]

[1] Griswold, xxxii.

There is in this letter no statement nor even any implication that the cause of Poe's temporary resignation, of which we know only from this source, was drunkenness. All that is said would be more obviously and naturally explained, both in substance and tone, on the supposition that when Burton refused to print the censorious criticism on Rufus Dawes Poe gave way to his anger, perhaps used high words, and in a moment of pique left his situation; on returning to himself, and under the strong pressure of poverty at home, it is not unlikely that he surprised Burton by one of his self-humiliating and bitter letters, and that Burton wrote to him the foregoing kindly reply. This supposition explains everything that is said, whereas the assumption that Poe had been on a drunken spree is not required by any phrase or sentence, and would fail to explain why the entire letter deals with the subject of Poe's criticism and the temperament out of which it sprang.

Independently of this letter, however, it is plain that Burton did charge Poe with the vicious habit which he would find most difficulty in denying. Dr. Snodgrass heard the story at second hand, and nearly nine months later wrote about it to Poe, who was then editor of " Graham's." The reply is at length and explicit: —

PHILADELPHIA, *April* 1, 1841.

MY DEAR SNODGRASS: — I fear you have been thinking it was not my design to answer your kind letter at all. It is now April Fool's Day, and yours is dated March 8th; but believe me, although, for good reason, I may occasionally postpone my reply to your favors, I am never in danger of forgetting them.

. . . .

In regard to Burton. I feel indebted to you for the kind interest you express; but scarcely know how to reply. My situation is embarrassing. It is impossible, as you say, to notice a buffoon and a felon, as one gentleman would notice another. The law, then, is my only resource. Now, if the truth of a scandal could be admitted in justification — I mean of what the law terms a *scandal* — I would have matters all my own way. I would institute a suit, forthwith, for his personal defamation of myself. He would be unable to prove the truth of his allegations. I could prove their falsity and their malicious intent by witnesses who, seeing me at all hours of every day, would have the best right to speak — I mean Burton's own clerk, Morrell, and the compositors of the printing office. In fact, I could prove the scandal almost by acclamation. I should obtain damages. But, on the other hand, I have never been scrupulous in regard to what I have said of him. I have always told *him* to his face, and everybody else, that I looked upon him as a blackguard and a villain. This is notorious. He would meet me with a cross action. The truth of the allegation — which I could [as] easily prove as he would find it difficult to prove the truth of his own respecting me — would not avail me. The law will not admit, as justification of my calling Billy Burton a scoundrel, that Billy Burton is really such. What then can I do? If I sue, he sues: you see how it is.

At the same time — as I may, after further reflection, be induced to sue, I would take it as an act of kindness — not to say *justice* — on your part, if you would see the gentleman of whom you spoke, and ascertain with accuracy all that may legally avail me; that is to say, what and when were the words used, and whether your friend would be willing for your sake, for my sake, and for the sake of truth, to give evidence if called upon. Will you do this for me?

So far for the matter inasmuch as it concerns Burton. I have now to thank you for your defence of myself, as stated. You are a physician, and I presume no physician can have difficulty in detecting the *drunkard* at a glance. You are, moreover, a literary man, well read in morals. You will never be brought to believe that I could write what I daily write, *as* I write it, were I as this villain would induce those who know me not, to believe. In fine, I pledge you, before God, the solemn word of a gentleman, that I am temperate even to rigor. From the hour in which I first saw this basest of calumniators to the hour in which I retired from his office in uncontrollable disgust at his chicanery, arrogance, ignorance and brutality, *nothing stronger than water ever passed my lips.*

It is, however, due to candor that I inform you upon what foundation he has erected his slanders. At no period of my life was I ever what men call intemperate. I never was in the *habit* of intoxication. I never drunk drams, &c. But, for a brief period, while I resided in Richmond, and edited the *Messenger* I certainly did give way, at long intervals, to the temptation held out on all sides by the spirit of Southern conviviality. My sensitive temperament could not stand an excitement which was an every day matter to my companions. In short, it sometimes happened that I was completely intoxicated. For some days after each excess I was invariably confined to bed. But it is now quite four years since I have abandoned every kind of alcoholic drink — four years, with the exception of a single deviation, which occurred shortly *after* my leaving Burton, and when I was induced to resort to the occasional use of *cider*, with the hope of relieving a nervous attack.

You will thus see, frankly stated, the whole amount of my sin. You will also see the blackness of that heart which could *revive* a slander of this nature. Neither can you fail to perceive how desperate the malignity of the slanderer must be — how resolute he must be to slander, and how slight the grounds upon which he would build up a defamation — since he can find nothing better with which to charge me than an accusation which can be disproved by each and every man with whom I am in the habit of daily intercourse.

I have now only to repeat to you, in general, my solemn assurance that my habits are as far removed from intemperance as the day from the night. My sole drink is water.

Will you do me the kindness to repeat this assurance to such of your own friends as happen to speak of me in your hearing?

I feel that nothing more is requisite, and you will agree with me upon reflection.

Hoping soon to hear from you, I am,
     Yours most cordially,
       EDGAR A. POE.[1]

DR. J. E. SNODGRASS.

[1] Poe to Snodgrass, *Baltimore American*, April, 1881.

Unfortunately, this disclaimer is traversed by a letter from Mr. C. W. Alexander, the publisher of the magazine, to Mr. T. C. Clarke, of Philadelphia. In answer to the question whether Poe's alleged irregularities at that time were such as to interfere with his work, Mr. Alexander writes: —

"The absence of the principal editor on professional duties left the matter frequently in the hands of Mr. Poe, whose unfortunate failing may have occasioned some disappointment in the preparation of a particular article expected from *him*, but never interfering with the regular publication of the "Gentleman's Magazine," as its monthly issue was never interrupted upon any occasion, either from Mr. Poe's deficiency, or from any other cause, during my publication of it, embracing the whole time of Mr. Poe's connection with it. That Mr. Poe had faults seriously detrimental to his own interests, none, of course, will deny. They were, unfortunately, too well known in the literary circles of Philadelphia, were there any disposition to conceal them. But he alone was the sufferer, and not those who received the benefit of his preëminent talents, however irregular his habits or uncertain his contributions may occasionally have been." [1]

It is possible that Mr. Alexander, writing ten years after the event, may have confused his recollections and antedated the intemperance of Poe, which became frequent and notorious during the next year. Were it not for this letter there would

[1] Alexander to Clarke, October 20, 1850, Gill, p. 97.

be no direct evidence that Poe was not, as he claimed to be, a sober man from the time he left Richmond to that of his wife's illness in 1841, and this would agree with Gowan's account of him in New York and with Mrs. Clemm's statement, reported by Mr. R. E. Shapley, of Philadelphia, — "For years I know he did not taste even a glass of wine." To no other period of his mature life are these words applicable. It should be noted, too, that Wilmer, who sometimes met him in Philadelphia, says that during their acquaintance he "did not see him inebriated; no, not in a single instance;"[1] but in his "Recollections" he asserts unqualifiedly that this fault was the cause of all of Poe's differences with his employers. Probably the true cause of the trouble was less Poe's habits than his acts; it was of a business nature, and in the affair each party seems to have had matter for complaint. Burton, who it will be remembered was a comic actor, had got into quarrels with the managers, and he determined to have a theatre of his own; to obtain this he needed funds, and by way of raising them he advertised his magazine for sale without mentioning his intention to Poe. The latter, on his part, arranged to issue a prospectus of a new and rival monthly, "The Penn Magazine," without advising Burton. He had long had a strong ambition to have a magazine of his own. In fact, he was always waiting to find some

[1] *Our Press Gang*, p. 284.

one with capital to embark in the enterprise, and while still on Burton's was constantly uneasy through the indulgence of this hope. In a letter to Snodgrass, written six months before, there occurs a characteristic passage: —

"I have heard, indirectly, that an attempt is to be made by some one of capital in Baltimore, to get up a Magazine. Have you heard anything of it? If you have, will you be kind enough to let me know all about it by *return of mail* — if you can spend the time to oblige me — I am particularly desirous of understanding how the matter stands — who are the parties, &c."[1]

He was now preparing his prospectus, and no doubt hoped that Burton's going out of the trade would help his own prospects. He might fairly expect that in the changes about to take place some of the subscribers to the "Gentleman's" would remain with him, who, as its real editor, had won position and respect, especially with the press of the city, and that they would form a nucleus for the circulation of the "Penn." Whether in fact he did, as was charged by Griswold, obtain transcripts of Burton's subscription-list and other valuable papers, for his own use, remains in doubt. It was an obvious thing for him to do; he was out of humor with Burton, and as he believed that the latter would soon sell he may not have regarded it as a dishonorable proceeding. Undoubtedly Burton looked on Poe's action in advertising his new

[1] Poe to Snodgrass, January 21, 1840. MS. copy.

enterprise at that moment as likely to diminish the selling value of his property; if in addition Poe attempted to secure his subscribers in an underhand way, he would have had cause to be offended, and if he remonstrated Poe may have told him that he "looked upon him as a blackguard and a villain," in the phrases of his letter to Snodgrass. That there is no explicit mention of the charge in the following letter, in which Poe makes his explanation to his employer, counts for nothing in view of the points that mark omissions; but the letter, as edited, proves with sufficient certainty that the "Penn Magazine" was the apple of discord, and it has, besides, interesting bearings as an indication of Poe's daily habits of business, his demeanor and temper.

SIR : — I find myself at leisure this Monday morning, June 1, to notice your very singular letter of Saturday. . . . I have followed the example of Victorine and slept upon the matter, and you shall now hear what I have to say. In the first place, your attempts to bully me excite in my mind scarcely any other sentiment than mirth. When you address me again, preserve, if you can, the dignity of a gentleman. . . . I shall feel myself more at liberty to be explicit. As for the rest, you do me gross injustice; and you know it. As usual, you have wrought yourself into a passion with me on account of some imaginary wrong; for no real injury, or attempt at injury, have you ever received at my hands. As I live, I am utterly unable to say why you are angry, or what true grounds of complaint you have against me. You are a man of impulses; have made yourself, in consequence, some enemies; have been in many respects ill-treated by those whom you had looked upon as friends — and these things have rendered you suspicious. You once wrote in your magazine a sharp critique upon a book of mine — a very silly book — Pym. Had I written a similar criticism upon a book of yours, you feel that you would have been my enemy for life, and you therefore imagine in my bosom a latent hostility towards yourself. This has been a mainspring in your whole conduct towards me since our first acquaintance. It has acted to prevent all cordiality. In a general view of human nature your idea is just — but you will find yourself puzzled in judging me by ordinary motives. Your criticism was essentially correct, and therefore, although severe, it did not occasion in me one solitary emotion either of anger or dislike. But even while I write these words, I am sure you will not believe them. Did I not still think you, in spite of the exceeding littleness of some of your hurried actions, a man of many honorable impulses, I should not now take the trouble to send you this letter. I cannot permit myself to suppose that you would say to me in cool blood what you said in your letter of yesterday. You are, of course, only mistaken, in asserting that I owe you a hundred dollars, and you will rectify the mistake at once when you come to look at your accounts.

Soon after I joined you, you made me an offer of money, and I accepted $20. Upon another occasion, at my request, you sent me enclosed in a letter $30. Of this 30, I repaid 20 within the next fortnight (drawing no salary for that period). I was thus still in your debt

$30, when not long ago I again asked a loan of $30, which you promptly handed to me at your own home. Within the last three weeks, three dollars each week have been retained from my salary, an indignity which I have felt deeply but did not resent. You state the sum retained as $8, but this I believe is through a mistake of Mr. Morrell. My postage bill, at a guess, might be $9 or $10 — and I therefore am indebted to you, upon the whole, in the amount of about $60. More than this sum I shall not pay. You state that you can no longer afford to pay $50 per month for 2 or 3 pp. of MS. Your error here can be shown by reference to the Magazine. During my year with you I have written —

In July   5 pp
" August   9 "
" Sept.   16 "
" Oct.   4 "
" Nov.   5 "
" Dec.   12 "
" Jan.   9 "
" Feb.   12 "
" March   11 "
" April   17 "
" May   14 " + 5 copied — Miss McMichael's MS.
" June   9 " + 3 "   Chandlers.

132 [*sic*]

Dividing this sum by 12, we have an average of 11 pp. per month — not 2 or 3. And this estimate leaves out of question everything in the way of extract or compilation. Nothing is counted but *bonâ fide* composition. 11 pp. at $3 per p. would be $33, at the usual Magazine prices. Deduct this from $50, my monthly salary, and we have left $17 per month, or $4 $\frac{25}{100}$ per week, for the services of proof-reading; general superintendence at the printing office; reading, alteration and preparation of MSS., with compilation of various articles, such as Plate articles, Field sports, &c. Neither has anything been said of my name upon your title page, a small item — you will say — but still something, as you know. Snowden pays his editresses $2 per week each for their names *solely*. Upon the whole, I am not willing to admit that you have greatly overpaid me. That I did not do four times as much as I did for the Magazine was your own fault. At first I wrote long articles, which you deemed inadmissible, and never did I suggest any to which you had not some immediate and decided objection. Of course I grew discouraged, and could feel no interest in the journal.

I am at a loss to know why you call me selfish. If you mean that I borrowed money of you — you know that you offered it, and you know that I am poor. In what instance has any one ever found me selfish? Was there selfishness in the affront I offered Benjamin (whom I respect, and who spoke well of me) because I deemed it a duty not to receive from any one commendation at your expense? . . . I have said that I could not tell why you were angry. Place yourself in my situation and see whether you would not have acted as I have done. You first "enforced," as you say, a deduction of salary: giving me to understand thereby that you thought of parting company. You next spoke disrespectfully of me behind my back — this as an habitual thing — to those whom you supposed your friends, and who punctually retailed me, as a matter of course, every ill-natured word which you uttered. Lastly, you advertised your magazine for sale without saying a word to me about it. I felt no anger at what you did — none in the world. Had I not firmly believed it your design to give up your journal, with a view of attending to the Theatre, I should never have dreamed of attempting one of my own. The opportunity of doing something for myself seemed a good one — (and I was about to be thrown out of business) — and I embraced it. Now I ask you, as a man of honor and as a man of sense — what is there wrong in all this? What have I done at which you have any right to take offence? I can give you no definitive answer (respecting the continuation of Rodman's Journal) until I hear from you again. The charge of $100 I shall not admit for an instant. If you persist in it our intercourse is at an end, and we can each adopt our own measures.

In the meantime, I am,
Yr. Obt. St.,
EDGAR A. POE.[1]

WM. E. BURTON, ESQ.

This letter seems meant to be conciliatory, but if the savageness of Poe's characterization of his old chief, already given, is any sign, it failed of its purpose. Burton suppressed six or seven criticisms still on hand, and wrote and spoke hard words about his former associate. Nor did Poe lag much behind in returning ill-will. Six months later he wrote to Snodgrass: —

[1] Poe to Burton, Ingram, i. 175–179.

"Mr. Burton, that illustrious 'graduate of St. John's College, Cambridge,' is going to the devil with the worst grace in the world, but with a velocity truly astounding. The press here in a body, have given him the cut direct. So be it — suum cuique. We have said quite enough about this genius." [1]

On the whole, the natural inference from all these papers is that the two editors quarreled over some incident connected with the "Penn Magazine," and afterwards, being angry, told their friends all the grievances they had against each other, as their justification.

Burton's road, wherever it lay, did not again cross Poe's. Within two weeks after the rupture, "The Penn Magazine" was publicly [2] announced to appear January 1, 1841, and prospectuses were sent to the press and to private friends. Previous to his quarrel with Burton, Poe contributed to "Alexander's Weekly Messenger," published by the same firm as the "Gentleman's," a series of articles on cryptography, in which he challenged his readers to invent ciphers which he could not interpret. According to his own statement, out of the hundred sent in he read all but one, and that he proved to be an imposture. He probably now wrote further for the same, and possibly for other papers, as he had done on first coming to Philadelphia, and perhaps it was now that he contrib-

[1] Poe to Snodgrass, January 17, 1841. MS. copy.
[2] *Philadelphia Saturday Chronicle*, June 13, 1840.

uted to the "United States Military Magazine,"[1] in which at one time he had articles of considerable length; but no work of his has been traced until the December "Gentleman's," in which he published one of the most striking of the tales of conscience, "The Man of the Crowd." With this number the magazine passed under the control of George R. Graham, editor of a feeble monthly, the "Casket," who had bought out Burton in October, and now merged the two under the name, soon to become famous, of "Graham's Magazine." He was also one of the proprietors of "The Saturday Evening Post," a weekly, in which Poe had been praised with increasing warmth and frequency for the past year. By such means, apparently, Poe and Graham came to a better acquaintance in the fall of 1840. As the winter came on Poe was attacked by an illness of undefined character, but presumably similar to those which continued to occur with increasing frequency until his death. In consequence of this the issue of the "Penn," which was to have taken place January 1, was postponed until March 1. The state of his affairs, as they seemed to himself on recovering his health, is displayed in his correspondence with Snodgrass. He writes, January 17: —

[1] P. S. Duval to the author, August 4, 1884. This magazine was printed in Duval's lithographing establishment, in which Wilmer, in his *Recollections*, says Poe at one time, despairing of literature as a means of support, undertook to learn lithography. Mr. Duval writes that there is no truth whatever in this statement.

"You write to know my prospects with the 'Penn.' They are *glorious*, notwithstanding the world of difficulties under which I labored and labor. My illness (from which I have now entirely recovered), has been, for various reasons, a benefit to my scheme rather than a disadvantage; and, upon the whole, if I do not eminently succeed in this enterprise the fault will be altogether mine own. Still, I am using every exertion to insure success, and, among other manœuvres, I have cut down the bridges behind me. I must now do or die — I mean in a literary sense.

. . . .

"In the literary way I shall endeavor, gradually, (if I cannot effect the purpose at once) to give the Magazine a reputation for the having *no articles but from* the best pens — a somewhat negative merit, you will say. In criticism I will be bold and sternly, absolutely just, with friend and foe. From this purpose nothing shall turn me. I shall aim at *originality* in the body of the work, more than at any other especial quality. I have one or two articles of my own in statu pupillari that would make you stare, at least, on account of the utter oddity of their conception. To carry out the conception is a difficulty which — may be overcome."

That the lack of capital was still a principal obstacle, however, appears from the conclusion of the letter: —

"And now, my dear Snodgrass, will you do me a favor? I have heard some mention of a new magazine to be started in Baltimore by a Virginian & a practical printer. I am *anxious* to know all the details of the project. Can you procure and send me (by return of mail) a Prospectus? If you cannot get one, will you write me all about it— the gentleman's name, &c., &c., &c.?

"I have underscored the word 'anxious' because I really mean what I say, and because, about a fortnight ago, I made to the Hon. N. C. Brooks, A. M. a request just such as I now make to yourself. *He did not reply;* and I, expecting of course the treatment which one gentleman naturally expects from another, have been put to the greatest inconvenience by the daily but fruitless expectation."[1]

On the back of this letter was printed the prospectus of "The Penn Magazine," which forms the basis of Poe's many subsequent notices of a similar kind, and explains the aims and purposes that he continued to cherish as peculiarly his own. It read as follows:—

PROSPECTUS

OF

THE PENN MAGAZINE,

A MONTHLY LITERARY JOURNAL,

To be edited and published in the city of Philadelphia,

By EDGAR A. POE.

TO THE PUBLIC. — Since resigning the conduct of the Southern Literary Messenger, at the commencement of its third year, I have always had in view the establishment of a Magazine which should retain some of the chief features of that journal, abandoning or greatly modifying the rest. Delay, however, has been occasioned by a variety of causes, and not until now have I

[1] Poe to Snodgrass. MS. copy.

found myself at liberty to attempt the execution of the design.

I will be pardoned for speaking more directly of the Messenger. Having in it no proprietary right, my objects too being at variance in many respects with those of its very worthy owner, I found difficulty in stamping upon its pages that *individuality* which I believe essential to the full success of all similar publications. In regard to their permanent influence, it appears to me that a continuous definite character, and a marked certainty of purpose, are requisites of vital importance; and I cannot help believing that these requisites are only attainable when one mind alone has the general direction of the undertaking. Experience has rendered obvious — what might indeed have been demonstrated *a priori* — that in founding a Magazine of my own lies my sole chance of carrying out to completion whatever peculiar intentions I may have entertained.

To those who remember the early days of the Southern periodical in question, it will be scarcely necessary to say that its main feature was a somewhat overdone causticity in its department of Critical Notices of new books. The Penn Magazine will retain this trait of severity insomuch only as the calmest yet sternest sense of justice will permit. Some years since elapsed may have mellowed down the petulance without interfering with the sight (?) of the critic. Most surely they have not yet taught him to read through the medium of a publisher's will, nor convinced him that the interests of letters are unallied with the interests of truth. It shall be the first and chief purpose of the Magazine now proposed to become known as one where may be found at all times, and upon all subjects, an honest and a fearless opinion. It shall be a leading object to assert in precept, and to maintain in practice, the rights, while in effect it demonstrates the advantages, of an absolutely independent criticism; — a criticism self-sustained; guiding itself only by the purest rules of Art; analyzing and urging these rules as it applies them; holding itself aloof from all personal bias; acknowledging no fear save that of outraging the right; yielding no point either to the vanity of the author, or to the assumptions of antique prejudice, or to the involute and anonymous cant of the Quarterlies, or to the arrogance of those organized *cliques* which, hanging on like nightmares upon American literature, manufacture, at the nod of our principal book-sellers, a pseudo-public-opinion by wholesale. These are objects of which no man need be ashamed. They are purposes, moreover, whose novelty at least will give them interest. For assurance that I will fulfill them in the best spirit and to the very letter, I appeal with confidence to those friends, and especially to those Southern friends, who sustained me in the Messenger, where I had but a very partial opportunity of completing my own plans.

In respect to the other characteristics of the Penn Magazine a few words here will suffice.

It will endeavor to support the general interests of the republic of letters, without reference to particular regions — regarding the world at large as the true audience of the author. Beyond the precincts of literature, properly so called, it will leave in better hands the task of instruction upon all matters of *very* grave moment. Its aim chiefly shall be *to please* — and this through means of versatility, originality, and pungency. It may be as well here to observe that nothing said in this Prospectus should be construed into a design of sullying the Magazine with any tincture of the buffoonery, scurrility, or profanity, which are the blemish of some of the most vigorous of the European prints. In all branches of the literary department, the best aid, from the highest and purest sources, is secured.

To the mechanical execution of the work the greatest attention will be given which such a matter can require. In this respect it is proposed to surpass, by very much, the ordinary Magazine style. The form will somewhat resemble that of The Knickerbocker; the paper will be equal to that of The North American Review; pictorial embellishments are promised only in the necessary illustration of the text.

The Penn Magazine will be published in Philadelphia, on the first of each month: and will form, half-yearly, a volume of about 500 pages. The price will be $5 per annum, payable in advance, or upon the receipt of the first number, which will be issued on the first of March, 1841. Letters addressed to the Editor and Proprietor,

EDGAR A. POE.

PHILADELPHIA, *January* 1, 1841.

These purposes and the sanguine hopes of Poe were balked by the coincidence of a good offer from Graham and a financial depression through the country. The "Saturday Evening Post," February 20, 1841, announced that the scheme of the "Penn Magazine" had been suspended, owing to the disturbance in monetary affairs, in which periodicals were always the first to suffer; it was added that its editor had the finest prospects of success, the press, and particularly the South and West, being warm in his cause, and an excellent list of subscribers having been already secured; this "stern, just, and competent critic," it concluded, would now take the editorial chair of "Graham's."

Poe's hand may be clearly seen in the critical department of "Graham's" as early as February, but his responsibility as editor in charge did not begin until the April issue. From that time until June of the next year he contributed to every number, much of what he wrote being of his best work. This period of his authorship is especially distinguished by a remarkable quickening of his powers of analytical reasoning, by virtue of which he struck out a new vein of fiction. The first notable sign of this mental development is in the articles contributed to " Alexander's Weekly Messenger," about January, 1840, while he was still engaged on Burton's magazine, on the subject of cryptography, to which reference has already been made. In July, 1841, he returned to the subject, in "Graham's," and again received and translated several intricate cryptographs. On the first of May previous, when Graham's weekly, the "Saturday Evening Post," appeared in an enlarged and improved form, he gave distinction to the number by an analogous exercise of his analytical powers, — his successful exposure of the plot of " Barnaby Rudge " from the material afforded by the introductory chapters. Dickens is said to have been so surprised as to ask Poe if he were the devil. It was in April, however, in the very first number of his editing, that "Graham's" contained his earliest story in which this interest, the employment of method in disentangling a plot by mere ratiocination, is principally involved. It was "The Murders of the Rue Morgue," perhaps the most famous of his tales. It has been objected that really there is no analysis in unraveling a web woven for that purpose; and, in a sense, this is true. Acute as Poe's penetrative powers were, the ratiocinative tales (with the possible exception of "The Mystery of Marie Roget") do not illustrate them. The primary gift employed in these ingenious narratives is constructiveness; they differ from their predecessors, from "The Fall of the House of Usher" for example, not in the intellectual faculties exercised, but in their aim and conduct. In the earlier group Poe gradually worked up to the *dénoûment* of a highly complicated series of facts and emotions; in the later one, stating only the *dénoûment* of a similar series, he gradually worked back to its origins; in both cases he first constructed the story, but in telling it he reversed in one the method used in the other. The main difference is that in the old process the emotional element counts for more, while in the new one the incidents are necessarily the important part; indeed, they almost absorb attention. That the ratiocinative tales are on a lower level than the imaginative ones hardly needs to be said, since it is so conclusively indicated by the fact that later writers have far surpassed Poe in the complexity of this sort of mechanism, and therefore in the apparent miracle of the solution. They come short of Poe only in the original invention of the plot; that is to say, they fail by defects of imagination in the selection, and of artistic power in the grouping, of their facts, for it would be a mistake to suppose that the interest in "The Murders of the Rue Morgue" is simply the puzzle of detection.

The other tales that appeared during this period are, in the "Post," the insignificant "A Succession of Sundays" ("Three Sundays in a Week"), and in "Graham's" "The Descent into the Maelström," which is to be classed with the "MS. Found in a Bottle," and is the best of its kind; "The Island of the Fay," the earliest of the simple landscape pieces, and a study, as it proved, for "Eleonora;" an arabesque in his old manner, "The Colloquy of Monos and Una," noticeable as the first open expression of dissatisfaction with modern institutions; the two inferior sketches, "Never Bet the Devil your Head," a satire on tales with a moral, and "Life in Death" ("The Oval Portrait"), a variation of an old theme; and, lastly, the fine color study, "The Masque of the Red Death," in which the plot is managed almost exclusively by merely decorative effects.

In nearly all these tales, and particularly in this last one, the constructive genius of their author is most distinctively exercised; they are thus admirable illustrations of his theory as he developed it in his critical writings of this period, and fully reach the high standard of literary art by which he measured the works of others. Poe preferred the form of the short story to that of the novel, for the same reason that he thought brevity an essential in purely poetic composition, because length is inconsistent with a single effect, or, as he termed it, with the unity or totality of interest. Both his aim and his method in narrative prose are succinctly described in his own words : —

"A skilful literary artist has constructed a tale. If wise, he has not fashioned his thoughts to accommodate his incidents; but having conceived, with deliberate care, a certain unique or single *effect* to be wrought out, he then invents such incidents — he then combines such events as may best aid him in establishing this preconceived effect. If his very initial sentence tend not to the outbringing of this effect, then he has failed in his first step. In the whole composition there should be no word written, of which the tendency, direct or indirect, is not to the one preëstablished design. And by such means, with such care and skill, a picture is at length painted which leaves in the mind of him who contemplates it with a kindred art, a sense of the fullest satisfaction. The idea of the tale has been presented unblemished, because undisturbed; and this is an end unattainable by the novel." [1]

[1] *Works,* ii. 197, 198.

In Poe's best tales it is this ideal absolutely realized that has made them immortal.

Of his old poetry he contributed to the "Post" "The Coliseum" and "The Bridal Ballad," and to "Graham's," "To Helen," "Israfel," and "To One Departed," the last two much revised. The bulk of his writing, however, was critical, and consisted of notices of new books. In the course of the fifteen months he passed in review, at greater or less length, and with various degrees of care, works by Bulwer, Dickens, Macaulay, Marryatt, Lever, and James, and, of American authors, Longfellow and Hawthorne, besides others of only local notoriety, such as Brainard, the Davidson Sisters, Seba Smith, Wilmer, and Cornelius Mathews. There were shorter notices of many others, both at home and abroad, contemporary and classic; and in particular there was a concise view of over a hundred native writers in three papers, entitled "Autography," an expansion of similar articles in the "Messenger" for 1836. Without entering in this place on the question of Poe's powers and influence as a critic (and throughout his life, it must always be kept in mind, he was far more distinguished in America as a critic than as either a romancer or a poet), his attitude toward his contemporaries cannot be even momentarily neglected at any stage of his career.

This attitude had not changed since he was editor of the "Messenger." He still remembered his review of "Norman Leslie" as inaugurating the new age in American criticism, and Theodore S. Fay continued to be his favorite example of the bepuffed literary impostor. His general view of our literary affairs at this time was expressed in a review of the scurrilous and filthy satire by his friend Wilmer, "The Quacks of Helicon," in which he had incorporated his article written two years before and revamped by the editor of the "Pittsburg Examiner" in that short-lived periodical: —

"We repeat it: — *it is* the truth which he has spoken; and who shall contradict us? He has said unscrupulously what every reasonable man among us has long known to be 'as true as the Pentateuch' — that, as a literary people, we are one vast perambulating humbug. He has asserted that we are *clique*-ridden; and who does not smile at the obvious truism of that assertion? He maintains that chicanery is, with us, a far surer road than talent to distinction in letters. Who gainsays this? The corrupt nature of our ordinary criticism has become notorious. Its powers have been prostrated by its own arm. The intercourse between critic and publisher, as it now almost universally stands, is comprised either in the paying and pocketing of blackmail, as the price of a simple forbearance, or in a direct system of petty and contemptible bribery, properly so-called — a system even more injurious than the former to the true interests of the public, and more degrading to the buyers and sellers of good opinion, on account of the more positive character of the service here rendered for the consideration received. We laugh at the idea of any denial of our assertions upon this topic; they are infamously true. . . .

"We may even arrive, in time, at that desirable point from which a distinct view of our men of letters may be obtained, and their respective pretensions adjusted, by the standard of rigorous and self-sustaining criticism alone. That their several positions are as yet properly settled; that the posts which a vast number of them now hold are maintained by any better tenure than that of the chicanery upon which we have commented, will be asserted by none but the ignorant, or the parties who have best right to feel an interest in the 'good old condition of things.' No two matters can be more radically different than the reputation of some of our prominent *littérateurs*, as gathered from the mouths of the people, (who glean it from the paragraphs of the papers), and the same reputation as deduced from the private estimate of intelligent and educated men. We do not advance this fact as a new discovery. Its truth, on the contrary, is the subject, and has long been so, of everyday witticism and mirth.

. . . "Is there any man of good feeling and of ordinary understanding — is there one single individual among all our readers — who does not feel a thrill of bitter indignation, apart from any sentiment of mirth, as he calls to mind instance after instance of the purest, of the most unadulterated quackery in letters, which has risen to a high post in the apparent popular estimation, and which still maintains it, by the sole means of a blustering arrogance, or of a busy wriggling conceit, or of the most bare-faced plagiarism, or even through the simple immensity of its assumptions — as sumptions not only unopposed by the press at large, but absolutely supported in proportion to the vociferous clamor with which they are made — in exact accordance with their utter baselessness and untenability? We should have no trouble in pointing out, to-day, some twenty or thirty so-called literary personages, who, if not idiots, as we half think them, or if not hardened to all sense of shame by a long course of disingenuousness, will now blush, in the perusal of these words, through consciousness of the shadowy nature of that purchased pedestal on which they stand — will now tremble in thinking of the feebleness of the breath which will be adequate to the blowing it from beneath their feet. With the help of a hearty good will, even *we* may yet tumble them down."[1]

From this general condemnation Poe excepted an editor or two, and he reminded Wilmer, in deprecating indiscriminate abuse, that there were a few poets among us: —

"Mr. Bryant is not *all* a fool. Mr. Willis is not *quite* an ass. Mr. Longfellow *will* steal, but, perhaps, he cannot help it (for we have heard of such things,) and then it must not be denied that *nil tetigit quod non ornavit.*"[2]

In his own glance at the literary republic, in the "Autography," he had dispensed praise very freely, nine tenths of the verdicts being favorable and many flattering. The principal exceptions were among the New England writers, especially those whom

[1] *Works,* iv. 542–547.   [2] Ibid. iv. 549.

he believed to belong to the clique of the "North American Review;" Emerson, in particular, as being, moreover, a transcendentalist, he treated contemptuously, and Longfellow, whom he generously declares "entitled to the first place among the poets of America," but adds, on jealous reflection, "certainly to the first place among those who have put themselves prominently forth as poets," he strikes at with the old cut, as being guilty of the sin of imitation, — "an imitation sometimes verging upon down-right theft." [1]

In more detailed criticisms of current books, Poe, as was to be expected, merely made specifications of his general strictures regarding the low character of our literature. Whether he dealt with poetry or prose, with the dunces or the geniuses, his estimate, after he had first asked the absorbing question, "Was the writer a literary thief?" was that of a craftsman, and had almost exclusive reference to the workmanship. It consisted, as he would have said, in the application of principles of composition, in minute detail, instead of in the enunciation of them. Consequently, the criticism is, as a rule, so bound up with the work to which it relates as to have no value by itself, and has now no vitality. He spoke the truth in describing his reviews as neither wholly laudatory nor wholly defamatory even in the most exasperating cases of stupidity. To the reader it will not infrequently

[1] *Works,* ii. xviii.

seem that he used a giant's force to crush a fly, or in too many passages was guilty of the worst taste, or even now and then became scurrilous, blustering, and vituperative, or, especially when he attempted humor, very flat. The traits of his style were always the same, whether he was pricking a reputation or confining himself to mere criticism; he attended to one, or another, or all, of certain points, the chief being originality in idea, handling, construction, keeping, rhetorical and grammatical rules; and he exemplified by citation whatever defects or merits he found. Very seldom he felt able to give unstinted praise, as to Hawthorne, whose tales he said belonged " to the highest region of Art — an Art subservient to genius of a very lofty order," and whose mind he declared " original in *all* points; "[1] but even this notice, in which his insight and his justice are both conspicuous, he could not forbear to blot with the suggested charge that in " Howe's Masquerade " the New Englander had stolen directly from some passages in his own " William Wilson."

In none of these articles does Poe develop any principles except in that on Longfellow's " Ballads and other Poems." He barely touched the old offense of plagiarism, but made his attack in a new quarter by attempting to show that Longfellow's " conception of the *aims* of poesy *is all wrong*," for the reason that " didacticism is the prevalent *tone*

[1] *Works*, ii. 199.

of his song." In his proof Poe restated his poetic theory, which had become freed from its metaphysics since five years before, and in the course of his argument he struck out the happy phrase that remained his pet definition of poetry ever after: —

"Its [Poetry's] first element is the thirst for supernal BEAUTY — a beauty which is not afforded the soul by any existing collocation of earth's forms — a beauty which, perhaps, *no possible* combination of these forms would fully produce. Its second element is the attempt to satisfy this thirst by *novel* combinations among those forms of beauty which already exist, — or by novel combinations *of those combinations which our predecessors, toiling in chase of the same phantom, have already set in order.* We thus clearly deduce the *novelty*, the *originality*, the *invention*, the *imagination*, or lastly, the *creation* of BEAUTY (for the terms as here employed are synonymous) as the essence of all Poesy."[1]

With a slight change (which summed up in one word a succeeding paragraph, embodying his view that music was a necessary constituent), this definition of poetry as being "the rhythmical creation of beauty" became the first principle of his poetic criticism, as indeed, however obscurely made out, it had always been. His former doctrine that a poem should have complete unity within itself he reiterated by reprinting unchanged the passage already quoted from the "Messenger" of 1836. In accordance with these canons, Longfellow, whom under all

[1] *Works,* ii. 366.

circumstances Poe ranked at the head of our poets, was judged to fail by making truth either a primary end or one secondary to mere beauty, and to succeed by confining his poems each to one idea.

Whether these piquant criticisms and powerful tales made "Graham's" popular, or whether its success was due to the shrewd business sagacity and generous advertisement of its owners, the magazine had at once a brilliant run. It had opened with a circulation of eight thousand in January, 1841; in July it had risen to seventeen thousand; in December (at which time the names of Mrs. Emma C. Embury and Mrs. Ann S. Stephens were added to those of George R. Graham, C. J. Peterson, and Edgar A. Poe, as editors) it was twenty-five thousand, and in March forty thousand, — in each case according to the public announcement in the magazine itself. Poe was the working editor during this time, and is fairly entitled to a considerable, if not the main, share in the success of the undertaking. At the same time he seems never to have been contented with his position, and especially he continued to cherish the plan of starting the "Penn Magazine." Shortly after assuming the editorship he wrote to Snodgrass, "The 'Penn,' I hope, is only 'scotched, not killed,'" and added that the project would "unquestionably be resumed hereafter;"[1] and a few months later he addressed his

[1] Poe to Snodgrass, April 1, 1841, *Baltimore American*, April, 1881.

old friend, Kennedy, then in Congress, on the same subject, as appears from a letter to Mr. F. W. Thomas, a Baltimore friend, poet and novelist, dated July 4, 1841: "I wrote to Mr. K. about ten days ago on the subject of a magazine, a project of mine in connection with Graham."[1] Poe doubtless referred to the same scheme when he wrote to Snodgrass, on September 19, what, in view of the success of "Graham's," seems a strange passage: —

"It is not impossible that Graham will join me in the 'Penn.' He has money. By the way is it impossible to start a first-class mag. in Baltimore? Is there no publisher or gentleman of moderate capital who would join me in this scheme? — publishing the work in the City of Monuments?"[2]

A more conclusive indication of restless dissatisfaction with his seeming good fortune as editor of the leading American magazine occurs in an earlier letter to Thomas, dated June 26, 1841: —

"I have just heard through Graham, who obtained his information from Ingraham, that you have stepped into an office at Washington, salary $1,000. From the bottom of my heart I wish you joy. You can now lucubrate at your ease, and will infallibly do something worthy yourself.

"For my own part, notwithstanding Graham's unceasing civility and real kindness, I feel more and more dis-

[1] Poe to Thomas, Stoddard, xcv.
[2] Poe to Snodgrass, MS. copy.

gusted with my situation. Would to God I could do as you have done. Do you seriously think that an application on my part to Tyler would have a good result? My claims, to be sure, are few. I am a Virginian — at least I call myself one, for I have resided all my life, until within the last few years, in Richmond. My political principles have always been, as nearly as may be, with the existing administration, and I battled with right good will for Harrison, when opportunity offered. With Mr. Tyler I have some slight personal acquaintance, although it is a matter which he has possibly forgotten. For the rest I am a literary man, and I see a disposition in Government to cherish letters. Have I any chance? I would be greatly indebted to you if you would reply to this as soon as you can, and tell if it would, in your opinion, be worth my while to make an effort; and, if so, put me on the right track. This could not be better done than by detailing to me your own mode of proceeding." [1]

On July 4, Poe followed this up by another more urgent request: —

"I received yours of the 1st, this morning, and have again to thank you for the interest you take in my welfare. I wish to God I could visit Washington, but — the old story, you know — I have no money; not enough to take me there, saying nothing of getting back. It is a hard thing to be poor; but as I am kept so by an honest motive I dare not complain.

"Your suggestion about Mr. Kennedy is well-timed, and here, Thomas, you can do me a true service. Call

[1] Poe to Thomas, Stoddard, xciii.

upon Kennedy — you know him, I believe; if not, introduce yourself — he is a perfect gentleman, and will give you cordial welcome. Speak to him of my wishes, and urge him to see the Secretary of War in my behalf, or one of the other Secretaries, or President Tyler. I mention in particular the Secretary of War, because I have been to W. Point, and this may stand me in some stead. I would be glad to get almost any appointment, even a $500 one, so that I have something independent of letters for a subsistence. To coin one's brain into silver, at the nod of a master, is, to my thinking, the hardest task in the world. Mr. Kennedy has been, at all times, a true friend to me — he was the first true friend I ever had — I am indebted to him *for life itself.* He will be willing to help me now, but *needs urging,* for he is always head and ears in business." [1]

Besides indulging in these plans Poe now remembered his old publishers, Lea & Blanchard, and entertained the hope that they would undertake a new edition of his "Tales," including the best of those written since 1839. A few weeks after their first publication, he had written to Snodgrass, "I am happy to say that the edition is already very nearly exhausted." [2] On June 17, 1840, he amplified this statement by saying, "Touching my Tales you will scarcely believe me when I tell you that I am ignorant of their fate, and have never spoken to the publishers concerning them since the day of their

[1] Poe to Thomas, Stoddard, xciv., xcv.
[2] Poe to Snodgrass, December 19, 1839. MS. copy.

issue. I have cause to think, however, that the edition was exhausted almost immediately." [1]

Perhaps it was still with this impression that he addressed the following letter: —

MESSRS. LEA & BLANCHARD, —
PHILADELPHIA.

GENTLEMEN: I wish to publish a new collection of my prose Tales with some such title as this: —

'*The Prose Tales of Edgar A. Poe, including " The Murders in the Rue Morgue," the " Descent into the Maelström," and all his later pieces, with a second edition of the " Tales of the Grotesque & Arabesque."*'

The later pieces will be eight in number, making the entire collection thirty-three, which would occupy two *thick* novel volumes.

I am anxious that your firm should continue to be my publishers, and, if you would be willing to bring out the book, I should be glad to accept the terms which you allowed me before, that is, you receive all profits, and allow me twenty copies for distribution to friends.

Will you be kind enough to give me an early reply to this letter, and believe me

Yours, very respectfully,

EDGAR A. POE.[2]

PHILADELPHIA,
Office Graham's Magazine, August 13, '41.

Whatever doubt he had regarding the matter was dissipated by the reply of the firm: —

[1] Poe to Snodgrass, MS. copy.
[2] *The Library of George W. Childs*, described by F. W. Robinson. Philadelphia, 1882: pp. 13, 14.

Aug. 16, 1841.

EDGAR A. POE

We have yrs of 15th inst in which you are kind enough to offer us a "new collection of prose Tales."

In answer we very much regret to say that the state of affairs is such as to give little encouragement to new undertakings. As yet we have not got through the edition of the other work and up to this time it has not returned to us the expense of its publication. We assure you that we regret this on your account as well as on our own — as it would give us great pleasure to promote your views in relation to publication.[1]

[Unsigned.]

But if Poe could not start his own magazine, nor get a public office, nor publish a new volume of "Tales," his lot was to all outward appearance fortunate; his prospects were brilliant, his reputation steadily growing, his associates friendly, and, especially, his home was in a condition of greater comfort than ever before. Whatever practical difficulties it was his lot to encounter, no shadow had crossed the threshold of the little cottage where he lived with his wife and her mother in a close privacy of watchful love and domestic happiness. Mrs. Clemm, a vigorous woman of about fifty years, who is said to have had the face, size, and figure of a man, was the head of the household, received and expended Poe's wages, and kept things in order. The few acquaintances who called on the family sometimes wondered, as did Mayne Reid,

[1] Letter-book of Lea and Blanchard.

how this masculine matron should have been the mother of the fragile girl, still under twenty-one, whose feminine beauty and charm was of so delicate an order that she seems nearly as sylph-like as one of Poe's imaginary creations. "She hardly looked more than fourteen," writes Mr. A. B. Harris, who knew her at this time, "fair, soft, and graceful and girlish. Every one who saw her was won by her. Poe was very proud and very fond of her, and used to delight in the round, child-like face and plump little finger [*sic. Q.* figure?], which he contrasted with himself, so thin and half-melancholy looking, and she in turn idolized him. She had a voice of wonderful sweetness, and was an exquisite singer, and in some of their more prosperous days, when they were living in a pretty little rose-covered cottage on the outskirts of Philadelphia, she had her harp and piano."[1] The third member of this strangely-consorted group, Poe himself, was the same reserved, isolated, dreamy man, of high-strung nerves, proud spirit, and fantastic moods, that he had been in youth. With senses excessively acute and a mind easily accessible to motives of dread, if he was not the monomaniac of fear he knew in Roderick Usher, he was always haunted by suggestions of evil to come; nor was he quite free from the vague apprehension that belongs to children's minds. He did not like to go out in the dark, and with such jocularity as he was

[1] *Hearth and Home.* Quoted in Ingram, i. 221.

capable of said that he believed evil demons had power then. In his home alone he found happiness, affection, and a refuge from contact with the world.

One evening when Virginia was singing she ruptured a blood-vessel; her life was despaired of, and although she partially recovered it was only to sink again and again. The sick-bed was now the centre of the secluded home. "She could not bear the slightest exposure," writes Mr. Harris, "and needed the utmost care; and all those conveniences as to apartment and surroundings which are so important in the case of an invalid were almost matters of life and death to her. And yet the room where she lay for weeks, hardly able to breathe, except as she was fanned, was a little place with the ceiling so low over the narrow bed that her head almost touched it. But no one dared to speak, Mr. Poe was so sensitive and irritable; 'quick as steel and flint,' said one who knew him in those days. And he would not allow a word about the danger of her dying; the mention of it drove him wild."[1] Mr. Graham also tells how he saw Poe hovering around the couch with fond fear and tender anxiety, shuddering visibly at her slightest cough; and he continues, "I rode out one summer evening with them, and the remembrance of his watchful eyes, eagerly bent upon the slightest change of hue in that loved face, haunts me yet as the memory of a sad strain."[2]

[1] *Hearth and Home.* Quoted by Ingram, i. 223, 224.
[2] *Works*, i. xcvii.

This was the beginning of the long suspense of years, with their racking alternations of hope and despair, which Poe called his worst misfortune.

But the subtle influence which preserves a poet's heart from the wounds of life touched him, and raised the transitory elements of his common story and transformed them, and made them a part of the world's tradition of love and loss. In "Eleonora," which was published in the "Gift" for 1842, his absorbing sorrow turned thought and affliction to favor and to prettiness. In this alone of all his tales is there any sign of the warmth, the vital sense of human love. The myth — for such it is — is pictorial, like a mediæval legend: the child-lovers are set in one of those preternatural landscapes which his genius built in the void; but on this sequestered Paradise there fell no shadow save that of loveliness curtaining in innocent peace, behind thick forests and innumerable flowers, the Valley of the Many-Colored Grass, through which the River of Silence flowed noiselessly, and watered the slender, white-barked trees that leaned toward the light, and mirrored the scented lawns besprinkled with lilies and a thousand bright blossoms. Here love came to the boy and girl, beneath the fantastic trees suddenly bursting into bloom with bright star-shaped flowers, and they wander, like a new Aucassin and Nicolette, along the river that now murmurs musically, and over the ruby-red asphodels that spring up ten by ten in the place of the fallen white lilies; and the valley is filled with marvelous light and life and joy, as if glory and sweetness were imprisoned within its vaporous limits. Symbolism has seldom been more simple and pure, more imaginative, childlike, and direct, more absolute master of the things of sense for the things of the spirit, than in this unreal scene. Burne Jones might paint it, for it is the very spirit that sang of the Romaunt of the Rose. Rossetti might have sung its sad conclusion; for now the lady died: —

"The star-shaped flowers shrank into the stems of the trees, and appeared no more. The tints of the green carpet faded; and, one by one, the ruby-red asphodels withered away; and there sprang up, in place of them, ten by ten, dark, eye-like violets, that writhed uneasily and were ever encumbered with dew. And Life departed from our paths; for the tall flamingo flaunted no more his scarlet plumage before us, but flew sadly from the vale into the hills, with all the gay glowing birds that had arrived in his company. And the golden and silver fish swam down through the gorge at the lower end of our domain and bedecked the sweet river never again. And the lulling melody that had been softer than the wind harp of Æolus, and more divine than all save the voice of Eleonora, it died little by little away, in murmurs growing lower and lower, until the stream returned, at length, utterly, into the solemnity of its original silence. And then, lastly, the voluminous cloud uprose, and, abandoning the tops of the mountains to the dimness of old, fell back into the regions of Hesper, and took away all its manifold golden and gorgeous glories from the Valley of the Many-Colored Grass." [1]

Poe's life was full of glaring contrasts, just such as there is between this exquisite foreboding of his widowhood in symbols and the hard reality. To this experience of the fragility of his hold on happiness, and to this first perception of it toward the fall of 1841, he attributed the worst of his failures, the loss of all power to resist the temptation to drink.

At a later time, in answer to the question whether he could hint the "terrible evil" which was the cause of his "irregularities," he wrote: —

"Yes, I can do more than hint. This 'evil' was the greatest which can befall a man. Six years ago, a wife, whom I loved as no man ever loved before, ruptured a blood-vessel in singing. Her life was despaired of. I took leave of her forever, and underwent all the agonies of her death. She recovered partially, and I again hoped. At the end of a year, the vessel broke again. I went through precisely the same scene. . . . Then again — again — and even once again, at varying intervals. Each time I felt all the agonies of her death — and at each accession of the disorder I loved her more dearly and clung to her life with more desperate pertinacity. But I am constitutionally sensitive — nervous in a very unusual degree. I became insane, with long intervals of horrible sanity. During these fits of absolute unconsciousness I drank — God only knows how often or how much. As a matter of course, my enemies

[1] *Works,* iii. 450.

referred the insanity to the drink, rather than the drink to the insanity." [1]

Whether this self-abandonment to temptation was sudden or gradual is not stated; it may be that Poe's troubles merely occasioned an increase in those irregularities which were said to be matter of common fame before this time. A cousin, who was intimate with the family at the time of Virginia's seizure, says that he then frequently refused wine in her presence, and adds the too significant words that at that time his fits of intoxication were due to the excessive use of opium.[2]

In the next spring (1842) he lost the editorship of "Graham's." The only explanation vouchsafed by the proprietor is that one day, on returning from an unusual absence from his duties, Poe found Mr. Rufus Wilmot Griswold in his chair, and at once turned and left the office never to return.[3] This could hardly have been more than an incident in the truth. A man even so impulsive as Poe does not thus surrender through pique his main source of support, especially when he has a sick wife and is poor; nor, on the other hand, would a business man like Graham allow an editor, who had placed his magazine easily at the head of all competitors and made it a paying property, to depart for any such trivial display of temper. Without making

[1] Poe to ———, January 4, 1848   Ingram, i. 215, 216.
[2] Miss A. F. Poe to the author, September 13, 1884.
[3] Gill, pp. 110, 111.

an assertion, it may fairly be inferred that, to use Mr. Kennedy's words in regard to Poe's failure on the "Messenger," his nature was too "eccentric, irregular, and querulous" for him to hold the position; furthermore, as has become clear enough, his heart was not in the work: he had been chafing as restlessly in this position as when on "Burton's," and had continually sought other modes of support. Mr. Graham had engaged Griswold temporarily, and the "Saturday Evening Post," May 14, 1842, now announced that he had become an associate editor of that paper and of "Graham's." In the magazine itself it was stated that his duties, as Poe's successor, would begin with the July number. Unfortunately, Griswold was to inherit Poe's desk once more as a biographer, and therefore some closer notice must be taken of him.

Rufus Wilmot Griswold, when he was thus publicly announced as the new editor of "Graham's" in May, 1842, was a young man of twenty-seven years, who had some time before left the Baptist ministry for the more attractive walks of literature. He had published both sermons and songs, and had served on several newspapers in Boston, New York, and Philadelphia; latterly he had been engaged in compiling his popular volume, "The Poets and Poetry of America," — that *Hic Jacet* of American mediocrities of the first generation. An unsupported statement by Griswold respecting Poe is liable to suspicion, but there is no improbability in his account of the beginning of the most unfortunate acquaintance of his life. Poe was the editor of "Graham's" when he heard of Griswold's intention to set in order the "American Parnassus;" but he was not widely known as a poet, — in fact, he had practically abandoned poetry in late years. He was, however, fond of his early verses, and he was never known to omit any opportunity of advertising himself. It was natural, therefore, that shortly after the announcement of Griswold's venture he should call on him for the purpose of securing admission among Apollo's candidates, and it is consistent with all that is known of his habits that he should furnish[1] in March, 1841, a selection from his own verses and material for a biography. When, a year later, the unexpected meeting in Graham's office took place, the incident caused no rupture in the friendly relations of the two men. In April Griswold's long-expected volume had been issued, and Poe offered to review it for him. The transaction which then occurred should be given in Poe's words. September 12, 1842, he wrote to his friend, Mr. F. W. Thomas, as follows: —

"Graham has made me a good offer to return. He is not especially pleased with Griswold, nor is any one else,

[1] Poe to Griswold, March 29, 1841. Griswold, xxi. The genuineness of these letters as printed has been doubted, but the author believes that they are unquestionably Poe's compositions, and in all probability exact copies of the originals. The grounds of this opinion involve too many minutiæ to be recounted.

with the exception of the Rev. gentleman himself, who has gotten himself into quite a hornet's nest by his 'Poets and Poetry.' It appears you gave him personal offence by *delay* in replying to his demand for information touching Mrs. Welby, I believe, or somebody else. Hence his omission of you in the body of the book; for he had prepared quite a long article from my MS., and had selected several pages for quotation. He is a pretty fellow to set himself up for an *honest* judge, or even as a capable one. About two months since, we were talking of the book, when I said that I thought of reviewing it in full for the *Democratic Review*, but found my design anticipated by an article from that ass O'Sullivan, and that I knew no other work in which a notice would be readily admissible. Griswold said, in reply: 'You need not trouble yourself about the *publication* of the review, should you decide on writing it, for I will attend to all that. I will get it in some reputable work, and look to it for the usual pay, in the meantime handing you whatever your charge would be.' This, you see, was an ingenious insinuation of *a bribe* to puff his book. I accepted his offer forthwith, and wrote the review, handed it to him, and received from him the compensation; he never daring to look over the MS. in my presence, and taking it for granted that all was right. But that review has not yet appeared, and I am doubtful if it ever will. I wrote it precisely as I would have written under ordinary circumstances, and be sure there was no predominance of praise." [1]

This does not read very consistently with another

[1] Poe to Thomas, Stoddard, xcvii., xcviii.

IN PHILADELPHIA. 175

letter,[1] belonging clearly to a later time, in which he informs Griswold that he has made use of his name with the publishers for a copy, and contemplates noticing it in Lowell's "Pioneer."

While these changes were going on, Poe had not relaxed his efforts to obtain an office under government, and in the letter to Thomas, just quoted, he expresses high hopes of success and great gratitude to his friend for his efforts in the matter. At the same time he was considering Graham's offer to return, and a proposal vaguely entertained by Foster, editor of the "Aurora," to start a magazine in New York under Poe's charge. None of these plans came to anything; and, as always when everything else failed, Poe returned to his scheme for starting a magazine of his own. He had at once advertised the "Penn" on leaving "Graham's,"[2] and addressed his friends and acquaintances through a new Prospectus, and besought them to obtain subscriptions, of which he needed five hundred. As before, "The Penn Magazine" was to be original, fearless, and independent, and would in particular open its columns to merit instead of mushroom reputations, and would be distinguished by criticism instead of puffery. To Washington Poe, the

[1] Poe to Griswold. Griswold, xxi. *Cf.* letter *circa* January, 1849, ibid. xxii., in which Poe speaks of the review in the *Pioneer* as having actually appeared in 1843, but it is not to be found there. Possibly Poe contributed it, and the sudden suspension of the *Pioneer* prevented its publication.

[2] *The New York Mirror*, July 30, 1842.

head of his Augusta relatives, he wrote in August that he would issue the first number in the next January, with the hope that he might serve truth and advance American literature, and that fortune and fame would now come to him hand in hand.[1] He succeeded in interesting Mr. Thomas C. Clarke, the owner of the "Saturday Museum," a weekly paper, in his plan, and the two entered into a partnership for the publication of the new periodical, which it was thought best to call "The Stylus."

The literary work of Poe during the last half of this year was slight. In October he contributed to "Graham's" his long-delayed article on "Rufus Dawes," in which at last he took satirical vengeance on that poetaster. A weaker and less prominent magazine, "Snowden's Lady's Companion," was his principal resource; in it he published in October "The Landscape Garden," and in November, December, and February "The Mystery of Marie Roget," in parts. In this fall, too, he addressed for the first time Mr. J. R. Lowell, who had several times been praised by him incidentally, and who was about to issue a new periodical in Boston. As the correspondence thus begun is the most interesting series of letters by Poe, and as it throws considerable light upon both his affairs and his character, it will be given in full: —

DR SIR,

Learning your design of commencing a Magazine, in

[1] Poe to Washington Poe, August 15, 1842. Gill, p. 114.

Boston, upon the first of January next, I take the liberty of asking whether some arrangement might not be made, by which I should become a regular contributor.

I should be glad to furnish a short article each month — of such character as might be suggested by yourself — and upon such terms as you could afford "in the beginning."

That your success will be marked and permanent I will not doubt. At all events, I most sincerely wish you well; for no man in America has excited in me so much admiration — and, therefore, none so much of respect and esteem — as the author of "Rosaline."

May I hope to hear from you at your leisure? In the meantime, believe me

Most Cordially Yours,

EDGAR ALLAN POE.[1]

JAMES RUSSELL LOWELL, ESQRE.
PHILADELPHIA *Novem:* 16, 1842.

The offer was gladly accepted, and articles were sent by Poe, as suggested, for each number. The two following letters continue the story of the acquaintance: —

[not dated — mailed *December* 25, 1842.]

MY DEAR FRIEND

I send you a brief poem for No 2, with my very best wishes.

I duly received yours of the 19th and thank you for reversing the judgment of Mr. Tuckerman — the author of the "Spirit of Poesy," — which, by the way, is somewhat of a misnomer — since no spirit appears.

[1] Poe to Lowell, MS.

Touching the "Miscellany" — had I known of Mr. T.'s accession, I should not have ventured to send an article. Should he, at any time, accept an effusion of mine, I should ask myself what twattle I had been perpetrating, so flat as to come within the scope of his approbation. He writes, through his publishers, — "if Mr. Poe would condescend to furnish more quiet articles he would be a most desirable correspondent." All I have to say is that if Mr. T. Persists in his *quietude*, he will put a quietus on the Magazine of which Mess. Bradbury and Soden have been so stupid as to give him control.

I am all anxiety to see your first number. In the meantime believe me,[1]

[Signature torn off.]

PHILADELPHIA *February* 4, 1843.

MY DEAR MR. LOWELL,

For some weeks I have been daily proposing to write and congratulate you upon the triumphant début of the "Pioneer," but have been prevented by a crowd of more worldly concerns.

Thank you for the compliment in the foot-note. Thank you, also, for your attention in forwarding the Magazine.

As far as a $3 Magazine can please me at all, I am delighted with yours. I am especially gratified with what seems to me a certain coïncidence of opinion and of taste, between yourself and your humble servant, in the minor arrangements, as well as in the more important details of the journal, for example — the poetry

[1] Poe to Lowell, MS.

in the same type as the prose — the designs from Flaxman — &c. As regards the contributors our thoughts are one. Do you know that when, some time since, I dreamed of establishing a Magazine of my own, I said to myself — "If I can but succeed in engaging, as permanent contributors, Mr. Hawthorne, Mr. Neal, and two others, with a certain young poet of Boston, who shall be nameless, I will engage to produce the best journal in America." At the same time, while I thought, and still think highly of Mr. Bryant, Mr. Cooper, and others, I said nothing of *them.*

You have many warm friends in this city — but the reforms you propose require time in their development, and it may be even a year before "The Pioneer" will make due impression among the Quakers. In the meantime, persevere.

I forwarded you, about a fortnight ago I believe, by Harnden's Express, an article called "Notes upon English Verse." A thought has struck me, that it may prove too long, or perhaps too dull, for your Magazine — in either case, use no ceremony, but return it in the same mode (thro' Harnden) and I will, forthwith, send something in its place.

I duly received from Mr. Graham, $10 on your account, for which I am obliged. I would prefer, however, that you would remit directly to myself through the P. Office.

I saw, not long ago, at Graham's, a poem without the author's name — but which for many reasons I take to be yours — the chief being that it was *very* beautiful. Its title I forget but it slightly veiled a lovely Allegory — in which "Religion" was typified, and the whole painted the voyage of some wanderers and mourners in search of some far-off isle. Is it yours?

Truly your friend   E. A. POE.[1]

Within a few weeks of the date of this letter, the Prospectus of "The Stylus" was first issued through the columns of the "Saturday Museum," which called attention to it in an editorial puff of Poe. The Prospectus is shorter than that of the "Penn Magazine," but the identity of the two is avowed, and in the important parts describing the aims of the editors the same sentences formerly used are incorporated. The "*chief purpose*" is still declared to be to found a journal distinguished by "a sincere and fearless opinion," and it is announced as earnest of this intention that "an important feature of the work, and one which will be introduced in the opening number, will be a series of 'Critical and Biographical Sketches of American Writers.'" "The Stylus" was to be illustrated also, like the "Penn," and an agreement, signed January 31, 1843, was entered into between Clarke and Poe on one side and F. O. C. Darley on the other, in accordance with which the latter was to furnish not less than three original designs per month to Clarke and Poe, at seven dollars each, until July 1, 1844, and was not to contribute similar designs for use in any other magazine during that period. The subjects were to be given by the editors, and the first work put into the artist's

[1] Poe to Lowell, MS.

hands for this purpose was "The Gold Bug," for which he made and delivered some designs. Poe himself took the story to Mr. Darley, with whom he held pleasant relations. "He impressed me," writes the latter, "as a refined and very gentlemanly man; exceedingly neat in his person; interesting always, from the intellectual character of his mind, which appeared to me to be tinged with sadness. His manner was quiet and reserved; he rarely smiled. I remember his reading his 'Gold Bug' and 'Black Cat' to me before they were published. The form of his manuscript was peculiar: he wrote on half sheets of note paper, which he pasted together at the ends, making one continuous piece, which he rolled up tightly. As he read he dropped it upon the floor. It was very neatly written, and without corrections, apparently."[1] Several of these small rolls still exist.

In aid of the new venture Poe's life and portrait were printed in the "Saturday Museum," of which it was announced that he was editor. The life was written by a young Philadelphia poet, H. B. Hirst, from materials furnished by T. W. White, of the "Messenger," and Thomas; and the portrait, which was said to be a mere caricature, was lithographed from a miniature.

Poe himself was shortly after sent to Washington to obtain subscriptions among his political friends, and, if possible, those of the President

[1] Darley to the author, February 26, 1884.

and Cabinet through his old acquaintance, Rob Tyler. He apparently also meant to lecture, and to look after his prospects of becoming an office-holder, the particular post in view being an Inspectorship. The visit was unfortunate. On the evening of his arrival he began to drink, and his host's "rummy coffee" following port wine made the beginning of a spree. On the next day, March 11, he so far lost his head as to write a contradictory and untrue letter,[1] plainly the composition of an intoxicated man, to his partner; and a day later, Mr. J. E. Dow, who was taking care of him, also dispatched a letter to Mr. Clarke, advising him to come on and take charge of his friend, as Mr. Thomas was too ill to do so, and he himself too much engaged, while they both felt afraid to send him off to Philadelphia alone, lest he should be led to stop at Baltimore, and there meet with some harm. "Mrs. Poe," says the writer pitifully, "is in a bad state of health, and I charge you, as you have a soul to be saved, to say not one word to her about him until he arrives with you."[2] Poe, however, was sent home by himself, and arrived at Philadelphia March 15, where he was met at the station by Mrs. Clemm. After going home he called on Clarke, who was greatly surprised to see him, but received him "cordially and made light of the matter;" at least, so Poe wrote to his two

[1] Poe to Clarke. Gill, p. 120.
[2] Dow to Clarke. Gill, p. 121.

friends, Thomas and Dow, the next day, in a long epistle,[1] in which, although treating the affair jocosely, and alarmed for its possible effects on Clarke's mind, he expresses his regret and sends his apologies, with many words of gratitude for the attention shown him. He remarks incidentally, "I would be glad, too, if you would take an opportunity of saying to Mr. Rob Tyler that if he *can* look over matters and give me the Inspectorship, I will join the Washingtonians forthwith;" but he seems to have made up his mind that his hopes of office were vain.

That Clarke was not implacably offended by this episode, which Poe accounted for as an attack of illness which had unduly alarmed Dow, appears from the following letter to Lowell, in which the project of the "Stylus" is announced to him. The "Pioneer" had already met its fate, and Lowell was himself ill with ophthalmia.

PHILADELPHIA, *March* 27, 43.

MY DEAR FRIEND,

I have just received yours of the 24th and am deeply grieved, first that you should have been so unfortunate, and, secondly, that you should have thought it necessary to offer me any apology for your misfortunes. As for the few dollars you owe me — give yourself not one moment's concern about *them.* I am poor, but must be very much poorer, indeed, when I even think of demanding them.

[1] Poe to Thomas and Dow, March 16, 1843. MS. copy.

But I sincerely hope all is not so bad as you suppose it, and that, when you come to look about you, you will be able to continue "The Pioneer." Its decease, just now, would be a most severe blow to the good cause — the cause of a Pure Taste. I have looked upon your Magazine, from its outset, as the best in America, and have lost no opportunity of expressing the opinion. Herewith I send a paper, "The Phil. Sat. Museum," in which I have said a few words on the topic.

I am *not* editing this paper, although an announcement was prematurely made to that effect; but have the privilege of inserting what I please editorially. On the first of July next I hope to issue the first number of "The Stylus," a new monthly, with some novel features. I send you, also, a paper containing the Prospectus. In a few weeks I hope to forward you a specimen sheet. I am anxious to get a poem from yourself for the opening number, but, until you recover your health, I fear that I should be wrong in making the request.

Believe me, my dear friend, that I sympathize with you *truly* in your affliction. When I heard that you had returned to Boston, I hoped you were entirely well, and your letter disappoints and grieves me.

When you find yourself in condition to write, I would be indebted to you if you could put me in the way of procuring a brief article (also for my opening number) from Mr. Hawthorne — whom I believe you know personally. Whatever you gave him, we should be happy to give. A part of my design is to illustrate, whatever is fairly susceptible of illustration, with finely executed wood-engravings — after the fashion of Gigoux's "Gil Blas" or "Grandville's Gulliver" — and I wish to get a tale from Mr. Hawthorne as early as possible (if I am so fortunate as to get one at all), that I may put the illustration in the hands of the artist.

You will see by the Prospectus that we intend to give a series of portraits of the American literati, with critical sketches. I would be glad if I could so arrange matters as to have you *first*, provided you yourself have no serious objection. Instead of the "full-length portraits" promised in the Prospectus (which will be modified in the specimen sheet), we shall have medallions about three inches in diameter. Could you put me in possession of any likeness of yourself? — or would you do me the same favor in regard to Mr. Hawthorne? — You perceive I proceed upon the ground that you are intimate with Mr. H., and that making these inquiries would not subject you to trouble or inconvenience.

I confess that I am by no means so conversant with your own compositions (especially in prose), as I should be. Could you furnish me with some biographical and critical data, and tell me when or how I could be put in possession of your writings generally? — but I fear I am asking altogether too much.

If the 4th number of "The Pioneer" is printed, I would be obliged if you would send me an early copy through the P. O.

Please remember me to Mr. Carter, and believe me
    Most sincerely your friend,
                EDGAR A. POE.[1]

J. RUSSELL LOWELL, ESQ**.

Before the "Pioneer" was discontinued, after its third number, Poe had contributed to it "The Tell-

[1] Poe to Lowell. MS.

Tale Heart," the third of the tales of conscience; "Lenore," a greatly revised version of his old "Pæan;" and "Notes upon English Verse," a purely metrical discussion, which he afterwards remoulded into the "Rationale of Verse." During the same time he published in Miss Leslie's annual, "The Gift," for 1843, "The Pit and the Pendulum," a tale of no striking originality; and in "Graham's" the fine poem entitled "The Conqueror Worm," and "Flaccus" (the second of the series called "Our Amateur Poets"), a satirical review of one Thomas Ward, which he himself regarded as in his best manner.

Meanwhile the "Stylus" had been abandoned, and when the first of July came it found Poe sick and poor. On June 11 he wrote to Griswold a characteristic note: —

DEAR GRISWOLD: — Can you not send me $5? I am sick and Virginia is almost gone. Come and see me. Peterson says you suspect me of a curious anonymous letter. I did not write it, but bring it along with you when you make the visit you promised to Mrs. Clemm. I will try to fix that matter soon. Could you do anything with my *note?* Yours truly,

E. A. P.[1]

It was probably in response to this letter that Griswold called upon him at his home, No. 7 Spring Garden, of which he gave a description: —

"When once he sent for me to visit him, during a

[1] Griswold, **xx**.

period of illness caused by protracted and anxious watching at the side of his sick wife, I was impressed by the singular neatness and the air of refinement in his home. It was in a small house, in one of the pleasant and silent neighborhoods far from the centre of the town, and though slightly and cheaply furnished everything in it was so tasteful and so fitly disposed that it seemed altogether suitable for a man of genius. For this and for most of the comforts he enjoyed, in his brightest as in his darkest years, he was chiefly indebted to his mother-in-law, who loved him with more than maternal devotion and constancy." [1]

To this same period of unusual poverty and suffering Mayne Reid's characterization of Mrs. Clemm probably belongs: —

"She was the ever-vigilant guardian of the home, watching it against the silent but continuous sap of necessity, that appeared every day to be approaching closer and nearer. She was the sole servant, keeping everything clean; the sole messenger, doing the errands, making pilgrimages between the poet and his publishers, frequently bringing back such chilling responses as 'The article not accepted,' or 'The check not to be given until such and such a day,' — often too late for his necessities. And she was also the messenger to the market; from it bringing back not 'the delicacies of the season,' but only such commodities as were called for by the dire exigencies of hunger." [2]

He remembered the house as "a lean-to of three

[1] Griswold, xxxiv.
[2] *Onward*, quoted in the *Brooklyn Daily Eagle*, March 30, 1869.

rooms (there may have been a garret with a closet), of painted plank construction, supported against the gable of the more pretentious dwelling," — the latter being a four story red-brick mansion of a wealthy Quaker. But Mr. T. C. Clarke, whose family visited the Poes more or less frequently, describes it as a cottage set back from the street amid luxuriant grape and other vines, and ornamented in winter with flowers. There he especially remembered the childish wife, slowly wasting away in consumption, but "wearing on her beautiful countenance the smile of resignation, and the warm, even cheerful look with which she ever greeted her friends."[1] The appearance of the house, however, and the simple hospitality which he and Mayne Reid and others enjoyed in it, must have varied materially with the rapacity of the pawnbroker; and it is said that the family now became the object of charity.

The principal income during these trying months was the one-hundred-dollar prize received by Poe from "The Dollar Newspaper," edited by Joseph Sailer, for the story of "The Gold Bug," which he had recovered from Graham by exchanging a critical article for it, and had sent in to the judges. This, the most widely circulated of his tales, was published in two parts: the first June 21, 1843, and the second (together with the first, which was reprinted) a week later. On July 12 it was pub-

[1] Gill, p. 101.

lished again with two other prize tales in a supplement. A charge that it was plagiarized from Miss Sherburne's "Imogene, or The Pirate's Treasure," was made in "The Spirit of the Times," and was widely circulated, but a refutation was quickly attempted in "The Dollar Newspaper," July 19. The only other stories of Poe's published during this year were the fearful tale of "The Black Cat" in the "United States Saturday Post" (as the old "Saturday Evening Post" was now called), August 19, and "Morning on the Wissahiccon," a quiet landscape sketch of the environs of Philadelphia (evidently "The Elk," mentioned hereafter), contributed to Willis's annual, "The Opal," for 1844. In criticism he published three reviews, all in "Graham's:" one, perhaps the most contemptuous he ever wrote, on William Ellery Channing, the transcendentalist poet, being the third of the series "Our Amateur Poets;" one on Fitz-Greene Halleck, being No. viii. of "Our Contributors," a series of which the plan seems to have been taken from that projected by Poe for the "Stylus;" and one of a perfunctory kind on Cooper's "Wyandotte." In the fall an edition of his "Tales," in parts, was undertaken, but only one issue, containing "The Murders of the Rue Morgue" and "The Man who was Used Up," is known.[1]

Poe still interested himself from time to time in the solution of cryptographs, an occupation which

[1] *The New Mirror*, September, 1843.

the following letter, with its side-lights upon other topics, sufficiently illustrates: —

PHILA., *Aug.* 28, 1843.

MY DEAR SIR, — I have just rec^d your letter, enclosing one in hieroglyphical writing from Mr. Meek, and hasten to reply, since *you* desire it; although, some months ago, I was obliged to make a vow that I would engage in the solution of no more cryptographs. The reason of my making this vow will be readily understood. Much curiosity was excited throughout the country by my solutions of these cyphers, and a great number of persons felt a desire to test my powers individually — so that I was at one time absolutely overwhelmed; and this placed me in a dilemma; for I had either to devote my whole time to the solutions, or the correspondents would suppose me a mere boaster, incapable of fulfilling my promises. I had no alternative but to solve all; but to each correspondent I made known my intentions to solve no more. You will hardly believe me when I tell you that I have lost, in time, which to me is money, more than a thousand dollars, in solving ciphers, with no other object in view than that just mentioned. A really difficult cipher requires vast labor and the most patient thought in its solution. Mr. Meek's letter is very simple indeed, and merely shows that he misapprehends the whole matter. It runs thus: —

[Here follows the solution.]

This is the whole of Mr. Meek's letter — but he is mistaken in supposing that I "pride myself" upon my solutions of ciphers. I feel little pride about anything.

It is very true, as he says, that cypher writing is "no

great difficulty if the signs represent invariably the same letters and are divided into separate words." But the fact is, that most of the criptographs sent to me (Dr. Frailey's for instance) were *not* divided into words, and moreover, the signs *never* represented the same letter twice.

But here is an infallible mode of showing Mr. Meek that he knows nothing about the matter. He says cipher writing "is no great difficulty if the signs represent invariably the same letters and are divided into separate words." This is true; and yet, little as this difficulty is, he cannot surmount it. Send him, as if from yourself, these few words, in which the conditions stated by him are rigidly preserved. I will answer for it, he cannot decipher them for his life. They are taken at random from a well-known work now lying beside me : —

[Here follows Poe's cryptograph.]

And now, my dear friend, have you forgotten that I asked you, some time since, to render me an important favor? You can surely have no scruples in a case of this kind. I have reason to believe that I have been maligned by some envious scoundrel in this city, who has written you a letter respecting myself. I believe I know the villain's name. It is Wilmer. In Philadelphia no one speaks to him. He is avoided by all as a reprobate of the lowest class. Feeling a deep pity for him, I endeavoured to befriend him, and you remember that I rendered myself liable to some censure by writing a review of his filthy pamphlet called the "Quacks of Helicon." He has returned my good offices by slander behind my back. *All* here are anxious to have him convicted — for there is scarcely a gentleman in Phila[a] whom he has not libelled, through the gross malignity of his nature. Now, I ask you, as a friend and as a man of noble feelings, to send me his letter to you. It is your *duty* to do this — and I am sure, upon reflection, you will so regard it.

I await your answer impatiently.

Your friend, E. A. POE.[1]

Wilmer probably ill deserved this tirade, since, after Poe's death, he was one of his most faithful defenders. Scandal, however, was busy with Poe's name, and found its way into print in one of the city papers, in an article of which Poe suspected Griswold to be the author. There is some evidence, as will be seen later on, that he visited Saratoga this summer; but the illness of himself and his wife, and the poverty of the family, together with his seemingly uninterrupted employment in Philadelphia, go to discredit the story.

After the fall came, the only information concerning him at this obscure period is derived from his letters to Lowell: —

PHILADELPHIA, *Oct.* 19, 1843.

MY DEAR FRIEND,

I was upon the point of fulfilling a long neglected duty and replying to Mr. Carter's letter, enclosing $5, when I received yours of the 13th, remitting $5 more. Believe me I am sincerely grateful to you both for your uniform kindness and consideration.

You say nothing of your health — but Mr. C. speaks of its perfect restoration, and I see, by your very MS., that you are well again, body and mind. I need not say that

[1] Poe to John Tomlin, Esq. MS.

I am rejoiced at this — for you must know and feel that I am. When I thought of the possible loss of your eyesight, I grieved as if some dreadful misfortune were about happening to myself.

I shall look with much anxiety for your promised volume. Will it include your "Year's Life," and other poems already published? I hope that it may; for these have not yet been fairly placed before the eye of the world. I am seeking an opportunity to do you justice in a review, and may find it in "Graham," when your book appears. No poet in America has done so much. I have maintained this upon all occasions. Mr. Longfellow has genius, but by no means equals you in the true spirit. He is moreover so prone to imitation that I know not how to understand him at times. I am in doubt whether he should not be termed an arrant plagiarist. You have read his "Spanish Student"? I have written quite a long notice of it for Graham's December number. The play is a poor composition, with some fine poetical passages. His "Hymn to the Night," with some strange blemishes, is glorious. — How much I should like to interchange opinions with you upon poems and poets in general! I fancy that we should agree, usually, in results, while differing, frequently, about principles. The day may come when we can discuss everything at leisure, in person.

You say that your long poem has taught you a useful lesson, — "that you are unfit to write narrative — unless in a dramatic form." It is not you that are unfit for the task — but the task for you — for any poet. Poetry must eschew narrative — except, as you say, dramatically. I mean to say that the *true* poetry — the highest poetry — must eschew it. The Iliad is *not* the highest. The connecting links of a narrative — the frequent passages which have to serve the purpose of binding together the parts of the story, are necessarily prose, from their very explanatory nature. To color them — to gloss over their prosaic nature — (for this is the most which can be done) requires great skill. Thus Byron, who was no artist, is always driven, in his narrative, to fragmentary passages, eked out with asterisks. Moore succeeds better than any one. His "Alciphron" is wonderful in the force, grace, and nature of its purely narrative passages: — but pardon me for prosing.

I send you the paper with my life and portrait. The former is true in general — the latter particularly false. It does not convey the faintest idea of my person. No one of my family recognized it. But this is a point of little importance. You will see, upon the back of the biography, an announcement that I was to assume the editorship of the "Museum." This was unauthorized. I never did edit it. The review of "Graham's Magazine" was written by H. B. Hirst — a young poet of this city. Who is to write your life for "Graham?" It is a pity that so many of these biographies were entrusted to Mr. Griswold. He certainly lacks independence, or judgment, or both.

I have tried in vain to get a copy of your "Year's Life" in Philadelphia. If you have one, and could spare it, I would be much obliged.

Do write me again when you have leisure, and believe me,   Your most sincere friend,

                              EDGAR A. POE.[1]

J. R. LOWELL, ESQRE.

[1] Poe to Lowell. MS.

At some time during the summer Poe is said to have made his début as a lecturer in the "Egyptian Hall," Baltimore. He appeared in Philadelphia in the same rôle, November 25, and made a favorable impression. His subject was "The Poets and Poetry of America," and, while the lecture was largely compiled from his former book-reviews, it was especially distinguished by an attack, which seems to have been unusually severe, on Griswold's volume. At some time before this date, and probably at the very beginning of the year, there had appeared in the "Saturday Museum" an anonymous review of the third edition of Griswold's work, in which that reverend gentleman was held up to public ridicule in the most scoffing and bitter style, and contrasted with Poe by name, much to the latter's praise and to his own degradation. This mingled expression of pique, wrath, and scorn, with its flaunting self-commendation, is indubitably Poe's own work, but as it was unacknowledged Griswold had no plain ground for a personal quarrel. About the utterances of the lecture, however, he could have no doubt, and the flagellation he received in it, which does not seem to have displeased his literary associates, caused an open breach between himself and Poe that was not closed, even in appearance, until a year and a half had elapsed. It is worthy of note that Griswold had left his place on "Graham's" about two months before the delivery of the address.

The receipts from the new profession of lecturing could not have been large, and for one cause or another the editors who were accustomed to publish Poe's work either would not buy it, or else delayed to print it. After Griswold's retirement from "Graham's," Poe seems to have held during the winter the post of assistant to Graham, by far the larger part of the reviews being from his hand. In March, 1844, appeared his only signed article for several months past, a lengthy review of the drama, "Orion," by Richard Hengist Horne, recently published in England. Of this work, which appealed strongly to Poe's delight in pictorial fancy and subdued mystical suggestion, he declared, "It is our deliberate opinion that in all that regards the loftiest and holiest attributes of the true Poetry, 'Orion' has *never* been excelled. Indeed, we feel strongly inclined to say that it has never been *equaled*." After comparing one passage of it with Milton's description of hell, the latter being "*altogether inferior* in graphic effect, in originality, in expression, in the true imagination," he concludes more calmly that "'Orion' will be admitted, by every man of genius, to be one of the noblest, if not the very noblest poetical work of the age."[1]

Whether or not Poe had been taken back by Graham to be his unacknowledged assistant, he had now formed a new scheme, which is as fine a piece of literary visionariness as was ever elabo-

[1] *Works*, ii. 437–444.

rated by a penniless author. He unfolds it in the following letter to Lowell, which also contains other matter of contemporary interest.

PHILADELPHIA, *March* 30, 1844.

MY DEAR FRIEND,

Graham has been speaking to me, lately, about your Biography, and I am anxious to write it at once, always provided you have no objection. Could you forward me the materials within a day or two? I am just now quite disengaged — in fact positively idle.

I presume you have read the Memoir of Willis, in the April number of G. It is written by a Mr. Landor — but I think it full of hyperbole. Willis is *no* genius — a graceful trifler — no more. He wants force and sincerity. He is very frequently far-fetched. In me, at least, he never excites an emotion. Perhaps the best poem he has written is a little piece called "Unseen Spirits," beginning "The Shadows lay — Along Broadway."

You inquire about my own portrait. It has been done for some time — but is better as an engraving, than as a portrait. It scarcely resembles me at all. When it will appear I cannot say. Conrad and Mrs. Stephens will certainly come before me — perhaps Gen. Morris. My Life is not yet written, and I am at a sad loss for a Biographer — for Graham insists upon leaving the matter to myself.

I sincerely rejoice to hear of the success of your volume. To sell eleven hundred copies of a bound book of American poetry, is to do wonders. I hope everything from your future endeavors. Have you read "Orion?" Have you seen the article on "American

Poetry " in the " London Foreign Quarterly ? " It has been denied that Dickens wrote it — but, to me, the article affords so strong internal evidence of his hand that I would as soon think of doubting my existence. He tells much truth — although he evinces much ignorance and more spleen. Among other points he accuses myself of "metrical imitation" of Tennyson, citing, by way of instance, passages from poems which were written and published by me long before Tennyson was heard of : — but I have at no time made any poetical pretention. I am greatly indebted for the trouble you have taken about the lectures, and shall be very glad to avail myself, next season, of any invitation from the " Boston Lyceum." Thank you, also, for the hint about the North American Review ; — I will bear it in mind. I mail you, herewith, a "Dollar Newspaper," containing a somewhat extravagant tale of my own. I fear it will prove little to your taste.

How dreadful is the present condition of our Literature! To what are things tending? We want two things, certainly : — an International Copy-Right Law, and a well-founded Monthly Journal, of sufficient ability, circulation, and character, to control and so give tone to, our Letters. It should be, externally, a specimen of high, but not too refined Taste : — I mean, it should be boldly printed, on excellent paper, in single column, and be illustrated, not merely embellished, by spirited wood designs in the style of Grandville. Its chief aims should be Independence, Truth, Originality. It should be a journal of some 120 pp, and furnished at $5. It should have nothing to do with Agents or Agencies. Such a Magazine might be made to exercise a prodigious in fluence, and would be a source of vast wealth to its proprietors. There *can* be no reason why 100,000 copies might not, in one or two years, be circulated; but the means of bringing it into circulation should be radically different from those usually employed.

Such a journal might, perhaps, be set on foot by a coalition, and, thus set on foot, with proper understanding, would be irresistible. Suppose, for example, that the élite of our men of letters should combine secretly. Many of them control papers, &c. Let each subscribe, say $200, for the commencement of the undertaking; furnishing other means, as required from time to time, until the work be established. The articles to be supplied by the members solely, and upon a concerted plan of action. A nominal editor to be elected from among the number. How could such a journal fail? I would like very much to hear your opinion upon this matter. Could not the "ball be set in motion?" If we do *not* defend ourselves by some such coalition, we shall be devoured, without mercy, by the Godeys, the Snowdens, *et id genus omne.*

Most truly your friend,

EDGAR A. POE.[1]

The next week after writing this letter Poe put in execution what seems a very sudden determination to leave Philadelphia. Possibly the discontinuance of his undefined connection with "Graham's," which now took place, finally discouraged him; but whatever was the immediate occasion of his decision, looking back over the five years of his

[1] Poe to Lowell. MS.

life in that city, with its delusively brilliant openings and sharp reverses of fortune, he must have felt that he obeyed the dictates of worldly prudence in deserting a scene where his repeated failures and their causes were well known to the whole literary fraternity. He seems to have broken up his home at the cottage before this time, and he had not much more than ten dollars in his pocket when he left. Mrs. Clemm remained behind to sell his books and settle up affairs, and with Virginia he went to New York, apparently with no more definite a view than to make a new start in a new community.

CHAPTER VI.

IN NEW YORK.

POE'S account of his departure is given in a letter to Mrs. Clemm, which stands by itself in his correspondence as of a purely domestic kind, illustrative of life within doors, and (the more forcibly by its indirectness) of the penury to which at times the family was accustomed. Its confiding and familiar tone explains somewhat, too, how he won the devotion of his mother-in-law to that degree which has secured for her the admiration of all who were intimately acquainted with Poe's home life.

{ NEW YORK, *Sunday Morning,*
April 7, just after breakfast.

MY DEAR MUDDY,

We have just this minute done breakfast, and I now sit down to write you about everything. I can't pay for the letter, because the P. O. won't be open to-day. In the first place we arrived safe at Walnut St. wharf. The driver wanted to make me pay a dollar, but I would n't. Then I had to pay a boy a levy to put the trunks in the baggage car. In the meantime I took Sis [Virginia] in the Depôt Hotel. It was only a quarter past six, and we had to wait till seven. We saw the Ledger and Times — nothing in either — a few words of no account in the Chronicle. We started in good spirits, but did not get here until nearly three o'clock. We went in the cars to Amboy, about forty miles from N. York, and then took the steamboat the rest of the way. Sissy coughed none at all. When we got to the wharf it was raining hard. I left her on board the boat, after putting the trunks in the Ladies' cabin, and set off to buy an umbrella and look for a boarding-house. I met a man selling umbrellas, and bought one for twenty-five cents. Then I went up Greenwich St. and soon found a boarding house. It is just before you get to Cedar St., on the west side going up — the left-hand side. It has brown stone steps, with a porch with brown pillars. "Morrison" is the name on the door. I made a bargain in a few minutes and then got a hack and went for Sis. I was not gone more than half an hour, and she was quite astonished to see me back so soon. She did n't expect me for an hour. There were two other ladies waiting on board — so she was n't very lonely. When we got to the house we had to wait about half an hour before the room was ready. The house is old and looks buggy [The letter is cut here for the signature on the other side.] the cheapest board I ever knew, taking into consideration the central situation and the *living*. I wish Kate [Catterina, the cat] could see it — she would faint. Last night, for supper, we had the nicest tea you ever drank, strong and hot — wheat bread and rye bread — cheese — tea-cakes (elegant), a great dish (two dishes) of elegant ham, and two of cold veal, piled up like a mountain and large slices — three dishes of the cakes and everything in the greatest profusion. No fear of starving here. The landlady seemed as if she could n't press us enough, and we were at home directly. Her husband is living with her — a fat, good-natured old soul. There are eight or ten boarders — two or three of them ladies — two servants. For breakfast we had excellent-flavored coffee, hot and strong — not very clear and no great deal of cream — veal cutlets, elegant ham and eggs and nice bread and butter. I never sat down to a more plentiful or a nicer breakfast. I wish you could have seen the eggs — and the great dishes of meat. I ate the first hearty breakfast I have eaten since I left our little home. Sis is delighted, and we are both in excellent spirits. She has coughed hardly any and had no night sweat. She is now busy mending my pants which I tore against a nail. I went out last night and bought a skein of silk, a skein of thread, two buttons, a pair of slippers, and a tin pan for the stove. The fire kept in all night. We have now got four dollars and a half left. To-morrow I am going to try and borrow three dollars, so that I may have a fortnight to go upon. I feel in excellent spirits, and have n't drank a drop — so that I hope soon to get out of trouble. The very instant I scrape together enough money I will send it on. You can't imagine how much we both do miss you. Sissy had a hearty cry last night, because you and Catterina were n't here. We are resolved to get two rooms the first moment we can. In the mean time it is impossible we could be more comfortable or more at home than we are. It looks as if it were going to clear up now. Be sure and go to the P. O. and have my letters forwarded. As soon as I write Lowell's article, I will send it to you, and get you to get the money from Graham. Give our best love to C.

[Signature cut out.]

Be sure and take home the "Messenger" to Hirst.
We hope to send for you *very* soon.[1]

The postscript of this letter, — "Be sure and take home the 'Messenger' to Hirst," — though a matter of the most trifling detail, is worth explanation, since the circumstance to which it relates is yet remembered to Poe's discredit in Philadelphia, while the whole paltry affair furnishes a capital illustration of the mean though natural misconstruction to which he was sometimes exposed. The story is completely told in the following papers. Willis Duane, to whom the letters are addressed, was at one time Secretary of the Treasury.

NEW YORK, *Oct.* 28, '44.

MY DEAR SIR,

Owing to my absence from this city, (where I am now residing) I did not receive your letter of the 15th until this morning.

I regret exceedingly that circumstances should have led you to think me negligent, or uncourteous, in not returning the volume of the "Messenger" — for one or the other (perhaps both) you must long since have considered me. The facts are these: Some eight months ago, I believe, I chanced to mention, in Mr. Hirst's hearing, that I wished to look over a particular article in the "Messenger." He immediately volunteered to procure me the desired volume from you. I would much rather have borrowed it personally — but he seemed to make a point of the matter and I consented. Soon afterwards he handed me the book, which I retained a very short

[1] Poe to Mrs. Clemm. MS.

time. It is now certainly more than seven months since I returned it to Mr. Hirst, through my mother-in-law (Mrs. Clemm) who informs me that she left it at his office, with one of his brothers. Most probably it was deposited in a book-case, and thus overlooked and forgotten. May I trouble you to send for it.

Very truly yours,
EDGAR ALLAN POE.

WILLIS DUANE, ESQR.

Endorsed by Duane: N. B. The statement contained in this letter that the volume of "The Southern Literary Messenger" in question was returned to Henry B. Hirst, Esqr. was pronounced by Mr. Hirst to be "a damned lie," and subsequent events showed that Mr. Hirst was right in denying it — Mr. Poe having sold the book — I hope unintentionally — to William A. Leary, the bookseller on Second St.

W. D.

NEW YORK, *Jan.* 28, '45.

SIR,

Richmond is the last place in which I should have hoped to find a copy of either the 1st, 2d, or 3d volumes of the "Messenger." For this reason I did not apply there. I have [been] putting myself, however, to some trouble in endeavoring to collect among my friends here the separate numbers of the missing volume. I am glad that your last letter relieves me from all such trouble in future. I do not choose to recognize you in this matter at all. To the person of whom I borrowed the book, or rather who insisted on forcing it on me, I have sufficient reason to believe that it was returned. Settle your difficulties with him, and insult me with no more of your communications.

EDGAR A. POE.

MR. DUANE.

Endorsed by Duane: Bombastes Furioso Poe. Dated January 28, 1845. Received January 31, 1845. Not to be answered. N. B. The volume of "The Southern Literary Messenger" to which this letter, and that of October 28, 1844, refer, was lent by me to E. A. Poe, through Henry B. Hirst, Esq., and was sold by the said Poe among a lot of books belonging to himself to William A. Leary, a bookseller on North Seventh Street. Mr. Leary sold it to a bookseller in Richmond, Va., who sold it to the publishers of the "Messenger," who sold it to a friend of mine who was visiting Richmond, and whom I had commissioned to purchase me a copy. My name was on the title page during all these sales.

Poe had the grace to be ashamed of himself, when he heard of the manner in which I had had to repurchase my own book. He remarked to H. B. Hirst, Esqr., "What must Mr. Duane think of me," on hearing of which, I sent him word that I thought he ought to send me the five dollars which the repurchase had cost me. He died without doing so, I suppose from inability.

W. D.[1]

Poe's innocence in the matter seems to be proved by the postscript to Mrs. Clemm, nor is there any reason to believe that the original mistake, by which the volume was included in the sale of Poe's books, was anything but a natural blunder made

[1] Poe to Duane. MSS.

in the confusion of the removal, — one, however, which Mrs. Clemm, probably out of short-sighted regard for Poe's feelings, may have been unwilling to acknowledge.

Poe's first business in New York after he got settled was presumably to call on the editor of "The Sun," and offer him the well-known "Balloon Hoax." At least on the following Saturday, April 13, "The Sun" contained a postscript, in double-leaded type, announcing that a balloon had crossed the Atlantic, bringing news, and had arrived at Charleston, S. C., and promising that an extra, giving full particulars, should be issued at ten o'clock on that morning. The extra duly appeared, with its narrative, in Poe's usual realistic manner, of a transatlantic voyage by a party of English aeronauts; and at a time when such journalistic fictions were more common and less easily detected than now, it achieved a momentary success. In the same month appeared the picturesque story of metempsychosis, "A Tale of the Ragged Mountains," in "Godey's Lady's Book." No other publications during this spring, except the poem "Dreamland" in "Graham's" for June, have been traced.

The only direct source of information regarding Poe during these first months in New York is his correspondence with Lowell, who now offered to write his life for the series, "Our Contributors," then appearing in "Graham's." Poe replied as follows: —

NEW YORK, *May* 28, '44.

MY DEAR FRIEND,

I received yours last night, forwarded from Philadelphia to this city, where I intend living for the future. Touching the Biography — I would be very proud, indeed, if you would write it, and did, certainly, say to myself, and I believe to Graham — that such was my wish; but as I fancied the job might be disagreeable, I did not venture to suggest it to yourself. Your offer relieves me from great embarrassment, and I thank you sincerely. You will do me justice; and that I could not expect at all hands.

Herewith, I mail you a Life written some time since by Hirst, from materials furnished principally by Thomas and Mr. T. W. White. It is correct, I think, in the main (barring extravagant eulogy), and you can select from it whatever you deem right. The limit is 6 pp. of Graham — as much less as you please. Besides the Tales enumerated in the foot-note, I have written "The Spectacles;" "*The Oblong Box;*" "A Tale of the Ragged Mountains;" "*The Premature Burial;*" "*The Purloined Letter;*" "*The System of Doctors Tar and Fether;*" "The Black Cat;" "The Elk;" "Diddling Considered as one of the Exact Sciences;" "*Mesmeric Revelation;*" "The Gold Bug;" "*Thou art the Man;*" about 60 altogether, including the "Grotesque and Arabesque." Those italicized are as yet unpublished — in the hands of different editors. Of the "Gold Bug" (my most successful tale), more than 300,000 copies have been circulated.

There is an article on "American Poetry" in a late number of the London Foreign Quarterly, in which some allusion is made to me, as a poet, and as an imitator of Tennyson. I would like you to say (in my defense) what is the fact: that the passages quoted as imitations were written and published, in Boston, before the issue of even Tennyson's first volume. Dickens (*I know*) wrote the article — I have private personal reasons for knowing this. The portrait prepared, does not in the least resemble me.

I wrote you a long letter from Philadelphia about seven weeks since — did you get it? You make no allusion to it. In great haste,

Your most sincere friend,

EDGAR A. POE.[1]

The list of the tales still in the hands of editors which this letter gives brings out strongly one source of the discouragement under which Poe had to bear up. He had been for ten years a writer of untiring industry, and in that time had produced an amount of work large in quantity and excellent in quality, much of it belonging in the very highest rank of imaginative prose; but his books had never sold, and the income from his tales and other papers in the magazines had never sufficed to keep the wolf from the door unless he eked out his support by editing. The fact that literature was not a paying profession, however, merely involved as its consequence that Poe was under the necessity of obtaining and keeping an editorial post, if he wished to escape poverty; that he did not realize

[1] Poe to Lowell. MS.

his situation with sufficient clearness, or had not sufficient force of character to govern himself for the sake of the comfort of his home, may have been his fault or his misfortune, but is in either case obvious enough. In spite of all this, nevertheless, it should be constantly kept in mind that Poe had difficulty in selling his work and was very poorly paid. In view of the whole mass of his writings, too, of which a large portion was perishable, what he says of his own indolence in the following letter ought to be taken with some allowance for the tendency he had to idealize his own nature. A poet's analysis of his original temperament, if it be sincere, is of the highest value; for a man's conception of his own character, particularly if he be of an introspective turn, counts often as one of the most powerful influences that shape his acts. In describing himself Poe was not unconscious of the presence of Lowell as his auditor, nor forgetful of the latter's relation to him as his biographer; but the account falls in with other more disinterested utterances by Poe regarding himself, and in general it has an idiosyncratic character that marks it as genuine. In reading it one involuntarily remembers the separate, slight intimations that Poe's life and works have already afforded of his use of drugs; more than once, to the reflective mind, a trait of the opium-eater must have already been startlingly distinct, and though the direct evidence of the habit is very scanty the indirect evidence is constant, varied, and convincing. In the light of this suggestion the following rhodomontade of philosophy and self-analysis may lose something of its seeming affectation: —

NEW YORK, *July* 2, '44.

MY DEAR MR. LOWELL, — I can feel for the "constitutional indolence" of which you complain — for it is one of my own besetting sins. I am excessively slothful and wonderfully industrious — by fits. There are epochs when any kind of mental exercise is torture, and when nothing yields me pleasure but solitary communion with the "mountains and the woods," — the "altars" of Byron. I have thus rambled and dreamed away whole months, and awake, at last, to a sort of mania for composition. Then I scribble all day, and read all night, so long as the disease endures. This is also the temperament of P. P. Cooke, of Virginia, the author of "Florence Vane," "Young Rosalie Lee," and some other sweet poems — and I should not be surprised if it were your own. Cooke writes and thinks as you — and I have been told that you resemble him personally.

I am *not* ambitious — unless negatively. I now and then feel stirred up to excel a fool, merely because I hate to let a fool imagine that he may excel me. Beyond this I feel nothing of ambition. I really perceive that vanity about which most men merely prate, — the vanity of the human or temporal life. I live continually in a reverie of the future. I have no faith in human perfectibility. I think that human exertion will have no appreciable effect upon humanity. Man is now only more active — not more happy — nor more wise, than he was 6,000 years ago. The result will never vary — and to suppose that it will, is to suppose that the foregone man has lived in vain — that the foregone time is but the rudiment of the future — that the myriads who have perished have not been upon equal footing with ourselves — nor are we with our posterity. I cannot agree to lose sight of man the individual in man the mass. — I have no belief in spirituality. I think the word a *mere* word. No one has really a conception of spirit. We cannot imagine what is not. We deceive ourselves by the idea of infinitely rarefied matter. Matter escapes the senses by degrees — a stone — a metal — a liquid — the atmosphere — a gas — the luminiferous ether. Beyond this there are other modifications more rare. But to all we attach the notion of a constitution of particles — atomic composition. For this reason only we think spirit different; for spirit, we say, is unparticled, and *therefore* is not matter. But it is clear that if we proceed sufficiently far in our ideas of rarefaction, we shall arrive at a point where the particles coalesce; for, although the particles be infinite, the infinity of littleness in the spaces between them is an absurdity. — The unparticled matter, permeating and impelling all things, is God. Its activity is the thought of God — which creates. Man, and other thinking beings, are individualizations of the unparticled matter. Man exists as a "person," by being clothed with matter (the particled matter) which individualizes him. Thus habited, his life is rudimental. What we call "death" is the painful metamorphosis. The stars are the habitations of rudimental beings. But for the necessity of the rudimental life, there would have been no worlds. At death, the worm is the butterfly — still material, but of a matter unrecognized by our organs — recognized occasionally, perhaps, by the sleep-waker directly — without organs — through the mesmeric medium. Thus a sleep-waker may see ghosts. Divested of the rudimental covering, the being inhabits *space*, — what we suppose to be the immaterial universe, — passing everywhere, and acting all things, by mere volition, cognizant of all secrets but that of the nature of God's volition, — the motion, or activity, of the unparticled matter.

You speak of "an estimate of my life," — and, from what I have already said, you will see that I have none to give. I have been too deeply conscious of the mutability and evanescence of temporal things to give any continuous effort to anything — to be consistent in anything. My life has been *whim* — impulse — passion — a longing for solitude — a scorn of all things present, in an earnest desire for the future.

I am profoundly excited by music, and by some poems, — those of Tennyson especially — whom, with Keats, Shelley, Coleridge (occasionally), and a few others of like thought and expression, I regard as the *sole* poets. Music is the perfection of the soul, or idea, of Poetry. The *vagueness* of exaltation aroused by a sweet air (which should be strictly indefinite and never too strongly suggestive) is precisely what we should aim at in poetry. Affectation, within bounds, is thus no blemish.

I still adhere to Dickens as either author, or dictator, of the review. My reasons would convince you, could I give them to you, but I have left myself no space. I had two long interviews with Mr. D. when here. Nearly everything in the critique, I heard from him, or suggested to him, personally. The poem of Emerson I read to him.

I have been so negligent as not to preserve copies of any of my volumes of poems — nor was either worthy of preservation. The best passages were culled in Hirst's article. I think my best poems "The Sleeper," "The Conqueror Worm," "The Haunted Palace," "Lenore," "Dreamland," and the "Coliseum," — but all have been hurried and unconsidered. My best tales are "Ligeia," the "Gold-Bug," the "Murders in the Rue Morgue," "The Fall of the House of Usher," the "Tell-Tale Heart," the "Black Cat," "William Wilson," and "The Descent into the Maelström." "The Purloined Letter," forthcoming in the "Gift," is perhaps the best of my tales of ratiocination. I have lately written for Godey "The Oblong Box" and "Thou art the Man," — as yet unpublished. With this I mail you the "Gold-Bug," which is the only one of my tales I have on hand.

Graham has had, for nine months, a review of mine on Longfellow's "Spanish Student," which I have "used up," and in which I have exposed some of the grossest plagiarisms ever perpetrated. I can't tell why he does not publish it. — I believe G. intends my Life for the September number, which will be made up by the 10th August. Your article should be on hand as soon as convenient.   Believe me your true friend,

E. A. POE.[1]

The philosophic lucubrations in the foregoing were taken from his metaphysical tale, "Mesmeric Revelations," about to be published in the "Columbian Magazine" for August, and were afterwards more fully developed. In his next letter he

[1] Poe to Lowell. MS.

returned to the subject, and gave the noticeable information that he was engaged on his "Critical History of American Literature," a book at which he kept working until death.

NEW YORK, *August* 18, 1844.
MY DEAR FRIEND,

With this letter I take the liberty to mail you a number of the "Columbian Magazine," in which you will find a paper on "Mesmeric Revelation." In it I have endeavored to amplify some ideas which I suggested in my last letter.

You will observe many corrections and alterations. In fact the article was wofully misprinted; and my principal object in boring you with it now, is to beg of you the favor to get it copied (with corrections) in the Brother Jonathan — I mean the Boston Notion — or any other paper where you have interest. If you can do this without trouble, I would be very deeply indebted to you. I am living so entirely out of the world, just now, that I can do nothing of the kind myself.

In what are you occupied? — or is it still the far niente? For myself I am very industrious — collecting and arranging materials for a Critical History of American Literature. Do you ever see Mr. Hawthorne? He is a man of rare genius. A day or two since I met with a sketch by him called "Drowne's Wooden Image" — delicious. The leading idea, however, is suggested by Michäel Angelo's couplet: —

> Non ha l' ottimo artista alcun concetto
> Chè un marmo solo in se non circonscriva.

To be sure Angelo half stole the thought from Socrates.

How fares it with the Biography? I fear we shall be late. Most truly your friend,

EDGAR A. POE.[1]

Two months later he acknowledges the receipt of the biography, which Lowell had sent, September 27, in care of his friend, Mr. C. F. Briggs, Poe's future partner, and again reverts to the scheme for the association of authors in a Magazine Company.

NEW YORK, *Oct.* 28, '44.

MY DEAR FRIEND,

A host of small troubles growing from the *one* trouble of poverty, but which I will not trouble you with in detail, have hitherto prevented me from thanking you for the Biography and all the well-intended flatteries which it contains. But, upon the principle of better late than never, let me thank you now, again and again. I sent it to Graham on the day I received it — taking with it only one liberty in the way of modification. This I hope you will pardon. It was merely the substitution of another brief poem for the last you have done me the honor to quote.

I have not seen your marriage announced, but I presume from what you said in your penultimate letter, that I may congratulate you now. Is it so? At all events I can wish you no better wish than that you may derive from your marriage as substantial happiness as I have derived from mine.

A long time ago I wrote you a long letter to which you have never replied. It concerned a scheme for pro

[1] Poe to Lowell. MS.

tecting ourselves from the imposition of publishers by a coalition. I will state it again in brief. Suppose a dozen of the most active or influential men of letters in this country should unite for the purpose of publishing a magazine of high character. Their names to be kept secret, that their mutual support might be the more effectual. Each member to take a share of the stock at $100 a share. Each, if required, to furnish one article each month — the work to be sustained altogether by the contributions of the members, or by unpaid contributions from others. As many of the members as possible to be taken from those connected otherwise with the press: — a black-ball to exclude any one suggested as a member by those already conjoined — this to secure unanimity. These, of course, are mere hints in the rough. But suppose that (the scheme originating with yourself and me) we write to any others or, seeing them personally, engage them in the enterprise. The desired number being made up, a meeting might be held, and a constitution framed. A point in this latter might be that an editor should be elected periodically from among the stockholders.

The advantages of such a coalition seem to me very great. The Magazine could be started with a positive certainty of success. There would be no expense for contributions, while we would have the best. Plates, of course, would be disdained. The aim would be to elevate without stupefying our literature — to further justice — to resist foreign dictation — and to afford (in the circulation and profit of the journal) a remuneration to ourselves for whatever we should write.

The work should be printed in the very best manner,

and should address the aristocracy of talent. We might safely give, for $5, a pamphlet of 128 pages, and, with the support of the variety of our personal influence, we might easily extend the circulation to 20,000, — giving $100,000. The expenses would not exceed $40,000, — if indeed they reached $20,000 when the work should be fairly established. Thus there would be $60,000 to be divided among twelve, — $5,000 per annum apiece.

I have thought of this matter long and cautiously, and am persuaded that there would be little difficulty in doing even far *more* than I have ventured to suggest.

Do you hear anything more about the Lectures?
           Truly yours,   E. A. POE.[1]

It was before the date of this letter that, according to Mr. N. P. Willis, Mrs. Clemm called upon him and solicited employment for Poe, who was then, she said, ill. Willis, who was just converting his weekly paper, the "New Mirror," into the "Evening Mirror," a daily, with a weekly issue in addition, was in need of a subordinate, and in consequence of Mrs. Clemm's visit, whose countenance, he says, in his falsetto style, was made " beautiful and saintly by an evident complete giving up of her life to privation and sorrowful tenderness," Poe was engaged as an assistant — "a mechanical paragraphist," to use Willis's phrase — in the "Mirror" office. There, at a desk in a corner, he sat from nine in the morning until the paper went to press, ready for whatever work might befall. Without a

[1] Poe to Lowell. MS.

smile, or a word of praise or blame, he discharged the duties of the daily routine punctually, listened good-humoredly to the request that he would dull the edge of a criticism or soften a misanthropic sentiment, and conformed with entire fidelity to the suggestions made. Such is Willis's sketch of his subordinate, and he adds in general terms that through a considerable period he saw only "one presentment of the man, — a quiet, patient, industrious, and most gentlemanly person, commanding the utmost respect and good feeling by his unvarying deportment and ability." It needs no keen eye to read between the lines of this highly respectable description the real facts, — that the pay was small, the labor perfunctory and uninteresting, and the spirit of the poet himself, compelled to subdue his saturnine temper to the geniality of his chief, was chafing and burning within. It was a striking instance of Pegasus in harness.

The first number of "The Evening Mirror" appeared October 7, 1844, and the next day the literary columns contained this passage upon Elizabeth Barrett Browning : —

"Miss Barrett is worth a dozen of Tennyson and six of Motherwell — equal perhaps in original genius to Keats and Shelley."

Two months later this was followed up by another unmistakable sentence on the same poetess: —

"We do not believe there is a poetical soul embodied

in this world that — as a centre of thought — sees further out toward the periphery permitted to angels, than Miss Barrett."[1]

These critical dicta could have been no one's but Poe's; and as his hand is readily discerned in the literary paragraphing at many other points, it is most likely that he was employed on the daily from its start. It is as certain, on the other hand, as internal evidence can make it that he never before this time, as has been stated,[2] made one of Willis's staff of writers.

Nothing of Poe's in the "Mirror" during the first three months requires notice; but meanwhile his old pieces in editors' hands had got published: the two inferior grotesques, "The Oblong Box" and "Thou art the Man," in "Godey's" for September and October; "The Literary Life of Thingum Bob," a satirical extravaganza, mainly ridiculous, on the ways of editors and the means of popularity, which had at last found its indulgent victim in the "Southern Literary Messenger" for December,

[1] *Evening Mirror*, December 7, 1844.
[2] Ingram, i. 248. The statement that Poe contributed translations from the French to the *New Mirror* from April, 1843, to its discontinuance (which is wrongly said to have taken place before Poe left Philadelphia), and signed them with his initials, rests on a negligent examination of the files. The translations referred to begin January 3, 1843 (i. 9), and are signed E. P.; they continue to the end, but afterwards they are also signed at the beginning of the articles "By a Lady." (For example, i. 307, 355, etc.) They are, moreover, from authors whom there is no evidence that Poe read.

where it appeared anonymously; "The Purloined Letter," in the "Gift" for 1845, closing the series of the ratiocinative tales. In the "Democratic Review" for November and December, too, the first installments of the miscellaneous notes called "Marginalia" were issued; and as one reads them and the later collections, which continued to be published until Poe died, one cannot but admire the audacity of their author, who could thus resell clippings from his old book reviews since the beginning of his career, by merely giving them a new title. It was a dexterous filching back from Time of the alms for oblivion already given and stored away in that capacious wallet. Doubtless Poe looked on editors as fair game, — if they would not buy his new tales, let them purchase his old criticisms. But now an event occurred that made any manuscripts by Poe treasure-trove. Probably the editors, who had almost emptied their pigeon-holes of his accumulated contributions, were sorry they had not delayed longer.

In the "Evening Mirror," January 29, 1845. "The Raven"[1] was published, with a highly com-

[1] The author is indebted to an unpublished paper by Professor W. E. Griffis for the earliest mention of "The Raven," which, on evidence satisfactory to Professor Griffis, was in the course of composition in the summers of 1842 and 1843. The legend, however, involves the assertion that Poe, at the time of his greatest poverty in Philadelphia, was visiting a pleasure resort near Saratoga Springs. Of this there is no documentary proof, and in the author's opinion it is highly improbable; the story is therefore not included in the text.

mendatory card from Willis; and a few days later "The American Whig Review" for February, from the advance sheets of which this poem had been copied, was the centre of literary interest and the prey of editorial scissors throughout the length and breadth of the country. In the magazine the author was masked under the pseudonym "Quarles," but in this journal he had been named as E. A. Poe. The popular response was instantaneous and decisive. No great poem ever established itself so immediately, so widely, and so imperishably in men's minds. "The Raven" became, in some sort, a national bird, and the author the most notorious American of the hour. It happened — and for this Godey and Graham must have blessed their stars — that in their respective magazines of this same month the former published "The 1002 Tale," the voyage of Sinbad among the wonders made known by modern science, and the latter Lowell's sketch of Poe.

One cannot help wondering whether Poe felt no misgiving when he read the latter, with its falsifications of fact, and in the first heat of an assured fame reflected that these might some day be inquired into. Not to mention minor representations, the third misstatement of his birth (1813), the romance of his expedition to St. Petersburg, and the assertion that he left West Point on account of the birth of a son and heir to Mr. Allan, he knew to be untrue; even if he were not responsible for the original errors (the assumption is absurd) in the previous sketches of him by Griswold and Hirst, he furnished the latter's biography as the source of information, and he himself revised Lowell's own article four months before its publication. Poe circulated, and so far as he could practically accredited, falsehoods concerning himself; moreover, he approved the report of his wildness in youth, and he took no pains to explain the questionable incidents of his career. One single poor defense for his conduct, in this particular instance, he left his biographer in the guarded sentence in his letter to Lowell, in which he describes the "Museum" Life as correct "in the main." Similar untruths, however, in regard to himself occur in his letters and other writings, although it has not been thought necessary to call special attention to them in each case. This failing casts suspicion upon all unsupported assertions by him that directly affect himself.

The first trial Poe made of the value of his popularity was to lecture in the library of the New York Historical Society, on February 28, when between two and three hundred persons gathered to hear him. His subject was, as before, American Poetry, and in substance the address was the old monologue, sharp, bitter, and grim, on the sins of editors and the stupidity of versifiers, relieved only by the recitation of a few fine poems and too generous praise where he thought praise was due.

He dealt with Mrs. Sigourney, Mrs. Welby, Mrs. Osgood, Seba Smith, the Davidsons, Bryant, Halleck, Longfellow, Sprague, and Dana. The inference is that the lecture was made up by piecing together his old book reviews, and was probably textually the same with that delivered at Philadelphia, except that he now omitted reference to Griswold, with whom he was endeavoring to renew his acquaintance, plainly from selfish motives. He was still playing the part of the fearless critic, and he found some listeners to follow Lowell's lead and commend him for his daring, while they acknowledged the usefulness of his ungracious service; but there were many more in whose minds his words rankled. He was a good speaker, having natural gifts of elocution and an effective manner. Willis, in noticing the lecture, sketches him with the elegant facility that now, to our changed taste, reads so much like nonsense: —

"He becomes a desk, — his beautiful head showing like a statuary embodiment of Discrimination; his accent drops like a knife through water, and his style is so much purer and clearer than the pulpit commonly gets or requires that the effect of what he says, besides other things, pampers the ear." [1]

The lecture over, Poe returned to his work upon the "Mirror," which he had already got into trouble by an attack on Longfellow's collection of minor fugitive poems, called "The Waif;" but in

[1] *Evening Mirror*, March 12, 1845.

the course of the month he withdrew from the paper, much to the regret of his employer. His contributions to the "Mirror" were of the slightest interest, and contain nothing novel. His connection with it had inured to his own benefit by the frequent puffs of himself, both direct and indirect, which it published, and by the literary introductions which his position afforded him. He was, however, always dissatisfied with his situation, and before half a year had passed practically used the "Mirror" to advertise for a better place. In the same issue that reprinted Lowell's critical estimate of him, he is editorially praised, his capacities as a magazine editor pointed out, and himself described as "ready for propositions."[1] No proposition of the kind was made, but an arrangement was entered into by which he became associated with Charles F. Briggs, then known as "Harry Franco," in the management of the "Broadway Journal," a weekly which had issued its first number on the 4th of January previous.

Briggs was a writer of light literature, from Nantucket, and ambitious of editing a paper. A month before this time he wrote to his friend Lowell, "I have made arrangements for publishing the first number of my long-talked-of paper in January. It will be published by John Bisco, a shrewd Yankee from Worcester, who has been a school-teacher in New Jersey, and was once the publisher of the

[1] *Evening Mirror*, January 20, 1845.

'Knickerbocker.'" Further on he adds, "If you know Poe's address, send it to me when you write."[1] In consequence of this introduction, Poe contributed to the first two numbers of the "Journal" a review of Mrs. Browning, and from that time was a regular writer, at the rate of $1 a column. The impression he made on Briggs is told in the following passages of the latter's correspondence with Lowell: —

"I like Poe exceedingly well; Mr. Griswold has told me shocking bad stories about him, which his whole demeanor contradicts."[2]

"Poe tells me that Graham refused to print his tale of the Gold Bug, and kept it in his possession nine months. I never read it before last week, and it strikes me as among the most ingenious pieces of fiction that I have ever seen. If you have not read it, it will repay you for the trouble when you do. He told me furthermore that the poem which you have quoted from the House of Usher,

> 'In a valley, fair and shady [sic]
> By good angels tenanted,' etc.,

he sent to O'Sullivan for the 'Democratic,' and it was returned to him. You see by these what the judgments of Magazine editors amount to. . . . I have always strangely misunderstood Poe, from thinking him one of the Graham and Godey species, but I find him as different as possible. I think that you will like him well when you come to know him personally."[3]

[1] Briggs to Lowell, December 7, 1844. MS.
[2] Briggs to Lowell, January 6, 1845. MS.
[3] Briggs to Lowell, January 27, 1845. MS.

At the beginning of March Poe was announced as a co-editor, with Henry G. Watson and Briggs, of the "Journal;" and for the sake of elucidation it should be added that by this time he was in the thick of the so-called "Longfellow war," in which he was endeavoring to sustain the charge of plagiarism against the poet, and that incidentally he occasionally glanced at Lowell as guilty of the same offense, whether knowingly or not. By following the correspondence, which is the only original authority for this portion of Poe's career, the relations between him and his chief are easily made out. On March 8 Briggs writes, —

"Poe is only an assistant to me, and will in no manner interfere with my own way of doing things. It was requisite that I should have his or some other person's assistance, on account of my liability to be taken off from the business of the paper, and as his name is of some authority I thought it advisable to announce him as an editor. Mr. Watson's name will command the support of a good portion of the musical interest in this city and in Boston, and by putting forth his name as musical editor I can gain his time for a *pro rata* dividend on the amount of patronage which he may obtain. He is the only musical critic in the country and a thorough good fellow. Poe has left the *Mirror*. Willis was too Willisy for him. Unfortunately for him (Poe) he has mounted a very ticklish hobby just now, Plagiarism, which he is bent on riding to death, and I think the better way is to let him run down as soon as possible by giving him no check. Wiley and Putnam are going to publish a new edition of his tales and sketches. Everybody has been raven-mad about his last poem, and his lecture, which W. Story went with me to hear, has gained him a dozen or two of waspish foes who will do him more good than harm." [1]

A week later, March 16, he returns to the same subject: —

"Poe is a monomaniac on the subject of plagiarism, and I thought it best to allow him to ride his hobby to death in the outset and be done with it. It all commenced with myself. When he was in the *Mirror* office he made what I thought a very unjustifiable charge against my friend Aldrich [James Aldrich], who is one of the best fellows in the world, and I replied to it as you saw. Somebody in Boston, 'Outis,' whose name I forget, replied to P. on behalf of Longfellow and Aldrich, and so the war began. It will end as it began, in smoke. But it will do us some good by calling public attention to our paper. Poe is a much better fellow than you have an idea of. . . . The 'Journal' gains strength every day, and I am very sanguine of success." [2]

Three days later he writes again more fully: —

"I thought it best to gain Poe's services as a critic because he already has a reputation for reviewing, and I could gain them by allowing him a certain portion of the profits of the paper. He thought it would gain the 'Journal' a certain number of subscribers immediately if his name were published in connection with it. I did

[1] Briggs to Lowell. MS.
[2] Briggs to Lowell. MS.

not much like the plan, but he had had more experience than myself in the matter, so I consented. . . . I retain precisely the same authority I did in the beginning. . . . Poe's fol-de-rol about plagiarism I do not like, but the replies which it provokes serve us as advertisements, and help us along. As he dealt more severely by me and my friend Aldrich than anybody else I do not think that anybody has any right to complain of his thumps. I think that you are too sensitive in regard to Longfellow; I really do not see that he has said anything offensive about him. . . . Poe has indeed a very high admiration for Longfellow, and so he will say before he is done. For my own part I did not use to think well of Poe, but my love for you and implicit confidence in your judgment, led me to abandon all my prejudices against him when I read your account of him. The Rev. Mr. Griswold, of Philadelphia, told me some abominable lies about him, but a personal acquaintance with him has induced me to think highly of him. Perhaps some Philadelphian has been whispering foul things in your ear about him. Doubtless his sharp manner has made him many enemies. But you will think better of him when you meet him." [1]

While Briggs was thus explaining his own position and defending Poe from the strictures of Lowell, who had now ceased to correspond with him, the "Broadway Journal" was becoming notorious by this "Longfellow war," which, as Briggs remarked at the time, was "all on one side." The attitude of Poe toward Longfellow has become suf-

[1] Briggs to Lowell. MS.

ficiently clear in the course of the preceding narrative; he was a jealous admirer. The present, and most notorious, embroglio was occasioned by the publication of "The Waif," a collection of fugitive pieces by minor authors, edited by Longfellow. In the "Evening Mirror" Poe had said, —

"We conclude our notes on the 'Waif' with the observation that, although full of beauties, it is infected with a *moral taint* — or is this a mere freak of our own fancy? We shall be pleased if it be so; — but there *does* appear, in this little volume, a very careful avoidance of all American poets who may be supposed especially to interfere with the claims of Mr. Longfellow. These men Mr. Longfellow can continuously *imitate* (*is* that the word?) and yet never incidentally commend."[1]

The discussion thus begun was followed up in succeeding issues with the protests of Longfellow's friends and the editorial comment in reply, extenuating on Willis's part, vindicatory on Poe's, until Willis withdrew from the discussion in a card in which he stated his entire dissent from "all the disparagement of Longfellow" that had been published in the "Mirror;" and soon after he admitted to its columns a lengthy defense of him by one "Outis," at just about the time that Poe left the office to join Briggs.

On March 1 the new editor of the "Broadway Journal" began his reply to "Outis," which was continued in weekly installments through five num-

[1] *Evening Mirror*, January 14, 1845.

bers. As far as it related to Longfellow it repeated textually the charge made in "Burton's" in regard to "The Midnight Mass for the Dying Year;" discredited a letter in which Longfellow had personally explained the error in consequence of which he had translated a song of Motherwell's back into English from the German of Wolff, under the impression that it was original with the latter; and finally charged new plagiarisms, particularly in the case of "The Spanish Student," some scenes of which he traced to his own "Politian" in a violent passage in which probably the old review is incorporated.

To sum up Poe's strictures as urged here and in earlier and later writings, Longfellow was a plagiarist, a didactic poet, and a writer of hexameters. In this there is so much truth as is involved in the milder statement that he belonged to the poets of cultivation rather than of irresistible original genius, that he frequently wrote to illustrate or enforce morality, and that his ear was too little refined to be offended by the spondaic weakness of an English hexameter. That Poe was sincere in his opinions, though he enforced them rudely and with the malicious pleasure of an envious rival, there can be little question; that Longfellow never pilfered from Poe, and that in the unconscious adaptations natural to a poet of culture he never imitated him, there can be no doubt at all. In the elusive search for motives in the case, it is best to remain content with Longfellow's charitable opinion: "The harshness of his criticisms I have never attributed to anything but the irritation of a sensitive nature, chafed by some indefinite sense of wrong." [1]

Poe's other contributions to the "Journal" during the time that he had "a third interest" (as he described to Griswold his salary of a third of the profits) were plentiful, but not original. The miserable grotesque "Peter Snooks," and the long-rejected tale "The Premature Burial," of which no earlier publication is found, were the only new stories; but of the old ones he reprinted, sometimes with slightly changed names and other revision, "Lionizing," "Berenice," "Bon-Bon," "The Oval Portrait," "The Philosophy of Furniture," "Three Sundays in a Week," "The Pit and the Pendulum," "Eleonora," "Shadow," "The Assignation," and "Morella;" and of his poems, "To F——," "The Sleeper," "To One in Paradise," and "The Conqueror Worm." He also utilized passages from old book-reviews by incorporating them in new notices. His new papers were for the most part hack-work articles on anastatic printing, street-paving, magazine literature, etc., etc.; the only noteworthy pieces being a critical baiting of one W. W. Lord, who had committed the unpardonable sin of plagiarizing from the author of "The Raven," and the exhaustive review of some volumes of Mrs. Browning's, already mentioned.

[1] *Southern Literary Messenger*, November, 1849.

In this last, although nearly all the space is taken up with unfavorable comment in detail, Miss Barrett is at the conclusion lifted to the highest pinnacle but one: "She has surpassed all her poetical contemporaries of either sex (with a single exception)," that exception being Tennyson.

Outside of the "Journal," Poe contributed to the April "Whig Review" "The Doomed City" and "The Valley Nis," revised, and "Some Words with a Mummy," a grotesque on the old theme that "there is nothing new under the sun," with some unusual satire on politics. Before the end of the year, it may be added here, he had published in the "Democratic" "The Power of Words," a metaphysical tale; in the "Whig," "The Facts in the Case of M. Valdemar," that tale which for mere physical disgust and foul horror has no rival in literature, though in writing it, Poe was much indebted to a romance, "The Seeress of Prevorst," and in the same magazine in July the new poem "Eulalie," and in August the review of "The American Drama" in which he dealt mainly with Willis's "Tortesa," and once more with Longfellow's "Spanish Student" at great length; in "Graham's," "The Imp of the Perverse," the last of the tales of conscience, and the absurd madhouse grotesque "Dr. Tarr and Prof. Fether;" and in "Godey's" two installments of the clippings from old magazines, called "Marginalia." These publications include all his new writings until 1846.

The history of the "Broadway Journal" in the mean time was interesting. When the first volume was approaching its end, Briggs wrote to Lowell, June 29, 1845, reviewing his plans: —

"I have arrangements on foot with a new publisher for the Journal who will enable me to give it a fresh start, and I trust very soon to be able to give you an earnest of its profits. I shall haul down Poe's name; he has latterly got into his old habits and I fear will injure himself irretrievably. I was taken at first with a certain appearance of independence and learning in his criticisms, but they are so verbal, and so purely selfish that I can no longer have any sympathy with him." [1]

Not long before, Lowell, being on his way from Philadelphia back to Cambridge, called on Poe; but as, in Mrs. Clemm's words to the former, "he was not himself" that day, none of those golden hopes, indulged in by Poe, and at an earlier date by Briggs also, were realized from this personal meeting. The interview, however, prepared Lowell for the following passage in Briggs's next letter, in explanation of what seemed a sudden demise of the "Journal:" —

"The non-appearance of the 'Broadway Journal' has probably surprised you. I had made arrangements with a new publisher, — a very good business man, — and had agreed upon terms with Bisco to buy his interest; but when I came to close with him he exacted more than I had stipulated for, and finding that he was determined

[1] Briggs to Lowell. MS.

to give me trouble I refused to do anything with the
'Journal.' I had the first number of the new volume all
ready to be issued, with a handsomely engraved title,
etc.; but, as I could not put the new publisher's name
upon it without Bisco's consent, I let it go a week, meaning to issue a double number — not doubting that I could
agree with him upon some terms; but he had fallen into
the hands of evil advisers, and became more extortionate
than ever. Poe in the meantime got into a drunken
spree, and conceived an idea that I had not treated him
well, for which he had no other grounds than my having
loaned him money, and persuaded Bisco to carry on the
'Journal' himself. As his doing so would give me a legal claim upon him, and enable me to recover something
from him, I allowed him to issue one number, but it is
doubtful whether he issues another. Mr. Homans, the
publisher, with whom I had agreed to undertake the
publication of the Journal, is an educated man and a
thorough good fellow, with a very extensive book-selling
connection. He is still desirous of taking hold of the
'Journal,' and has made me a very liberal offer to go on
with him if he can purchase Bisco's share. But I do not
yet know how the affair will terminate.

"Poe's mother-in-law told me that he was quite tipsy
the day that you called upon him, and that he acted
very strangely; but I perceived nothing of it when I
saw him in the morning. He was to have delivered a
poem before the societies of the New York University
a few weeks since, but drunkenness prevented him. I
believe he had not drank anything for more than eighteen months until within the past three months, but in
this time he has been very frequently carried home in a

wretched condition. I am sorry for him. He has some good points, but, taken altogether, he is badly made up. I was deceived by his superficial talents when I first met him, and relied too much upon the high opinion which you had expressed of him. His learning is very much like that of the famous Mr. Jenkinson in the 'Vicar of Wakefield.' He talks about dactyls and spondees with surprising glibness; and the names of metres being caviare to nine men out of ten, he has gained a reputation for erudition at a very cheap rate. He makes quotations from the German, but he can't read a word of the language." [1]

Some further explanation of the matter was given August 1: —

"I did not give you sufficient particulars to enable you to understand my difficulties with Bisco and Poe. Neither has done anything without my full consent, and I have nothing to complain of but their meanness, which they could n't help. I had told P. a month before that I should drop his name from the 'Journal.' He said I might keep it there if I wanted to, although he intended to go into the country and devote his time to getting up books, and would not therefore be able to assist me. I had also told Bisco that I would have nothing more to do with him after the close of the first volume, and that I would not carry it on unless I could find a publisher to my mind. I did find such a publisher, and Bisco, thinking that I was very anxious to go on with it, was more exacting in his demands for his share of the 'Journal' than I thought just, so I told him

[1] Briggs to Lowell, July 16, 1845. MS.

IN NEW YORK. 237

I would not take it; and he, thinking to spite me, and Poe, thinking to glorify himself in having overmastered me, agreed to go on with it. I laughed at their folly, and told them to go ahead; but I still hold the same right that I ever did, and could displace them both if I wished to do so. But seeing so much poltroonery and littleness in the business gave me a disgust to it, and I let them alone, hoping to get back from Bisco some money which I had advanced him." [1]

Three weeks later he wrote a characterization of Poe more in detail: —

"You have formed a correct estimate of Poe's characterless character. I have never met a person so utterly deficient of high motive. He cannot conceive of anybody's doing anything, except for his own personal advantage; and he says, with perfect sincerity, and entire unconsciousness of the exposition which it makes of his own mind and heart, that he looks upon all reformers as madmen; and it is for this reason that he is so great an egoist. He cannot conceive why the world should not feel an interest in whatever interests him, because he feels no interest himself in what does not personally concern him. Therefore, he attributes all the favor which Longfellow, yourself, or anybody else receives from the world as an evidence of the ignorance of the world, and the lack of that favor in himself he attributes to the world's malignity. It is too absurd for belief, but he really thinks that Longfellow owes his fame mainly to the ideas which he has borrowed from his (Poe's) writings in the 'Southern Literary Messenger.' His presumption is

[1] Briggs to Lowell. MS.

beyond the liveliest imagination. He has no reverence for Homer, Shakespeare, or Milton, but thinks that 'Orion' is the greatest poem in the language. He has too much prudence to put his opinions into print, — or, rather, he can find nobody impudent enough to print them, — but he shows himself in his private converse. The Bible, he says, is all rigmarole. As to his Greek, — you might see very well if it were put in your eye. He does not read Wordsworth, and knows nothing about him." [1]

As has been incidentally mentioned above, the "Journal" was suspended for one week; and when the first number of the second volume appeared, a week later, it bore Poe's name as sole editor. Since he describes himself as "one third proprietor," in his old terms, it seems probable that he agreed to go on with Bisco for one third of the profits, just as before, but having entire charge. Bisco himself declares that he meant to get rid of Briggs, and, in order to do so, took up with Poe. There was from the first some financial tangle between the parties, which, fortunately, there is no need to unravel. The result of the difference was to install Poe in full control. One of his acts was to have a fling at Briggs, in connection with which our last extract from the latter's correspondence has its interest: —

"You take Poe's *niaiseries* too seriously. I only cared for his unhandsome allusion to me in the B. J. because it proved him a baser man than I thought him before.

[1] Briggs to Lowell, August 21, 1845. MS.

... The truth is that I have not given him the shadow of a cause for ill-feeling; on the contrary he owes me now for money that I lent him to pay his board and keep him from being turned into the street. But he knows that I am possessed of the secret of his real character and he no doubt hates me for it. Until it was absolutely necessary for me to expose some of his practices to save myself from contempt I never breathed a syllable of his ill habits, but I tried in vain to hide them from observation out of pure compassion, for I had not known him long before I lost all respect for him and felt a loathing disgust for his habits. I did not much blame him for the matter of his remarks about Jones, although the manner of them was exceeding improper and unjust; the real cause of his ire was Jones' neglecting to enumerate him among the humorous writers of the country, for he has an inconceivably extravagant idea of his capacities as a humorist. The last conversation I had with Poe he used all his power of eloquence in persuading me to join him in the joint editor-ship of the 'Stylus.' "[1]

Poe remained simply editor, with his third interest for pay, until October. In the first number of his editing was a review of his own "Tales,"[2] just published by Wiley and Putnam as No. 2 in their

[1] Briggs to Lowell, October 13, 1845. MS.
[2] *Tales.* By Edgar A. Poe. New York: Wiley and Putnam. 1845. Pp. 228. The contents are, in order: The Gold Bug, The Black Cat, Mesmeric Revelations, Lionizing, The Fall of the House of Usher, The Descent into the Maelström, The Colloquy of Monos and Una, The Conversation of Eiros and Charmion, The Murders of the Rue Morgue, the Mystery of Marie Roget, The Purloined Letter, The Man in the Crowd.

"Library of American Books," and edited by Duyckinck, who certainly had selected from Poe's numerous and uneven stories those on which his fame has proved itself to be founded. Poe, however, declared in private, "Those selected are *not* my best, nor do they fairly represent me in any respect."[1] He meant that they were too much of one kind, whereas he had aimed at diversity in his writings; in other words, the grotesque tales were slighted, and hence the universality of his genius and the versatility of his talents were not illustrated. During the first months of his editorship he reprinted, as before, his old tales, occasionally somewhat revised: "How to Write a Blackwood Article," "The Masque of the Red Death," "The Literary Life of Thingum-Bob," "The Business Man," "The Man who was Used Up," "Never Bet the Devil your Head," "The Tell-Tale Heart," "William Wilson," "Why the Little Frenchman wears his Hand in a Sling," "The Landscape Garden," "The Tale of Jerusalem," "The Island of the Fay," "MS. Found in a Bottle," "The Duc d'Omelette,"[2] "King Pest,"[2] "The Power of Words," and "Diddling Considered as one of the Fine Arts." Of his poetry he used "The Coliseum," "Zante," "Israfel," "Silence,"[3] "Science," "Bridal Ballad," "Eulalie," "Lenore,"[2] "A Dream,"[3] "Catholic Hymn,"[4] "Romance,"[3] "City in the

---

[1] Poe to ———. Ingram, ii. 24.
[2] Signed "Littleton Barry." [3] Signed P. [4] Signed ‡.

Sea," "To the River ——," "The Valley of Unrest," "To F——," "To ——"[1] ("The bowers whereat"), "Song"[1] ("I saw thee"), and "Fairyland;"[2] of criticism there was nothing noteworthy except a flattering review of Hirst and a satirical one of Hoyt, both poetasters.

In October occurred one of the best known incidents of Poe's life. In the summer he had visited Boston, and now was invited to give a poem before the Boston Lyceum (it will be remembered that Lowell had at Poe's request formerly interested himself to obtain an engagement for him to lecture before the same organization), and he accepted. On the evening appointed, October 16, a lecture, which was the second of the course, having been given by Caleb Cushing, Poe came forward on the platform of the Odeon, and after some prefatory remarks about the foolishness of didacticism read "Al Aaraaf." The audience, the hour being late, began to disperse, but enough persons remained to enjoy his recitation of "The Raven," with which the entertainment closed. Whatever was the cause, Poe disappointed his audience, and afterwards some Boston papers commented somewhat severely on the performance, especially when the truth came out that the poem given was a juvenile production, written years before. Poe, when he returned to New York, declared that he had acted of malice prepense.

[1] Unsigned.   [2] Signed ++

"It would scarcely be supposed that we would put ourselves to the trouble of composing for the Bostonians anything in the shape of an *original* poem. We did not. We had a poem (of about five hundred lines) lying by us — one quite as good as new — one at all events, that we considered would answer sufficiently well for an audience of transcendentalists. *That* we gave them — it was the best that we had — for the price — and it *did* answer remarkably well. Its name was *not* "The Messenger Star" — who but Miss Walter would ever think of so delicious a little bit of invention as that? We had no name for it at all. The poem is what is occasionally called a 'juvenile poem' — but the fact is, it is anything but juvenile now, for we wrote it, printed it, and published it, in book form, before we had fairly completed our tenth year. We read it *verbatim*, from a copy now in our possession, and which we shall be happy to show at any moment to any of our inquisitive friends."[1] . . .

The audacity of this last claim to precocity of genius, which would make Poe ten years younger than he was, is almost burlesque. He goes on to say, "Over a bottle of champagne that night, we confessed to Messrs. Cushing, Whipple, Hudson, Field, and a few other natives who swear not altogether by the frog-pond — we confessed, we say, the soft impeachment of the hoax."

This was Poe's explanation, given in the course of an article, destitute of any gentlemanly trait, in reply to Miss Walter, of the "Transcript," whose name had before been the target for his

[1] The *Broadway Journal*, November 1, 1845.

shafts. One would say that pique rather than delight was roused in him by the success of what has been called his "mischief-making" expedition to Boston. The fact probably was, as originally stated by Griswold, that Poe had undertaken an engagement, and being unable to write a poem for such an occasion he resorted to his old compositions, and selected "Al Aaraaf" as the most available. He may have felt some doubt as to how the audience would take it, but he had none as to the excellence of his poem. His elaborate explanation of his motives was an afterthought.

Just at this time occurred the singular transaction by which Poe became sole proprietor of the "Journal" October 24. Mr. Bisco says that he made over his rights to Poe for the consideration of a promissory note for $50, signed by Poe, and indorsed by Horace Greeley, who had at one time written on political topics for the paper; and when it came due Bisco collected it, as was to be anticipated, from the indorser. Greeley himself refers to this incident, with sharp pleasantry: —

"A gushing youth once wrote me to this effect:

'DEAR SIR, — Among your literary treasures, you have doubtless preserved several autographs of our country's late lamented poet, Edgar A. Poe. If so, and you can spare one, please inclose it to me, and receive the thanks of yours truly.'

I promptly responded as follows: —

'DEAR SIR, — Among my literary treasures, there

happens to be exactly *one* autograph of our country's late lamented poet, Edgar A. Poe. It is his note of hand for fifty dollars, with my indorsement across the back. It cost me exactly $50.75 (including protest), and you may have it for half that amount. Yours, respectfully.'

That autograph, I regret to say, remains on my hands, and is still for sale at first cost, despite the lapse of time and the depreciation of our currency."[1]

Thus Poe at last owned and edited the "Journal," but he needed capital to run it. In August he had written to Neilson Poe,[2] with whom he had reëstablished connections, that he should start a magazine in January; but this was probably only a chance reference to the "Stylus," which he was always trying to float. At present he devoted himself to raising further funds to pay the current bills of the paper. Among Griswold's letters, the authenticity of which cannot be fairly doubted, is one written two days after the "Journal" passed into Poe's hands. But before citing this it should be remarked that Poe and his future biographer had now become reconciled, and wore at least the show of amity until Poe's death. The occasion of their renewal of acquaintance was Griswold's "Prose Writers of America," in which Poe wished for notice. Soon after the first exchange of letters

[1] *Recollections of a Busy Life.* By Horace Greeley: pp. 196. 197.

[2] Poe to Neilson Poe, August 8, 1845. MS.

Poe sent him his poems to be edited, and at a later date he reminded him of the many times he had spoken favorably of him, and gave as the reason for the personal attack in the Philadelphia lecture the fact that some one had ascribed to Griswold the "beastly article" to which reference has already been made.

On October 26, 1845, at any rate, Poe felt sufficiently sure of Griswold's favor to make a request:

MY DEAR GRISWOLD: *Will* you aid me at a pinch — at one of the greatest pinches conceivable? If you will, I will be indebted to you for life. After a prodigious deal of manœuvering, I have succeeded in getting "The Broadway Journal" entirely within my own control. It will be a fortune to me if I can hold it — and I can do it easily with a very trifling aid from my friends. May I count you as one? Lend me $50, and you shall never have cause to regret it.

Truly yours,
EDGAR A. POE.[1]

In reply to this he apparently received twenty-five dollars at once, and as much more on the first of December; but, the lack of capital continuing to be a pressing trouble, he wrote to his cousin, George Poe, touching the same matter: —

NEW YORK, *November 30, '45.*

DEAR SIR, —

Since the period when (no doubt for good reasons) you declined aiding me with the loan of $50, I have

[1] Griswold, xxi., xxii.

perseveringly struggled against a thousand difficulties, and have succeeded, although not in making money, still in attaining a position in the world of letters, of which, under the circumstances, I have no reason to be ashamed.

For these reasons — because I feel that I have exerted myself to the utmost — and because I believe that you will appreciate my efforts to elevate the family name — I now appeal to you once more for aid.

With this letter, I send you a number of "The Broadway Journal," of which, hitherto, I have been merely editor, and one third proprietor. I have lately purchased the whole paper, and, if I can retain it, it will be a fortune to me in a short time; — but I have exhausted all my resources in the purchase. In this emergency I have thought that you might not be indisposed to assist me.

I refrain from saying any more — for I feel that if your heart is kindly disposed toward me, I have already[1]

[Rest, with signature, cut off.]

While these embarrassments were annoying him, Poe used his paper for the reproduction of his works as formerly, and before the end of the year he had reprinted "Some Words with a Mummy," "The Devil in the Belfry," "A Tale of the Ragged Mountains," "Four Beasts in One," "The Oblong Box," "Mystification," "Loss of Breath,"[2] and one not elsewhere published, so far as is known, "The Spectacles," an extremely weak piece of humor, which Horne had tried to get printed in Eng-

[1] Poe to George Poe, November 30, 1845. MS.
[2] Signed "Littleton Barry."

land without success. The poetry had been exhausted before this date, all of it having been put into the printer's hands in September.

The "Journal" showed vigorous management; its advertisements had been largely increased, and its circulation is said to have doubled. The last numbers of December are full of promises regarding the future; but George Poe not responding, the Greeley note becoming due, and obliging friends being now obdurate, the demise of the paper suddenly took place. On December 26 was published the following: —

VALEDICTORY.

Unexpected engagements demanding my whole attention, and the objects being fulfilled so far as regards myself personally, for which "The Broadway Journal" was established, I now, as its editor, bid farewell — as cordially to foes as to friends.

EDGAR A. POE.

What other objects Poe achieved, except the republication of nearly all the narrative prose he had ever written, and of a considerable portion of his poems, it is hard to see. One more number is said to have been issued, January 3, under the editorship of Thomas Dunn English, with which the "Journal" expired.

Just at the close of the year, apparently on December 31, Poe's collected poems had been issued by Wiley and Putnam, under the title "The Raven and Other Poems." [1] The volume contained nearly all the poetry he had ever written, and the versions are those now established in the text. In the preface he speaks in dispraise of his work, saying that he thinks nothing in this volume of much value to the public, or very creditable to himself. "Events not to be controlled," he continues, in the well-known words, "have prevented me from making at any time any serious effort in what, under happier circumstances, would have been the field of my choice. With me poetry has been not a purpose, but a passion; and the passions should be held in reverence; they must not — they cannot at will be excited, with an eye to the paltry compensations, or the more paltry commendations, of mankind." [2]

The poems which this proud apology prefaced comprise the poetic labors of their author up to the

---

[1] *The Raven and Other Poems.* By Edgar A. Poe. New York: Wiley and Putnam. 1845. The contents were, in order, The Raven, Valley of Unrest, Bridal Ballad, The Sleeper, The Coliseum, Lenore, Catholic Hymn, Israfel, Dream-land, Sonnet — To Zante, City in the Sea, To One in Paradise, Eulalie — A Song, To F——s S. O——d, To F——, Sonnet — Silence, The Conqueror Worm, The Haunted Palace, Scenes from "Politian." Then followed, with the foot-note still published, Poems in Youth: Sonnet — To Science, Al Aaraaf, Tamerlane, A Dream, Romance, Fairy-land, To ——, To the River ——, The Lake — To ——, Song, To Helen. It is scarcely necessary to add that the youthful poems are not printed exactly "*verbatim,* without alteration from the original edition," but the changes, nevertheless, are not important.

[2] *Works,* i. 4.

close of this year, and although a few were to be added before his death, they illustrate fully his poetic powers. In attempting an estimate of their worth, it is only just to recur once more to the theory which Poe had now completely developed regarding the aims and scope of poetry; for it is his own comment on his own text. To put it in the fewest words, Poe believed that of the pleasures that spring from Truth, which satisfies the intellect, or from Passion, which excites the heart, or from Beauty, which elevates the soul, the latter is the most pure, keen, and absorbing; and this because it appeals to that sense of harmony and feeds that yearning for its manifestation which belongs to the immortal part of man. In the moods aroused through the sentiment of beauty man is most clearly conscious of his eternal nature, and in the lifting up of his spirit under such influences penetrates (so Poe thought) to the divine. This subtle power is possessed by all beauty in its sensible forms as built by God in nature; but the suggestions of something fairer beyond and above nature, which arise in its presence, stimulate man to attempt to reach this unknown loveliness by recombining the elements he perceives, and thus in imagination (which repeats the creative act of God) to fashion by art, under the guidance of his own instinct, an ideal beauty which shall be a new and purer source of spiritual emotion. This creation of beauty is the end of all the fine arts, but in music and in poetry it is most directly accomplished. It would, however, be an error to suppose that Poe, in thus adopting the doctrines of Coleridge and rejecting passion and truth and morality as poetic themes, meant to sever poetry by distinct boundaries from those regions of life; on the contrary, he expressly states that "the incitements of Passion, the precepts of Duty, and even the lessons of Truth" may be advantageously introduced into a poem, if they are only subordinated and blended in by the skill of the artist who understands how to use them for the heightening of the effect of mere beauty; and furthermore, it should be observed that to beauty itself Poe assigns both a moral value, as lending attraction to virtue, and an intellectual value, as leading out to the mystical province of that truth which, withdrawn from the probing of the reason, is fathomed by the imagination alone. Such a speculation may be regarded as a baseless reverie or as profound philosophy; but it is essential to keep in mind the fact not only that Poe made beauty the theme of poetry, but also that he found its value in intimations of the divine; or, in other words, that he was devoted to a mystical æstheticism. Of the minor articles of his creed it is necessary to recall only those which assert that a poem should be brief; should aim at a single artistic effect, but not to the exclusion of a secondary suggested meaning; and should be touched, if possible, by a certain quaintness, grotesqueness, or peculiarity of rhythm or metre, to give it tone.

One who reflects upon the character of mind implied by the holding of this theory, the elements of which assimilated and united only very slowly in Poe's case, cannot be surprised at the objections ordinarily urged against Poe's verses. They are said to be vague, destitute of ideas, insubstantial, unreal, full of artifice, and trenching on the domain of music. That these phrases accurately describe the impression made by the poems on many minds by no means strangers to the poetic sentiment may be granted without hesitation; and if any one maintains that from certain points of view such words are justly applied, it would be futile to dissent. The diversity of criticism upon Poe's verse is largely due to the assumption that it can be measured intelligibly by any other than his own standard. The poet strives, Poe thought, to bring about in others the state felt in himself; and in his own case that was one of brooding reverie, a sort of emotional possession, full of presentiment, expectancy, and invisible suggestion, the mood that is the habitat of superstition; vagueness was the very hue in which he painted. Again, if in his prose tales he declares repeatedly that he meant not to tell a story, but to produce an effect, much more is it to be thought that in poetry he aimed not to convey an idea, but to make an impression. He was not a philosopher nor a lover; he never served truth nor knew passion; he was a dreamer, and his life was, warp and woof, mood and sentiment instead of act and thought. When he came to poetic expression which must needs be the genuine manifestation of the soul's secret, he had no wisdom and no romance to disclose, of any earthly reality, and he was forced to bring out his meagre store of visionary facts, to which his random and morbid feelings alone gave credibility. To say of such works that they are destitute of ideas and insubstantial is not criticism, — it is mere description. Even for that slight framework of the things of sense which Poe had to shape in order to allegorize his moods at all, he seems but little indebted to nature. The purely imaginary character of his landscape has been touched on, again and again, hitherto; it is indicative of the obvious fact that he never regarded nature as anything but the crucible of his fancies. To qualify his conceptions as unreal is merely to gather into a colorless word the quivering eastern valley, the flaming city isled in darkness, the angel-thronged, star-lighted theatre of the Worm's conquest, the wind-blown kingdom by the sea, the Titanic cypress alley, the night's Plutonian shore, or any other of those dim tracts,

"Out of space, out of time,"

where his spirit wandered. So, too, if any one presses the charge of artifice home, it must be allowed just, though it attaches only to the later poems and is the excess of art. No poet was ever less spontaneous in excellence than Poe. When one reads, at successive stages of his career, the same old stanzas in new versions, and notices how they grew out of rudeness of many different descriptions into such perfection as they reached, he perceives before him an extraordinary example of growth in the knowledge and exercise of the poetic art, — the pulse of the machine laid bare. The changes are minute and almost innumerable, the approaches to perfection are exceedingly gradual, the last draft is sometimes only slightly related to the earliest; but — and this is the point that proves Poe primarily a careful artist rather than an inspired poet — in every instance the alteration is judicious, the step is a step forward. One who achieves success mainly by self-training in art comes to rely on art overmuch; and so he degenerates into artifice, or visible art, puts his faith in mechanism, and trusts his fame to cogs and levers of words and involutions of sounds; or it may happen, as was perhaps finally the case with Poe, that a weakened mind keeps facility with the tools when the work slips from its grasp. At least, so much truth lies in this last objection of the artificiality of Poe's work as to justify the more generous statement that he was, in verse as in prose, essentially a skillful literary artist. And furthermore, music was an essential element of his art. It is true that his ear for verbal melody was at first very defective, and was never perfect, but in much of his best work the rhythmic movement is faultless in its flow and its simplicity. This is not, however, all that is meant by saying that he borrowed effects from music. In his verses sonorousness counts independently of its relation to the meaning of the words, and the poem seems at intervals to become merely a volume of sound, in which there is no appeal to the mind at all, but only a stimulation of the feelings as by the tones of an instrument. In the management of the theme, too, particularly in his later verse, the handling of the refrain, the recurrence to the same vocal sounds and the same order of syllabic structure, the movement of the whole poem by mere new presentations of the one idea, as in "The Raven," or of the same group of imagery, as in "Ulalume," partakes of the method of musical composition. In these ways Poe did appropriate the effects of music, and they blended with the other characteristics of his art as sound and color in nature, to make that vague impression on the mind of which he sought the secret. It belongs to his originality that he could thus exercise his mastery in the borderland between poetry and music, where none before him had had power.

After all, to meet the last circumscription of his praise, he did not write a dozen poems of the best rank. Those of his youth, already sufficiently characterized, were works of promise in a boy, but they would not have made a bubble as they sank in the waters of oblivion. Of those composed in manhood (and as such should be reckoned the present versions of "The Sleeper," "The Valley of

Unrest," "The City in the Sea," "To One in Paradise," and possibly "Israfel") the first fine one was "The Haunted Palace," nor was that to be free from later improvements; and from its appearance until his death Poe's poems of the same level can be counted on the fingers. To the world, indeed, he is the genius of one poem only, "The Raven;" unless, to support his name, the fame of "The Bells" and of "Ulalume" be added. There is no occasion to examine either these three or any others of the dozen that are justly immortal; they all belong to the class of poems that make their way at once or not at all. Yet it may serve to define and possibly to elucidate Poe's nature if it be incidentally noticed that, except in his single lyric "Israfel," the theme of his imagination is ruin; and that in the larger number of these few best poems it is the special case of ruin which he declared the most poetic of all, — the death of a beautiful woman. It is of no concern that the treatment was radically different, so that in each instance a poem absolutely unique was created; the noteworthy fact is, at present, that Poe's genius was developed in its strength by brooding over a fixed idea, as the insane do; and when, under great excitement, some other mode of expression was imperative, it was found only in such objective work as the marvelous allegory of "The Conqueror Worm," so terrible in the very perfection of its flawless art, or in such spirit-broken confession as that other allegory of "The Haunted Palace," which in intense, imaginative self-portraiture is scarcely excelled in literature. The secret life, the moments of strongest emotion, the hours of longest reach, implied by such motives as these, make that impenetrable background of shadow against which in these poems the poet stands relieved forever, — the object of deep pity, whether his sufferings were imaginary or real, inevitable or self-imposed, the work of unregarding fate or the strict retribution of justice.

But when the utmost has been said adversely, the power of these dozen poems is undiminished even over those who admit their vagueness, their lack of ideas, their insubstantial and unreal quality, their sometimes obvious artifice, their likeness to musical compositions, and their scant number. Poe would himself have considered such censures as praises in disguise, and scoffed at their authors as dull-mettled rascals, like Partridge at the play. The power, after all, remains; first and foremost a power of long-practiced art, but also of the spell itself, of the forms evoked independently of the magic that compels them, — a fascination that makes the mind pause. If one is not subdued by this, at least at moments, there are some regions of mortality unknown to him; he will never disembark on No Man's Land. If one is not sensible of the exquisite construction here shown, the poetic art is as much a mystery to him as was Prospero's to Caliban. But if one with the eye to see and the heart to understand, being once overcome by these poems, continues to inhabit with the ill things that dwell there, he forgets Poe's own gospel of the ends of art, and perceives not the meaning of the irony that made the worshiper of beauty the poet of the outcast soul. If it be the office of poetry to intimate the divine, it must be confessed these works of Poe intimate the infernal; they are variations struck on the chord of evil that vibrates in all life, throbs of the heart of pain, echoes of ruin that float up from the deep within the deep, the legend and pæan and ritual of hopeless death; they belong to the confusions of a superstitious mind, the feebleness of an unmanned spirit, the misery of an impotent will. Profound in knowledge of the obscure sources of feeling; almost magical in the subtlety of their art; bold, clear, and novel in imagination; ideal, absolutely original, married to music of the most alluring charm, these poems fulfill all conditions of Poe's standard save one, and that the supreme one. They deserve their fame; but, seeing the gifts of genius involved in their creation, one turns from the literary result, and scans more narrowly the life in which they were involved.

At this time Poe first began to frequent, sometimes in company with his invalid wife, but more often alone, the receptions at which the *littérateurs* of the metropolis, particularly the ladies, used to meet. These gatherings took place commonly at Dr. Orville Dewey's, the eloquent preacher; or at

James Lawson's, distinguished in Poe's mind as a man interested in our literature although a Scotchman, and as an enthusiast in all matters of taste although himself devoid of it; or at Miss Anne Charlotte Lynch's, a poetess of the Willis group, whose weekly receptions in Waverley Place were thronged by literary men, artists, poetesses, and others of like pursuits. At such resorts, in the midst of a variously constituted company, Poe would sit, dressed in plain black, but with the head, the broad, retreating white brow, the large, luminous, piercing eyes, the impassive lips, that gave the visible character of genius to his features; and if the loud, bluff pleasantry of the humorist physician, Dr. Francis, or the high-keyed declamation of Margaret Fuller in her detested transcendentalist Boston dialect, would permit, he would himself, in his ordinary subdued, musical tones exercise the fascination of his talk on women of lesser note, among whom — to mention only those that come within the scope, of this narrative — were Mrs. Elizabeth Oakes-Smith, once known as the author of "The Sinless Child"(which Poe thought the most original long American poem excepting Maria del Occidente's "Bride of Seven"); Mrs. Elizabeth Frieze Ellet, whose hand Poe took in an evil hour; and Mrs. Mary Gove, afterwards Mrs. Nichols, "a Mesmerist, a Swedenborgian, a phrenologist, a homœopathist, and a disciple of Priessnitz," and, adds Poe, "what more I am not prepared to say."[1] Notwithstanding his natural reserve his manners were pleasing, and his conversation, although best when but one or two were present, must have been engaging and impressive even in the constraint and inconsequence of general talk. Upon women, especially in these last years, his voice and look had a magical power, although this was probably only the extraordinary charm peculiar to the Virginia society in which he was bred; and, on his side, Poe had long indulged a habit of idealizing women and worshiping them in secret. An attachment of this sort he had formed for Mrs. Francis Sargent Osgood (a poetess of thirty and the wife of an American artist), who on publishing her first volume, seven years before, in London had been taken up as a *protégée* by Mrs. Norton. Poe had noticed her verses many times with great favor, and in his New York lecture, especially, eulogized her in warm terms. Shortly after this latter incident Willis one day handed her "The Raven," with the author's request for her judgment on it, and for an introduction to herself. She assented, and a few days later Poe called at the Astor House to see her.

"I shall never forget," she wrote, "the morning when I was summoned to the drawing-room by Mr. Willis to receive him. With his proud and beautiful head erect, his dark eyes flashing with the electric light of feeling and of thought, a peculiar, an inimitable blending of

[1] *Works,* ii. 65.

sweetness and hauteur in his expression and manner, he greeted me, calmly, gravely, almost coldly, yet with so marked an earnestness that I could not help being deeply impressed by it. From that moment until his death we were friends; although we met only during the first year of our acquaintance." [1]

The friendship, so signed, was sealed by some verses addressed to Poe, in the character of Israfel, by Mrs. Osgood, and published in the "Broadway Journal;" and to these Poe replied with a third version of his old stanzas, originally written for little Eliza White, and now transparently rededicated "To Mrs. F——s S——t O——d." The young poetess soon became intimate with the household in Amity Street, then the place of their settlement, and to her pen is due the only description of the family, at this time, that has been preserved: —

"It was in his own simple yet poetical home that to me the character of Edgar Poe appeared in its most beautiful light. Playful, affectionate, witty, alternately docile and wayward as a petted child, for his young, gentle, and idolized wife, and for all who came, he had, even in the midst of his most harassing literary duties, a kind word, a pleasant smile, a graceful and courteous attention. At his desk beneath the romantic picture of his loved and lost Lenore, he would sit, hour after hour, patient, assiduous, and uncomplaining, tracing, in an exquisitely clear chirography and with almost superhuman swiftness, the lightning thoughts — the 'rare and radiant fancies' — as they flashed through his wonderful and

[1] Griswold, liii.

ever-wakeful brain. I recollect, one morning, toward the close of his residence in this city, when he seemed unusually gay and light-hearted. Virginia, his sweet wife, had written me a pressing invitation to come to them; and I, who never could resist her affectionate summons, and who enjoyed his society far more in his own home than elsewhere, hastened to Amity Street. I found him just completing his series of papers entitled 'The Literati of New York.' 'See,' said he, displaying in laughing triumph several little rolls of narrow paper (he always wrote thus for the press), 'I am going to show you by the difference of length in these the different degrees of estimation in which I hold all you literary people. In each of these one of you is rolled up and fully discussed. Come, Virginia, help me!' And one by one they unfolded them. At last they came to one which seemed interminable. Virginia laughingly ran to one corner of the room with one end, and her husband to the opposite with the other. 'And whose lengthened sweetness long drawn out is that?' said I. 'Hear her!' he cried. 'Just as if her little vain heart did n't tell her it's herself!'"[1]

Mrs. Osgood was a kind friend, and while her indulgence in sentimentality is sufficiently evident in these reminiscences, and plainly affected her more than she was conscious of, she was pleased to think, with Virginia, that her influence over Poe was for his good. If on his part there were in this Platonic friendship, as she declares, "many little poetical episodes, in which the impassioned

[1] Griswold, lii.-liii.

romance of his temperament impelled him to indulge," they were powerless to disturb the love and confidence between himself and Virginia; and on her own part, his devoted admirer obtained from him a solemn promise not to use stimulants, and, she naively states, he so far observed his word as never to appear before her when affected by them.

At Virginia's request a correspondence arose between the two, but fraught with evil consequences; for, one day, after the Poes had removed to the village of Fordham, whither they went when the cherry-trees blossomed in 1846, Mrs. Ellet, who was calling on them, saw an open letter from Mrs. Osgood to Poe, couched in language which in her judgment required friendly interference. This lady consulted with her friends, and the scandalized bevy of interlopers prevailed on Mrs. Osgood to commission some of them to demand the return of her portion of the too sugared correspondence. It seems strange that Mrs. Osgood did not herself make the request quietly, if she thought she had committed herself improperly; instead of doing so, however, she sent Margaret Fuller and a companion, who astonished the poet with their credentials. In a moment of exasperation he is said to have remarked that Mrs. Ellet had better come and look after her own letters, — a chance word that seems to have canceled all his considerate flattery of that versifier in the past ten years. The ladies returned to New York with their precious bundle; and Poe says that he gave Mrs. Ellet her own packet without awaiting her application, and hence was surprised when her brother demanded of him, a few days later, what he had no longer in his possession. Mrs. Osgood did not meet Poe after this, but her testimony to his good qualities was never lacking on occasion. She wrote these reminiscences on her death-bed to defend his memory. "I have never *seen* him," she said, "otherwise than gentle, generous, well bred, and fastidiously refined. To a sensitive and delicately nurtured woman, there was a peculiar and irresistible charm in the chivalric, graceful, and almost tender reverence with which he invariably approached all women who won his respect. It was this which first commanded and always retained my regard for him."[1]

While this romance was verging to its catastrophe, Poe's literary work was the series of papers already mentioned, "The Literati of New York." It was published in "Godey's Lady's Book," which had now become the mainstay of his support, although he still occasionally contributed to "Graham's," which in March published an installment of "Marginalia," and in April "The Philosophy of Composition," with its notorious analysis of the genesis of "The Raven."

In "Godey's" he had written criticisms in each number since the previous November, noticing Mathews, Mrs. Smith, Simms, Mrs. Hewitt, Mrs.

[1] Griswold, lii.

Osgood, and Bryant; but "The Literati" was a series of papers, not called forth by current books, but a sort of "Autography" expanded, and probably made up all he had yet written of his projected work on our literature. "The Literati" proper, which began to appear in May and continued through six numbers, dealt with thirty-eight authors resident in New York, and Poe professed to give in the main not merely his own opinion of them, but that of literary society as expressed in private. The sketches themselves are distinctly the work of a magazinist, both in conception and execution; in fact, they are simply somewhat hurriedly recorded impressions of literary people and their works, interspersed, according to Poe's inveterate habit, with extracts from, or paraphrases of, his old book-reviews since the time of the "Messenger." Being written with perfect frankness, and in that spirit of oblivious indifference to what the world would say which had won a hearing for Poe's criticism, the series was the literary hit of the season. Few of these characterizations (they include personal as well as literary qualities) are in any way humiliating to their subjects. None, it is true, not even that of Mrs. Osgood, is unreservedly laudatory; but if limitations of capacity are marked out sharply and freely, praise is, as a rule, generously given within the bounds. Against Lewis Gaylord Clark, of "The Knickerbocker," Poe had an old grudge, and just at this time Briggs had succeeded to Fay and Griswold as the peculiar object of his spleen; but with these exceptions, although some of the nobodies might have been nettled at the cavalier manner in which their merits were circumscribed or themselves patronized, there were very few with any just cause for complaint, since Poe was not so much the prince of critics as to anticipate exactly the judgment of posterity by ignoring them. In respect to the more important ones, Willis, Halleck, and Margaret Fuller, his decisions were final and have been sustained. There was a good deal of discussion, however, among the disturbed mediocrities; Godey was implored by the honey-tongued and brow-beaten by the loud-mouthed, but he refused to be intimidated by either method, as he assured the public in a card; and, in particular, Thomas Dunn English was roused to open combat.

This individual, whom Poe facetiously called "Thomas Dunn Brown," was a doctor, lawyer, novelist, editor, and poet of twenty-seven years of age, whom Poe, despite his foolish disclaimer of personal acquaintance, had met in Philadelphia, and had allowed to lounge about his office and run errands for him when he was editing the "Broadway Journal." No mortal ever held a pen who would not resent such a shameless exposure of his ears as was Poe's article in this instance, — a sort of grotesque in criticism. English secured forthwith the columns of the "Mirror" (which had changed hands), and poured out on Poe, June 23, a flood of scurrility; besides a plentiful use of billingsgate and the easy charge of intoxication, there was in particular a specific accusation of obtaining money under false pretenses and of downright forgery. Poe replied four days later in the Philadelphia "Saturday Gazette," and exercised his powers of recrimination at a length and with an effect that makes one think of the lion and the jackal. Of course he confessed his poverty and his excesses, with the pitiful extenuation that the latter were the unavoidable result rather than the cause of his misfortune; but he exculpated himself from the charges affecting his integrity, and had he not in his turn indulged in intemperate personal abuse there would have been nothing to desire in his rejoinder. Poe also brought suit against the "Mirror," and, no witnesses appearing to justify the libel, he was adjudged damages, February 17, 1847, in the sum of $225, with costs to the defendant.

Notwithstanding the wrath of a few manikins, Poe's "Literati" was not a prose Dunciad; and the impression that his criticism in general was an anathema on American mediocrity is an entirely false one. Not infrequently, indeed, he exposed some fool's folly with the raillery and zest of a boy's untroubled enjoyment in the low comedy of the situation; now and then, in a more bitter mood, he could with deliberate leisure pull some insect of the hour to pieces, or impale a Bavius or two upon the highway. He looked on himself as a public executioner, and was proud of the office. On the whole, however, his commendation equaled, if it did not exceed, his condemnation, and more than one of those whom he extolled to the skies has long since sunk back to the dust. The peculiarity of his position was, not that he was an unjust judge, but that he was the only one; not that his censures were undeserved, but that he alone pronounced a sentence without fear or favor. He thus drew about himself a swarm of enemies; and as his life offered only too fair an opportunity they used their advantage to take revenge in slander, as did Dr. English, but in secret. In these critical decisions of Poe's, speaking generally, he does not seem to have been himself actuated by any unworthy motive, any personal consideration of friendliness or enmity, or any hope of gain or fear of loss; if such matters affected his judgment, it was ordinarily either in an unconscious or an involuntary way. Now and then, as in the case of Griswold, he was stung into telling truth when he might otherwise have held his peace; or he apologized, as to Mathews, for the violence of some earlier critique, or lowered the key of his laudation when friendship ceased, as with Lowell. Worldly motives swayed his mind, now more, now less; personal feelings entered into his verdicts; but he was not governed by them. His open claim to impartiality, sincerity, and integrity seems to be sustained; or, if shaken at all, to be invalidated by the praise he gave to his feminine friends rather than by the contempt he poured out on his masculine foes.

It is thought in some quarters that Poe's criticism, and particularly its destructive portions, was very valuable. It is even said that he raised the level of our current literature. The race of chameleon poets, however, is not yet extinct, and they feed on the green trees of Tennyson, Browning, and Swinburne as once on those of Moore, Mrs. Hemans, and Keats. Reputations are still made by the coteries of a publisher's anteroom and sustained by judicious advertising. The motives that influence the editorial judgments of the press have changed but little in a generation. If, as is true, the mediocrities of our time are more clever in their imitation and more painstaking in their drudgery, this is rather to be ascribed to the general rise of the standard of literary excellence, due to the intellectual movement of the age, than to the influence of a single free lance like Poe. The good that criticism can do to the producers of literature is trifling; its work is to improve the popular taste, and to make the best that is written widely known and easily apprehensible; to authors it is, for many reasons, well-nigh useless. Destructive criticism of imaginative work, especially, is ordinarily futile, and in Poe's case no exception need be made. The good he did was infinitesimal; it would have been far better to leave such work to the scythe of Time.

Of the excellence of Poe's criticism in itself, however, there can be no question. He was the disciple of Coleridge; and, being gifted with something of Coleridge's analytic powers, he applied the principles he thus derived with skill and effect. No one, too, could subject himself to so long a self-training, and become so perfect in his own subtle art, without developing a refined taste of the highest value in criticism. The test of his ability as a critic, the severest test to which a man can be put, is the quickness and certainty of his recognition of unknown genius. In this Poe succeeded; the rank he gave to the American poets, young and old (and in the case of the best of them he had only their earliest work to judge by), is the rank sustained by the issue, and his success in dealing with the English reputations of the future was not less marked. To Tennyson, Dickens, and Longfellow he brought early applause; Mrs. Browning, Lowell, and Hawthorne were foreknown by him when their names were still in doubt. It is no diminution of his just praise that he so far shared in human weakness as to obey an obscure jealousy, notably in Longfellow's case; or to be misled by a prejudice, as with Emerson or any other transcendentalist; or to hail many a poetaster, particularly in petticoats, as of Apollo's band. He was as extreme in eulogy as in denunciation; and, especially in the case of Southern writers, he sometimes indulged in so laudatory a strain as to be guilty of absurdity. His decisions in more than one instance, like those on Moore, and in a less degree on Dickens, were merely contemporary; and in other cases, like that of Horne's "Orion," were esoteric and whimsical. His silence, too, regarding the great men of the past, such as Shakspere, and the unanimous report of his violent depreciation of them in conversation, must count in settling his own virtues as a critic. He was, it is easy to see now, prejudiced here and partial there; foolish, or interested, or wrong-headed; carping, or flattering, or contemptuous. Yet he was the first of his time to mark the limitations of the pioneer writers, such as Irving, Bryant, and Cooper, and to foresee the future of the younger men who have been mentioned; he was, too, though he originated no criterion, the first to take criticism from mere advertising, puffery, and friendship, and submit it to the laws of literary art. This was much to do, and in his lifetime, whatever were his deficiencies, was regarded as his great distinction; it was the more honorable because of the offense that was now and then bound to be given, even if Poe had been the wisest and kindest of men instead of the reckless, erratic, and unscholarly judge he was. For, to come to the rationale of the matter, it was by no means learning, in which he was a charlatan, nor inborn sense, nor intellectual honesty, nor moral insight, nor power of imaginative sympathy, that gave his criticism value, — in all these he was deficient; but it was merely the knowledge of the qualities and methods of artistic effect, which came to him in the development of his own genius under the controlling influence of Coleridge's reason and imagination. His criticism is thus largely a series of illustrations of literary art as he himself practiced it.

For weeks before English's libel Poe had been ill at Fordham, whither he had lately removed, and henceforth his constitution may be regarded as hopelessly broken. This premature exhaustion may be in part ascribed to continuous overwork, repeated disappointments, and the humiliations of poverty; but his shattered health must also be traced to the use of liquor, his indulgence in which, since, after his year of abstinence, he broke down in 1845, had been extreme. In addition to this cause, too, must be recorded the more insidious and mortal influence of the use of opium, which, vampire-like, had sucked the vitality out of the whole frame of his being, mental, moral, and physical.

The cottage to which he had retired in the spring of 1846, although at the best a mean dwelling, was the pleasantest retreat he had known. It was a one story and a half house, still standing on King's Bridge Road, at the top of Fordham Hill. Within, on the ground-floor, were two small apartments, a kitchen and sitting-room; and above, up a narrow stairway, two others, one — Poe's room — a low, cramped chamber, lighted by little square windows like port-holes, the other a diminutive closet of a bedroom, hardly large enough to lie down in. The furniture was of the simplest: in the clean, white-floored kitchen, says Mrs. Gove, who visited the family during this first summer, were a table, a chair, and a little stove; and in the other room, which was laid with checked matting, were only a light stand with presentation volumes of the Brownings upon it, some hanging shelves with a few other books ranged on them, and four chairs. Outside, however, the broad views, in contrast with the dwarfed interior, must have had, as is now the case, a fine spaciousness. The old cherry-trees are still rooted in the grassy turf, out of which crops here and there the granite of the underlying rock; and a stone's throw to the east of the veranda, then as now overgrown with vines, rises the ledge itself, overhung by sighing pines, and looking off far across the meadows, woods, and villages, to the glimmer of ocean on the dim horizon. Of this little home in the pleasant country there are many reminiscences, curiously intermingling the beauty of nature with the charm of the three occupants. Mrs. Clemm, now over sixty, with her large, benevolent features and white hair, in a worn black dress, made upon all who saw her an impression of dignity, refinement, and especially of deep motherly devotion to her children; Virginia, at the age of twenty-five, retained her beauty, but the large black eyes and raven hair contrasted sadly with the white pallor of her face; Poe himself, poor, proud, and ill, anticipating grief, and nursing the bitterness that springs from helplessness in the sight of suffering borne by those dear to us, was restless and variable, the creature of contradictory impulses, alternating between the eagerness of renewed hope and the dull maze of the ever-recurring disappointment. Friends called on him, and found him anxious over the one great trouble of his poverty, or inspirited by the compliment of a letter from Mrs. Browning, or endeavoring to distract his mind with his pets,— a bobolink he had caught and caged, or a parrot some one had given him, or his favorite cat. If he went away to the city, he came back at once to his home; once, when he was detained, he sent a note to Virginia, which is unique in his correspondence: —

June 12, 1846.

MY DEAR HEART — My Dear Virginia — Our mother will explain to you why I stay away from you this night. I trust the interview I am promised will result in some *substantial good* for me — for your dear sake and hers — keep up your heart in all hopefulness, and trust yet a little longer. On my last great disappointment I should have lost my courage *but for you* — my little darling wife. You are my *greatest* and *only* stimulus now, to battle with this uncongenial, unsatisfactory, and ungrateful life.

I shall be with you to-morrow [illegible] P. M., and be

assured until I see you I will keep in *loving remembrance* your *last words*, and your fervent prayer!

Sleep well and may God grant you a peaceful summer with your devoted

EDGAR.[1]

As the summer went on Poe grew no better, and daily Virginia failed and faded, and the resources of the household were being slowly reduced to the starving point. Autumn came, the snow and the cold and the winter seclusion, and affairs grew desperate; the wolf was already at the door when by happy chance this same Mrs. Gove, whose kind heart could prompt her to something better than her verses, called on the Poes, and found the dying wife in the summer sitting-room, which had been taken for her use. The scene requires her own description:—

"There was no clothing on the bed, which was only straw, but a snow-white counterpane and sheets. The weather was cold, and the sick lady had the dreadful chills that accompany the hectic fever of consumption. She lay on the straw bed, wrapped in her husband's great-coat, with a large tortoise-shell cat in her bosom. The wonderful cat seemed conscious of her great usefulness. The coat and the cat were the sufferer's only means of warmth, except as her husband held her hands, and her mother her feet. Mrs. Clemm was passionately fond of her daughter, and her distress on account of her illness and poverty and misery was dreadful to see."[2]

[1] Ingram, ii. 88, 89.   [2] Ingram, ii. 97.

On her return to New York, Mrs. Gove applied to Mrs. Maria Louise Shew, the daughter of a physician, who had given his child a medical education, and thus had helped to make her the useful friend of the poor to whom she devoted her life. Relief was immediately sent, and by Mrs. Shew's efforts a subscription of sixty dollars was soon made up. "From the day this kind lady first saw the suffering family of the poet," adds Mrs. Gove, whose narrative is here closely followed, "she watched over them as a mother watches over her babe. She saw them often, and ministered to the comfort of the dying and the living."

Under the influence of this glimpse of kindliness, Poe roused his faculties to new work. The "Literati," which had come to an end in October, was followed in the next month in "Godey's" by a tale of Italian vengeance, in the traditional style, "The Cask of Amontillado;" but with this and an installment of "Marginalia" in the December "Graham's" his publications for this year came to an end.

In December, much to his mortification, the necessitous condition of his family was made public by a paragraph in "The Express," which appears to have been kindly meant, since it merely appealed to his friends in his behalf: —

"We regret to learn that Edgar A. Poe and his wife are both dangerously ill with the consumption, and that the hand of misfortune lies heavy upon their temporal affairs. We are sorry to mention the fact that they are so far reduced as to be barely able to obtain the necessaries of life. This is indeed a hard lot, and we hope that the friends and admirers of Mr. Poe will come promptly to his assistance in his bitterest hour of need." [1]

Willis, who saw this notice, gave greater currency to the facts by an article in his own paper, "The Home Journal," in which he made his friend's destitution the text of a plea for an authors' house of refuge. Poe, who felt humiliated by these disclosures, wrote an open letter to Willis, December 30, 1846, in which he tried hard to deny the actual misery of his condition, but only succeeded in forcing his pen to the guarded assertion that he had indeed been in want of money in consequence of his long illness, but that it was not altogether true that he had materially suffered from privation beyond the extent of his capacity for suffering. This labored statement, however, which is given in nearly his exact words, was soon afterwards privately acknowledged, in a letter to Mrs. Locke, of Lowell, who sent him some verses, and apparently followed them with more solid expressions of her interest, to be only an indulgence of his natural pride, which impelled him, he wrote, "to shrink from public charity, even at the cost of truth in denying those necessities which were but too real." [2]

Within a month, however, all his new hopes and

[1] Griswold, xl.   [2] Griswold, xli.

old troubles were lost sight of in view of the rapidly approaching death of his wife. On January 29, 1847, he wrote to Mrs. Shew, whose attention had been unremitting during all these winter weeks, the following note: —

KINDEST — DEAREST FRIEND, — My poor Virginia still lives, although failing fast and now suffering much pain. May God grant her life until she sees you and thanks you once again! Her bosom is full to overflowing — like my own — with a boundless — inexpressible gratitude to you. Lest she may never see you more — she bids me say that she sends you her sweetest kiss of love and will die blessing you. But come — oh come tomorrow! Yes, I *will* be calm — everything you so nobly wish to see me. My mother sends you, also, her "warmest love and thanks." She begs me to ask you, if possible, to make arrangements at home so that you may stay with us To-morrow night. I enclose the order to the Postmaster. Heaven bless you and farewell!

EDGAR A. POE.[1]

FORDHAM, *Jan.* 29, '47.

In response, Mrs. Shew called to take a last leave of the invalid, who asked her to read some letters from the second Mrs. Allan, exculpating Poe from causing any difficulty at his old home, and gave her Poe's picture and his mother's jewel-case as keepsakes. On the next day, Saturday, January 30, Virginia died. Her husband, wrapped in the military cloak that had once served to cover her, followed the body to the tomb, to which it was consigned in the presence of a few friends.

[1] Ingram, ii. 107.

CHAPTER VII.

THE END OF THE PLAY.

Poe became very ill after this event; and although in the middle of March he seems to have partially recovered under the nursing of Mrs. Shew and his mother-in-law, he again sank, and his life was believed to be endangered. It was necessary to raise fresh funds for his relief, and by the interest of various friends one hundred dollars were collected at once, and afterwards other sums were contributed. Mrs. Shew, who, as has been said, had received a medical education, decided that Poe "in his best health had lesion of one side of the brain;" and she adds in her diary, "As he could not bear stimulants or tonics, without producing insanity, I did not feel much hope that he could be raised up from brain fever, brought on by extreme suffering of mind and body, — actual want and hunger and cold having been borne by this heroic husband in order to supply food, medicine, and comforts to his dying wife, until exhaustion and lifelessness were so near at every reaction of the fever that even sedatives had to be administered with extreme caution."[1] It was at this time that

[1] Ingram, ii. 115.

he dictated, in half-delirious states of mind, the romantic and unfounded story, which he obliged Mrs. Shew to write down, of his voyage to France, his duel, and his French novel, which has been accepted as sober truth.

On recovering from this prolonged illness sufficiently to resume work in some degree, he confined himself to his home. He rose early, ate moderately, drank only water, and took abundance of exercise in the open air. From time to time he visited Mrs. Shew in the city, and she in turn called upon him, and would frequently advise him to contract marriage, with the warning that he could be saved from sudden death only by a prudent, calm life with a woman who had sufficient strength and affection to manage his affairs for him. On his part, he restrained his reply to remarks, which she termed ironical, regarding her ignorance of the world's evil. In this summer and autumn he entertained more than one acquaintance who carried away bright recollections of his home. He had still the caged birds to pet, and now in addition he amused his leisure with cultivating a flower garden, in which were beds of mignonnette, heliotrope, and dahlias. Frequently he would walk some miles to the westward, along uneven country roads lined with orchards, to the High Bridge, on whose lofty granite arches, a hundred and forty-five feet above high-water, the great aqueduct crosses Harlem River; and there on the elevated grassy causeway, used only by foot-passengers, he would pace by day or night, or would lean on the low parapet, alone, musing on his own life, or speculating on the constitution of the universe, or merely enjoying the beauty of the picturesque scenes up and down the river. The ledge, too, back of his house, with its pines and the wide prospect, was one of his haunts, and thither he would retreat to escape literary callers, or to dream out the metaphysical rhapsody over which he was brooding; for it was in such solitary places that he planned "Eureka."

This year, particularly in its earlier part, was necessarily one of comparative inactivity, yet Poe's name did not pass out of the public notice. Willis, who remained his faithful literary friend, took pains to copy his poems, advertise his plans, and commend his genius whenever opportunity offered; and Poe on his part kept him informed in regard to his doings. In the "Home Journal," March 13, appeared the lines "To M. L. S——," addressed to Mrs. Shew, of inferior poetic merit, and characterized by the peculiar and sometimes dissonant cadences of the later unrhymed poems. A week later the same paper announced as soon to be published "The Authors of America, in Prose and Verse, by Edgar A. Poe," but the work did not appear, though the review of Hawthorne in the November "Godey's," in which Poe decides that Hawthorne is not original, after all, but only peculiar, may be regarded as an extract from it. In December the ballad "Ulalume," having been rejected by the "Union Magazine," was published in the "Whig," and reprinted by Willis in accordance with the following request from Poe, which may serve as an example of several such letters: —

FORDHAM, *Dec.* 8.

MY DEAR MR. WILLIS, — Many thanks for the kind expressions in your note of three or four weeks ago.

I send you an "American Review" — the number just issued — in which is a ballad by myself, but published anonymously. It is called "Ulalume" — the page is turned down. I do not care to be known as its author just now; but I would take it as a great favor if you would copy it in the H. J., with a word of *inquiry* as to who wrote it: — provided always that you think the poem worth the room it would occupy in your paper — a matter about which I am by no means sure.

Always yours gratefully, EDGAR A. POE.[1]

Willis prefaced his reprint with the desired inquiry as to the authorship of "Ulalume," and described it, in words that may not have seemed to Poe indicative of sympathetic insight, as an "exquisitely piquant and skillful exercise of rarity and niceness of language," and "a curiosity in philologic flavor." Since this extraordinarily inane characterization, the best opinion has differed widely in regard to this ballad, and still most men of poetic sensibility would say no more in its favor than did Willis. It is built out of the refrain, the

[1] Poe to Willis. MS.

most difficult mode of construction, and consequently it requires in the reader not only a willingness to accept monotony as a means of expression, but a content with it; the thought moves so slowly, with such slight advances from its initial stage, with such difficult increments of meaning and indistinguishable deepening of tone, that, like the workings of an expiring mind, it only just keeps wearily in action; its allegorizing, moreover, is further from nature than is usual even with Poe, and implies by its very simplicity that long familiarity with its imagery that Poe possessed. For these and other reasons, the sympathetic mood, without which no such poem is comprehended, must be of rare occurrence in this case; but if ever that mood comes, — that physical exhaustion and mental gloom and dreaming upon the dark, in which the modes of expression in this poem are identical with those of nature, — then, in spite of jarring discords, cockney rhymes, and coarse types of mystery and horror, this poem may well seem the language of a spirit sunk in blank and moaning despair, and at every move beaten back helplessly upon itself. It was written at the period of Poe's lowest physical exhaustion and probably of most poignant self-reproach. During these months he was not far from insanity. The criticism that finds in the ballad he thus wrote merely a whimsical experiment in words has little to go on; it is more likely that, taking into consideration, too, the lack of finish in conjunc-

THE END OF THE PLAY. 283

tion with the justness of touch in its essential structure, we have, in this poem, the most spontaneous, the most unmistakably genuine utterance of Poe, the most clearly self-portraying work of his hand. That, to most readers, it is unintelligible, and is suggestive of humor rather than of pathos, only marks how far Poe was now removed, through one and another influence, from normal humanity.

Before the publication of "Ulalume," which thus marks the extreme development of Poe's original genius, occurred the first sign that he was to be widely recognized in foreign lands, unless the theft of some of his writings by English magazines may be regarded as an indication of fame. In the "Revue des Deux Mondes," October 15, 1846, was a lengthy and appreciative review of the last edition of his tales, and attention having been already called to him in Paris by the legal proceedings between some of the city journals that had stolen, either from the original or from each other, "The Murders of the Rue Morgue," Madame Isabelle Meunier translated his best stories.

But while, unknown to himself, his reputation was thus growing in France, where it was destined to be wide-spread and enduring, he was engaged in thinking out what he thought would prove his best title to the remembrance of posterity, "Eureka." As the winter advanced he applied himself wholly to this speculation; night after night in the coldest weather he would wrap himself in his great military cloak, and pace the little veranda of the cottage through long hours of solitary meditation, elaborating thought by thought his theory of the eternal secret. At the opening of the new year, 1848, he had practically completed the work, and he now set himself with new vigor to the old task of establishing the "Stylus," with the hope that "Eureka" would furnish him with the necessary funds. He sent out the old prospectus, with its well-worn announcements that the management was to bear the mark of individuality, the contributions to be selected solely on the ground of merit, the criticism to be independent, sincere, and fearless ; all that five years had added to the advertisement was the promise of "Literary America," by the editor, being "a faithful account of the literary productions, literary people, and literary affairs of the United States," to be begun in the first number. Poe's plan was to make a personal canvass through the country, as had been so successfully done by his friend Mr. Freeman Hunt in launching his "Merchants' Magazine" a few years previous. With the view of raising the money for this journey he advertised a lecture in the Society Library, on the "Cosmogony of the Universe," and at his request Willis besought public favor for it in his paper, the "Home Journal," and added a good word for the projected "Stylus," the founding of which was said to be the ultimate object of the lecture. On February 3, in response to these notices, about sixty persons assembled, the night unfortunately being stormy, and, it is said, were held entranced for two hours and a half by an abstract of "Eureka," although the charm must have been exercised by the personality of the poet rather than the substance of what he uttered; and indeed Poe seems to have been an eloquent and impressive speaker, as he had good right to be both by inheritance and by the natural endowments of his voice and person.

The lecture was imperfectly reported by a few of the city papers, but made no impression. Financially it had failed of its purpose, and therefore Poe, seeing no better means of obtaining funds, determined to publish the entire work, and at once offered it to Mr. Putnam, who many years afterward wrote an account[1] of the interview which, though doubtless essentially true, seems to be colored. He says that Poe was in a tremor of excitement and declared with intense earnestness and solemnity that the issue of the book was of momentous interest, that the truths disclosed in it were of more consequence than the discovery of gravitation, and that an edition of 50,000 copies would be but a beginning. Mr. Putnam confesses that he was impressed, and two days later accepted the manuscript. An edition of 500 copies was printed without delay and published early in the summer, in good form, under the title "Eureka; A Prose

[1] *Putnam's Magazine*, iv. 471. N. S. (October, 1869.)

Poem,"[1] and introduced by the well-known preface: —

"To the few who love me and whom I love — to those who feel rather than to those who think — to the dreamers and those who put faith in dreams as in the only realities — I offer this Book of Truths, not in its character of Truth-Teller, but for the Beauty that abounds in its Truth; constituting it true. To them I present the composition as an Art-Product alone: — let us say as a Romance; or, if I be not urging too lofty a claim, as a Poem.

"*What I here propound is true:* — therefore it cannot die: — or if by any means it be now trodden down so that it die, it will 'rise again to the Life Everlasting.' Nevertheless it is as a Poem only that I wish this work to be judged after I am dead."

It is obviously impossible to grant Poe's request. He has written a physical explanation of the universe and based it on metaphysical principles; he has declared it a true account, and he must stand by his words. Moreover, the speculative activity of Poe's mind grew out of its analytical activity; the metaphysical essays virtually begin when the ratiocinative tales end, in 1845, and thus in the history of Poe's mental development, "Eureka," the principal work of his last years, necessarily occupies an important place. The earliest indication that such topics occupied his mind occurs in the review

[1] *Eureka: A Prose Poem.* By Edgar A. Poe. New York· Geo. P. Putnam. 1848: pp. 143.

of Macaulay's Essays: "That we know no more to-day of the nature of Deity — of its purposes — and thus of man himself — than we did even a dozen years ago — is a proposition disgracefully absurd; and of this any astronomer could assure Mr. Macaulay. Indeed, to our own mind, the *only* irrefutable argument in support of the soul's immortality — or, rather, the only conclusive proof of man's alternate dissolution and rejuvenescence *ad infinitum* — is to be found in analogies deduced from the modern established theory of the nebular cosmogony."[1] Shortly after this utterance the metaphysical tales begin, but the speculations of Poe were not fully developed until the publication of "Eureka." In the following criticism, which necessarily partakes somewhat of the abstract nature of its subject, only what is peculiar to Poe will be dwelt on; and it may as well be premised that the end in view is not the determination of abstract truth, but simply the illustration alike of Poe's genius and character by the light of his speculations.

Poe's hypothesis is as follows: The mind knows intuitively — by inductive or deductive processes which escape consciousness, elude reason, or defy expression — that the creative act of Deity must have been the simplest possible; or, to expand and define this statement, it must have consisted in willing into being a primordial particle, the germ of all things, existing without relations to aught, or,

[1] *Works,* ii. 447.

in the technical phrase, unconditioned. This particle, by virtue of the divine volition, radiated into space uniformly in all directions a shower of atoms of diverse form, irregularly arranged among themselves, but all, generally speaking, equally distant from their source; this operation was repeated at intervals, but with decreased energy in each new instance, so that the atoms were impelled less far. On the exhaustion of the radiating force, the universe was thus made up of a series of concentric hollow spheres, like a nest of boxes, the crusts of the several spheres being constituted of the atoms of the several discharges. The radiating force at each of its manifestations is measured by the number of atoms then thrown off; or, since the number of atoms in any particular case must have been directly proportional with the surface of the particular sphere they occupied, and since the surfaces of a series of concentric spheres are directly proportional with the squares of their distances from the centre, the radiating force in the several discharges was directly proportional with the squares of the distances to which the several atomic showers were driven.

On the consummation of this secondary creative act, as the diffusion may be called, there occurred, says Poe, a recoil, a striving of the atoms each to each in order to regain their primitive condition; and this tendency, which is now being satisfied, is expressed in gravitation, the mutual attraction of atoms with a force inversely proportional with the squares of the distances. In other words, the law of gravitation is found to be the converse of the law of radiation, as would be the case if the former energy were the reaction of the latter as is claimed; furthermore, the distribution of the atoms in space is seen to be such as would result from the mode of diffusion described. The return of the atoms into their source, however, would take place too rapidly, adds Poe, and without accomplishing the Deity's design of developing out of the original homogeneous particle the utmost heterogeneity, were it not that God, in this case a true *Deus ex machina*, has interposed by introducing a repelling force which began to be generated at the very inception of the universal reaction, and ever becomes greater as the latter proceeds. Poe names this force electricity, while at the same time he suggests that light, heat, and magnetism are among its phases, and ascribes to it all vital and mental phenomena; but of the principle itself he makes a mystery, since he is intuitively convinced that it belongs to that spiritual essence which lies beyond the limits of human inquiry. In the grand reaction, then, the universe is through attraction becoming more condensed, and through repulsion more heterogeneous. Attraction and repulsion taken together constitute our notion of matter; the former is the physical element, the Body, the latter is the spiritual element, the Soul. Incidentally it should be remarked that since in a divine design, being perfect, no one part exists for the sake of others more than the others for its sake, it is indifferent whether repulsion be considered, as hitherto, an expedient to retard the attractive force, or, on the other hand, the attractive force as an expedient to develop repulsion; in other words, it is indifferent whether the physical be regarded as subordinate to the spiritual element, or *vice versa*. To return to the main thread, Poe affirms that repulsion will not increase indefinitely as the condensation of the mass proceeds, but when in the process of time it has fulfilled its purpose — the evolution of heterogeneity — it will cease, and the attractive force, being unresisted, will draw the atoms back into the primordial particle in which, as it has no parts, attraction will also cease; now, attraction and repulsion constituting our notion of matter, the cessation of these two forces is the same thing with the annihilation of matter, or in other words, the universe, at the end of the reaction which has been mentally followed out, will sink into the nihility out of which it arose. In conclusion Poe makes one last affirmation, to wit, that the diffusion and ingathering of the universe is the diffusion and ingathering of Deity itself, which has no existence apart from the constitution of things.

It is difficult to treat this hypothesis, taken as a metaphysical speculation, with respect. To examine it for the purpose of demolition would be a tedious, though an easy task; but fortunately there is no need to do more than point out a few of its confusions in order to illustrate the worthlessness of Poe's thought in this field, and to indicate the depth of the delusion under which he labored in believing himself a discoverer of new truth. For this purpose it will be best to take the most rudimentary metaphysical ideas involved. The primordial particle is declared to be unconditioned — " my particle proper is absolute Irrelation," — or in other words it is the Absolute ; but this is incompatible with its being willed into being by Deity, to which it would then necessarily stand related as an effect to its cause; on the contrary, it must itself, being the Absolute, be Deity with which Poe at last identifies it. In other words, when Poe has reached the conception of the primordial particle as first defined by him, he is just where he started, that is, at the conception of Deity, and at that point, as has been seen, he had to end. The difficulty which bars inquiry — the inconceivability of creation — remains as insuperable as ever, although Poe may have cheated himself into believing it overcome by the legerdemain of a phrase from physics; in the attempt to describe the generation of the phenomenal universe out of the unknowable, he has been foiled by the old obstacles — the impossibility of making an equation between nothing and something, of effecting a transformation of the absolute into the conditioned. If the primordial particle be material, it is only the scientific equivalent of the old turtle of the Hindoos, on which the elephant stands to support the globe; if it be immaterial, it is the void beneath.

Such a criticism as the above belongs to the primer of thought in this science; but objections as obvious, brief, and fatal may be urged against every main point of the argument. Without entering on such a discussion it is sufficient to observe, as characteristic illustrations of the density of Poe's ignorance in this department of knowledge, that he regards space not as created but as given, explains the condensation of the universe as being a physical reaction upon the immaterial will of God (for the original radiating force cannot be discriminated from and is expressly identified with the divine volition, just as the primordial particle cannot be discriminated from and is expressly identified with the divine essence), and lastly so confuses such simple notions as final and efficient causes that he contradistinguishes the force of repulsion from that of attraction as arising and disappearing in obedience to the former instead of the later sort. In a word, Poe's theory belongs to the infancy of speculation, to the period before physics was separated from ontology; in this sense, and in no other, Kennedy's remark that Poe wrote like "an old Greek philosopher," was just.

What Poe himself most prized in this hypothesis was its pantheistic portion. The sentence of Baron Bielfeld, — " nous ne connaissons rien de

THE END OF THE PLAY.

la nature ou de l'essence de Dieu; — pour savoir ce qu'il est, il faut être Dieu même," — had made a deep impression on his mind early in life; it is one of the half-dozen French quotations that he introduces at every opportunity into his compositions; in "Eureka" he translates it, "We know absolutely *nothing* of the nature or essence of God; in order to comprehend what he is, we should have to be God ourselves," — and he immediately adds, "I nevertheless venture to demand if this our present ignorance of the Deity is an ignorance to which the soul is *everlastingly* condemned."[1] Now after reflection he boldly took the only road to such knowledge that was left open by the apothegm, and affirmed that he was God, being persuaded thereto by his memories of an ante-natal and his aspiration for an immortal existence, and in particular by his pride. "My whole nature utterly *revolts*," he exclaimed, "at the idea that there is any Being in the Universe superior to *myself!*"[2] On reading so violent an expression of belief one involuntarily examines the matter more closely and pushes home the question whether Poe did actually so fool himself to the top of his bent; and after some little investigation one finds that, if he was his own dupe, the reason is not far to seek. It is necessary here to summarize the speculations which were put forth elsewhere by Poe, especially in the metaphysical tales, and either led up to or supplemented the views of "Eureka."

[1] *Works*, i. 132.   [2] Ingram, ii. 144.

According to these other statements, the Universe is made up of gross matter sensibly perceived and of fine matter so minutely divided that the atoms coalesce (this is, of course, a contradiction in terms) and form an unparticled substance which permeates and impels all things. This unparticled substance or imperceptible coalescent matter is the universal mind (into such unintelligible phraseology is the keen analyst forced) ; its being is Deity ; its motion, regarded on the material or energetic side, is the divine volition, or, regarded on the mental or conscious side, is the creative thought. Deity and its activity, being such in its universal existence, is individualized, by means of gross matter made for that end, into particular creatures, among which are men; the human being, in other words, is a specialization of the universal, or is God incarnate, as is every other creature whatsoever. It is superfluous to follow Poe in his fantastic conception of the universe as the abode of countless rudimentary incarnations of the Deity, each a divine thought and therefore irrevocable ; the peculiar form of his pantheism would not be more defined thereby. At the first glance one sees that his theory is built out of Cartesian notions, crudely apprehended, and rendered ridiculous by the effort to yoke them with thoroughly materialistic ideas. In fact, Poe's scraps of speculative philosophy came from such opposite quarters that when his mind began to work on such contradictory information he could not well help falling into inextricable confusion. On the one hand he had derived, early in life, from obscure disciples of the French *philosophes*, the first truth that a materialist ever learns, — the origin of all knowledge in experience, and the consequent limitation of the mind to phenomena; on the other hand he had at a later period gleaned some of the conceptions of transcendentalism from Coleridge, Schlegel, and other secondary sources; from the union of such principles the issue was naturally monstrous, two-natured, like the Centaur. Essentially Poe was a materialist; whether, by gradually refining and subdividing matter, he reaches the unparticled substance, or by reversing the evolution of nature he arrives at the fiery mist and the primordial particle, he seeks to find out God by searching matter; and even in adopting the radically spiritual idea of pantheism, he is continually endeavoring to give it a materialistic form. He persuaded himself, as it is easy for ignorance to do; subtle as his mind was, well furnished for metaphysical thought both by his powers of abstraction and of reasoning, he wrote the jargon that belongs to the babbling days of philosophy because he did not take the pains to know the results of past inquiry and to train himself in modern methods. By his quick perception and adroit use of analogies, and especially by his tireless imagination, he gave his confused dogmatism the semblance of a reasoned system; but in fact his metaphysics exhibit only the shallowness of his scholarship and the degrading self-delusion of an arrogant and fatuous mind.

It is probable that few readers of "Eureka" ever seriously tried to understand its metaphysics. Its power — other than the fascination which some readers feel in whatever makes of their countenances " a foolish face of wonder " — lies in its exposition of Laplace's nebular theory and its vivid and popular presentation of astronomical phenomena. In this physical portion of the essay it has been fancied that Poe anticipated some of the results of later science; but this view cannot be sustained with candor. His own position that matter came from nihility and consisted of centres of force had been put forth as a scientific theory by Boscovich in 1758-59, had been widely discussed, and had found its way into American text-books. The same theory in a modified form had just been revived and brought to the notice of scientists by Faraday in his lecture in 1844. It has not, however, occupied the attention of first-class scientific men since that time. There may be, in the claim that " the recent progress of scientific thought runs in Poe's lines," some reference to Sir William Thomson's vortex theory of the constitution of atoms, but its resemblance to Poe's theory of vortices is only superficial, for what he puts forth was merely a revival of one of the earliest attempts to explain the Newtonian law, long since abandoned by science. It is true that in several particulars, such as the doctrine of the evolution of the universe from the simple to the complex, Poe's line of thought has now been followed out in detail; these suggestions, however, were not at the time peculiar to Poe, were not originated or developed by him, but on the contrary were common scientific property, for he appropriated ideas, just as he paraphrased statements of fact, from the books he read. He was no more a forerunner of Spencer, Faraday, and Darwin than scores of others, and he did nothing to make their investigations easier.

Poe's purely scientific speculations are mainly contained in the unpublished *addenda* to a report of his lecture on " The Universe " sent to a correspondent, and consist either of mathematical explanations of Kepler's first and third laws; or of statements, " that the sun was condensed at once (not gradually according to the supposition of Laplace) into his smallest size," and afterwards " sent into space his substance in the form of a vapor " from which Neptune was made; or of similar theories. They exhibit once more Poe's tenacity of mind, the sleuth-hound persistence of his intellectual pursuit; but, like his metaphysics, they represent a waste of power. They are, moreover, characterized by extraordinary errors. Some of the data are quite imaginary, it being impossible to determine what are the facts; some of them are quite wrong. The density of Jupiter, for example, in a long and important calculation, is constantly reckoned as two and one half, whereas it is only something more than one fifth, and the densities of the planets are described as being inversely as their rotary periods, whereas in any table of the elements of the solar system some wide departures from this rule are observable. Again, it is stated that Kepler's first and third laws "cannot be explained upon the principle of Newton's theory;" but, in fact, they follow by mathematical deduction from it. Poe's own explanation of them is merely a play upon figures. A striking instance of fundamental ignorance of astronomical science is his statement at various places that the planets rotate (on their own axes) in elliptical orbits, and the reference he frequently makes to the *breadth* of their orbits (the breadth of their paths through space) agreeably to this supposition. Such a theory is incompatible with the Newtonian law of gravitation, according to which any revolution in an elliptical orbit implies a source of attraction at the focus of the ellipse. Examples of bodies which have breadth of orbit in Poe's sense are found in the satellites of all the planets, each of which, however, has its primary as a source of attraction to keep it in its elliptical orbit; the primary by its revolution round the sun gives then the satellite a breadth of orbit. But to make the proper rotation of the planets themselves take place about a focus, which would be merely a point moving in an elliptical orbit about the sun, would be to give them an arbitrary motion with no force to produce it.

So far was Poe from being a seer of science, that he was fundamentally in error with regard to the generalizations which were of prime importance to his speculations. The one grand assumption of his whole speculation is the universality of the law of inverse squares as applied to attraction and repulsion, whereas it has been known since the beginning of study regarding them that that law does not explain all the forces involved, as, for example, molecular forces; and for this Boscovich himself had provided. Again, to illustrate his scientific foresight, he reproaches Herschel for his reluctance to doubt the stability of the universe, and himself boldly affirms, consistently with his theory, that it is in a state of ever swifter collapse; than this nothing could be more at variance with the great law of the conservation of energy. Undoubtedly Poe had talents for scientific investigation, had he been willing to devote himself to such work; but, so far as appears from this essay, he had not advanced farther in science that the elements of physics, mathematics, and astronomy, as he had learned them at school or from popular works, such as Dr. Nichol's "Architecture of the Heavens," or from generalizations, such as the less technical chapters of Auguste Comte's "La Philosophie Positif." Out of such a limited stock of knowledge Poe could not by mere reflection generate any Newtonian truth; that he thought he had done so, measures his folly. In a word, for this criticism must be brought to a close, "Eureka" affords one of the most striking instances in literature of a naturally strong intellect tempted by overweening pride to an Icarian flight and betrayed, notwithstanding its merely specious knowledge, into an ignoble exposure of its own presumption and ignorance. The facts are not to be obscured by the smooth profession of Poe that he wished this work to be looked on only as a poem; for, though he perceived that his argument was too fragmentary and involved to receive credence, he was himself profoundly convinced that he had revealed the secret of eternity. Nor, were "Eureka" to be judged as a poem, that is to say, as a fictitious cosmogony, would the decision be more favorable; even then so far as it is obscure to the reader it must be pronounced defective, so far as it is understood, involving as it does in its primary conceptions incessant contradictions of the necessary laws of thought, it must be pronounced meaningless. Poe believed himself to be that extinct being, a universal genius of the highest order; and he wrote this essay to prove his powers in philosophy and in science. To the correspondent to whom he sent the *addenda* he declared, "As to the lecture, I am very quiet about it — but if you have ever dealt with such topics, you will recognize the novelty and *moment* of my views. What I have propounded will (in good time) revolutionize the world of Physical and Metaphysical science. I say this calmly, but I say it."[1] Poe succeeded only in showing how egregiously genius may mistake its realm.

Besides "Eureka," Poe's publications for the first half year were of the slightest, consisting only of "Marginalia," in January and February, and "Fifty Suggestions," in May and June (a paper of the same character), in "Graham's," and "An Enigma," an anagrammatic poem to Sarah Ann Lewis, commonly called "Estelle," in the "Union," in March.

A glimpse of his life at home is afforded by an affectionate reminiscence of Mrs. Clemm's, which was reported by Mr. R. E. Shapley, of Philadelphia, in a newspaper, and has by chance been preserved; in the main parts it seems to apply to the whole period of his widowerhood: —

"He never liked to be alone, and I used to sit up with him, often until four o'clock in the morning, he at his desk, writing, and I dozing in my chair. When he was composing 'Eureka,' we used to walk up and down the garden, his arm around me, mine around him, until I was so tired I could not walk. He would stop every few minutes and explain his ideas to me, and ask if I understood him. I always sat up with him when he was writing, and gave him a cup of hot coffee every hour or two. At home he was simple and affectionate as a

[1] Poe to ———. Ingram, ii. 141.

child, and during all the years he lived with me I do not remember a single night that he failed to come and kiss his 'mother,' as he called me, before going to bed."

The principal event of his private life, when "Eureka" was being published, was the termination of his social intercourse with Mrs. Shew. Since the death of Virginia, this lady had maintained her intimacy with the family, and had actively befriended him in his literary projects. In the earlier part of the year she had asked him to furnish the music room and library of a new house which she was to occupy, and she made him at home when he visited her. One such visit is especially of interest, since to it has been ascribed the first suggestion of Poe's second great popular poem, "The Bells." It was early in the summer that he one day called and complained that he had to write a poem, but felt no inspiration. Mrs. Shew persuaded him to drink some tea in a conservatory whose open windows admitted the sound of church-bells, and gave him some paper, which he declined, saying, "I so dislike the noise of bells to-night, I cannot write. I have no subject — I am exhausted." Mrs. Shew then wrote, "The Bells, by E. A. Poe," and added, "The bells, the little silver bells;" on the poet's finishing the stanza thus suggested, she again wrote, "The heavy iron bells," and this idea also Poe elaborated, and then copying off the two stanzas, headed it, "By Mrs. M. L. Shew," and called it her poem.

Such, nearly in Mr. Ingram's own words, is the story which he derived from Mrs. Shew's diary. But although the incident is, without doubt, truly related, it may be questioned whether this was the original genesis of the poem. It will be remembered that Poe derived several suggestions from Châteaubriand at the very beginning of his career. The parallelism that exists between the completed poem of "The Bells" and a brief chapter of the "Génie du Christianisme" is at least worth noticing, and it is not likely to be a fortuitous coincidence. The following extract will sufficiently illustrate the matter.

"Il nous semble que si nous étions poëte, nous ne dédaignerions point cette cloche *agitée par les fantômes* dans la vieille chapelle de la forêt, ni celle qu'une religieuse frayeur balançoit dans nos campagnes pour écarter le tonnerre, ni celle qu'on sonnoit la nuit, dans certains ports de mer, pour diriger le pilote à travers les écueils. Les carillons des cloches, au milieu de nos fêtes, sembloient augmenter l'allégresse publique; dans des calamités, au contraire, ces mêmes bruits devenoient terribles. Les cheveux dressent encore sur la tête au souvenir de ces jours de meurtre et de feu, retentissant des clameurs du tocsin. Qui de nous a perdu la mémoire de ces hurlements, de ces cris aigus, entrecoupés de silences, durant lesquels on distinguoit de rares coups de fusil, quelque voix lamentable et solitaire, et surtout le bourdonnement de la cloche d'alarme, ou le son de l'horologe qui frappoit tranquillement l'heure écoulée?"[1]

[1] *Génie du Christianisme.* Par M. le Vicomte de Châteaubriand Paris, P. Pourrat Frères, 1836: tome ii., 261.

In view of Poe's known habits of composition, it is most likely that this poetic suggestion in a work to which he was in early years under considerable obligations, was one of the ideas that haunted him for years, and this is sustained by his frequent reference to the magical sounds of bells throughout his literary life. It may well be that this is the poem referred to in Griswold's memoir as the subject on which he meant to write for the Boston Lyceum — " a subject which he said had haunted his imagination for years." [1] If there be any plausibility in this inference, the likelihood is that Mrs. Shew, who pleads guilty to Poe's reproach that she never read his tales or poems, merely recalled to him thoughts and words which she already knew had been running in his mind.

The events immediately subsequent to this incident also deserve mention. Word was sent to Mrs. Clemm that Poe would remain in the city, and, going to his room, he slept twelve hours, after which he only faintly remembered what he had done. "This showed," says the diary, "that his mind was injured, nearly gone out for want of food and from disappointment. He had not been drinking, and had only been a few hours from home. Evidently his vitality was low and he was nearly insane. While he slept we studied his pulse, and found the same symptoms which I had so often noticed before. I called in Dr. Francis (the old man

[1] Griswold, xxxviii.

was odd, but very skillful), who was one of our neighbors. His words were, 'He has heart disease and will die early in life.'"[1] On the next day he was taken home by his friend, but did not seem to understand that he was ill.

It must have been very soon after this that Mrs. Shew, finding that her *protégé* was too irresponsible and too romantic to be allowed such freedom with her as he had been accustomed to, broke off the acquaintance. Poe, who was never very sensible of the social realities of life, seems in these last years to have been unable to observe the limits set by the world to even the most genuine and pure devotion in such a case. The consequence which, although he had foreseen it, must, in his state of health, have been hard to endure, was the sudden and complete cessation of intercourse between the families. In June Mrs. Shew wrote an explanatory letter to him, and he replied as follows, but they never afterwards met on the old terms: —

"Can it be true, Louise, that you have the idea fixed in your mind to desert your unhappy and unfortunate friend and patient? You did not say so, I know, but for months I have known you were deserting me, not willingly, but none the less surely — my destiny —

'Disaster, following fast and following faster, till his song one burden bore —
Till the dirges of his Hope that melancholy burden bore —
Of "Never — nevermore."'

[1] Ingram, ii. 156.

So I have had premonitions of this for months. I repeat, my good spirit, my loyal heart! must this follow as a sequel to all the benefits and blessings you have so generously bestowed? Are you to vanish like all I love, or desire, from my darkened and 'lost soul'? I have read over your letter again and again, and cannot make it possible, with any degree of certainty, that you wrote it in your right mind. (*I know you did not without tears of anguish and regret.*) Is it possible your influence is lost to me? Such tender and true natures are ever loyal until death; but you are not dead, you are full of life and beauty! Louise, you came in, ... in your floating white robe — 'Good morning, Edgar.' There was a touch of conventional coldness in your hurried manner, and your attitude as you opened the kitchen door to find Muddie, is *my last remembrance of you.* There was love, hope, and *sorrow* in your smile, instead of love, hope, and *courage*, as ever before. O Louise, how many sorrows are before you! Your ingenuous and sympathetic nature will be constantly wounded in its contact with the hollow, heartless world; and for me, alas! unless some true and tender, and pure womanly love saves me, I shall hardly last a year longer alive! A few short months will tell how far my strength (physical and moral) will carry me in life here. How can I believe in Providence when *you* look coldly upon me? Was it not you who renewed my hopes and faith in God? ... and in humanity? Louise, I heard your voice as you passed out of my sight leaving me ...; but I still listened to your voice. I heard you say with a sob, 'Dear Muddie.' I heard you greet *my Catarina*, but it was only as a memory ... nothing escaped *my ear*,

and I was convinced it was not your generous self ...
repeating words so foreign to your nature — to your
tender heart! I heard you sob out your sense of duty
to my mother, and I heard her reply, 'Yes, Loui ...
yes.' ... Why turn your soul from its true work for the
desolate to the thankless and miserly world? ... I felt
my heart stop, and I was sure I was then to die before
your eyes. Louise, it is well — it is fortunate — you
looked up with a tear in your dear eyes, and raised the
window, and talked of the guava you had brought for
my sore throat. Your instincts are better than a *strong
man's reason for me* — I trust they may be for *yourself*. Louise, I feel I shall not prevail — a shadow has
already fallen upon your soul, and is reflected in your
eyes. It is *too late* — you are floating away with the
cruel tide ... it is not a common trial — it is a fearful
one to me. Such rare souls as yours so beautify this
earth! so relieve it of all that is repulsive and sordid.
So brighten its toils and cares, it is hard to lose sight of
them even for a short time ... but you must know and
be assured of my regret and sorrow if aught I have
ever written has hurt you. *My heart never wronged
you.* I place you in *my esteem* — in *all solemnity* —
beside the friend of my boyhood — the mother of my
school-fellow, of whom I told you, and as I have repeated
in the poem ... as the truest, tenderest of this world's
most womanly souls, and an angel to my forlorn and
darkened nature. I will not say 'lost soul' again, for
your sake. I will try to overcome my grief for the sake
of your unselfish care of me in the past, and in life or
death, I am ever yours gratefully and devotedly,

"EDGAR A. POE."[1]

[1] Ingram, ii. 157-159.

Poe was not to remain long in this forlorn condition. He had indulged for some years one of his silent ideal adorations for Mrs. Sarah Helen Whitman, a poetess of Providence, Rhode Island, to whom he had been attracted by a verbal description of her eccentricities and sorrows. Of this ideal passion no words except his own can convey an adequate idea, although it must be premised that the following passages were not written until after he had met the lady.

"She [his informant] had referred to thoughts, sentiments, traits, *moods*, which I knew to be my own, but which, until that moment, I had believed to be my own solely — unshared by any human being. A profound sympathy took immediate possession of my soul. I cannot better explain to you what I felt than by saying that your unknown heart seemed to pass into my bosom — there to dwell forever — while mine, I thought, was translated into your own. From that hour I loved you. Since that period I have never seen nor heard your name without a shiver, half of delight, half of anxiety. — The impression left upon my mind was that you were still a wife, and it is only within the last few months that I have been undeceived in this respect. For this reason I shunned your presence and even the city in which you lived. You may remember that once when I passed through Providence with Mrs. Osgood I positively refused to accompany her to your house, and even provoked her into a quarrel by the obstinacy and seeming unreasonableness of my refusal. I dared neither go nor say why I could not. I dared not speak of you —

much less see you. For years your name never passed my lips, while my soul drank in, with a delirious thirst, all that was uttered in my presence respecting you. The merest whisper that concerned you awoke in me a shuddering sixth sense, vaguely compounded of fear, ecstatic happiness, and a wild inexplicable sentiment that resembled nothing so nearly as a consciousness of guilt." [1]

Mrs. Whitman, on her part, had been informed of frequent commendatory allusions to herself made by Poe, and was prevailed upon to address some verses to him for the entertainment of what was termed a valentine party given by some literary friends in New York. The two did not meet on this occasion; but the verses, published in the "Home Journal," March 18 (now entitled "The Raven," in Mrs. Whitman's "Poems") were sent to Poe. He says, in the continuation of the letter just quoted, that he was thrown into a state of ecstasy by this proof of her regard, and, as he could not express his emotion in spontaneous lines, took down a volume of his old poems and read "To Helen," with the result that the identity of name and the aptness of the sentiment, which to one accustomed to the Calculus of Probabilities wore an air of positive miracle, overwhelmed him with the belief that their destinies were conjoined. He was, at least, aroused to the point of composition, and replied to her valentine with the lines "To ——," afterwards elaborated into the beautiful, if not impassioned poem "To Helen," which is supposed to

[1] Poe to Mrs. Whitman, no date. Ingram, ii 161, 162.

commemorate his first sight of this lady when, on his way back from his first visit to Boston, in the summer of 1845, he had observed her among the roses of her garden in the moonlight. Whether this legend be true or not — and there is no reason to doubt it — the scene of the lines is clearly a mere elaboration of that suggested in the seventh stanza of Mrs. Whitman's "The Raven," in connection with the vista obviously repeated from his lines of the previous year to Mrs. Shew. This poem was afterwards printed in the "Union Magazine" for November; but as at this time it drew no acknowledgment from its object, to whom, although he had not as yet been introduced, he sent a written copy still without his name, he soon after, June 10, applied to his visitor of the previous autumn, Miss Anna Blackwell, who was then at Providence, and begged her to write him something about Mrs. Whitman, and added "*keep my secret* — that is to say, let no one know I have asked you to do so."[1] This lady did not answer his note; on the contrary, hearing Miss Maria McIntosh, another literary woman, tell Mrs. Whitman that one evening at Fordham a month previously Poe had talked only of her, Miss Blackwell gave the letter at once to Mrs. Whitman herself, who continued to observe an obstinate silence towards her admirer.[2]

[1] Ingram, ii. 165.

[2] Cf. Mrs. Whitman to R. H. Stoddard, September 30, 1872. Stoddard, cxxxiv. - cxxxix.

In the following month Poe went to Lowell, Mass., the residence of his old correspondent, Mrs. Locke, and lectured on "The Poetic Principle." There he made acquaintance with a family who became his devoted friends. Immediately upon his return to New York, being furnished with funds for his long-delayed journey in behalf of the "Stylus," derived possibly from this lecture or the two advances made on "Eureka," he started for Richmond. In that city he made the acquaintance of Mr. John R. Thompson, editor of the "Southern Literary Messenger," of whose office he made a resort, and among his old friends he met his boyish flame, Miss Royster, now the widow Shelton, well supplied with worldly goods and well disposed toward himself. He was on the point of taking up the youthful romance and proposing marriage to her, when he received from Mrs. Whitman, who had begun to question the propriety of her neglect, two stanzas of her poem, "A Night in August," unsigned, and sent, she says, after a lapse of more than two months, in "playful acknowledgment" of his own anonymous lines. In the letter already quoted, Poe represents his state of mind during her silence as a hoping against hope culminating in a spirit far more reckless than despair; and he concludes, referring to his intention of offering his hand to Mrs. Shelton at this stage, "your lines reached me in Richmond on the very day in which I was about to enter on a course which would have borne me far, far away, from *you*, sweet, sweet Helen, and from the divine dream of your love." He left with Mr. Thompson for publication in "The Messenger," a criticism of Mrs. Lewis's poems, printed in the September number, and "The Rationale of Verse," printed in the October and November numbers, and immediately returned to Fordham. There he found time to write an open letter, September 20, to Mr. C. F. Hoffman, of "The Literary World," in reply to a criticism on "Eureka" which had appeared during his absence, and in which he observes that the ground covered by Laplace compares with that covered by his own theory as a bubble with the ocean on which it floats; and, on the next day, if Mrs. Whitman's date be correct, having obtained a letter of introduction from Miss McIntosh, he presented himself to his poetical correspondent, passed two evenings in her company, and with a characteristic choice of place, asked her, as they were walking in the cemetery, to marry him. Mrs. Whitman, who had delayed her reply, wrote to him a letter in which, as may be gathered from Poe's indignant protest against confounding so spiritual a love as his with merely mortal matters, she referred to her age — she was forty-five and had been widowed for the past fifteen years — her personal appearance, and her illness; but such objections could not withstand the high style of Poe's vein, and she was forced to acknowledge, though rather by suggestion than confession, the real ground of her refusal, which was the representations of her friends in regard to Poe's character. To this he replied, October 18, with a protestation that "with the exception of occasional follies and excesses which I bitterly lament but to which I have been driven by intolerable sorrow, and which are hourly committed by others without attracting any notice whatever — I can call to mind no act of my life which would bring a blush to my cheek — or to yours."[1] He reminded her of the enemies he had made by his published criticisms, of the result of his libel case, and of her distance from his friends, and concluded with a sketch of the secluded Eden he had fancied for their abode (out of "Landor's Cottage" which he was then writing), and expressions of his sorrow that his dream was not to be realized, of his deep devotion to herself, his utter hopelessness and the agony of his determination to abandon his fruitless wooing.

Soon after dispatching this letter, however, being on his way to Lowell to deliver a new lecture, he stopped at Providence, and, calling upon Mrs. Whitman, he again urged her to accept his hand and realize the last and brightest hope that remained to him in life. She promised still to entertain his proposal, and to write to him at Lowell the decision at which she should arrive. Thither he went, and though he did not deliver his lecture,

[1] Ingram, ii. 171.

cemented his acquaintance with his new friends and spent some days at the village of Westford, where he rested; waited, strolled off 'to look at the hills,' and enjoyed the society of "Annie," whom he had taken into his confidence, and of her sister. The latter, who was then a school-girl, in her reminiscences of Poe, draws the familiar portrait of him, self-possessed, serious, deferential to all women, distinguished by the large, deep eyes and low baritone voice that charmed so many of them; but she adds nothing of novel interest except a quiet indoor scene, curiously illustrative of the speed with which he established a habit of intimacy with married women.

"My memory photographs him, sitting before an open wood fire, in the early autumn evening, gazing intently into the glowing coal, holding the hand of a dear friend — 'Annie' — while for a long time no one spoke, and the only sound was the ticking of the tall old clock in the corner of the room." [1]

About the second of November, having received an indecisive letter from Mrs. Whitman, who seems to have been always struggling between her inclination and her prudence, and having replied that he would call at her house on Saturday, November 4, he left this pleasant home.

Two weeks later he wrote to his friend at Lowell, referring to what happened after he bade her farewell, as follows: —

[1] Ingram, ii. 190.

THE END OF THE PLAY. 315

"I remember nothing distinctly from that moment until I found myself in Providence. I went to bed and wept through a long, long, hideous night of Despair — When the day broke, I arose and endeavored to quiet my mind by a rapid walk in the cold, keen air — but all *would* not do — the Demon tormented me still. Finally, I procured two ounces of laudanum, and without returning to my hotel, took the cars back to Boston. When I arrived I wrote you a letter, in which I opened my whole heart to you — to *you*. . . . I told you how my struggles were more than I could bear. . . . I then reminded you of that holy promise which was the last I exacted from you in parting — the promise that, under all circumstances, you would come to me on my bed of death. I implored you to come *then*, mentioning the place where I should be found in Boston. Having written this letter, I swallowed about half the laudanum, and hurried to the Post Office, intending not to take the rest until I saw you — for, I did not doubt for one moment, that Annie would keep her sacred promise. But I had not calculated on the strength of the laudanum, for, before I reached the Post Office my reason was entirely gone, and the letter was never put in. Let me pass over — my darling *sister* — the awful horrors that succeeded. A friend was at hand, who aided, and (if it can be called saving) saved me, but it is only within the last three days that I have been able to remember what occurred in that dreary interval. It appears that, after the laudanum was rejected from the stomach, I became calm, and to a casual observer, sane — so that I was suffered to go back to Providence." [1]

[1] Poe to "Annie," November 16, 1848. Ingram, ii. 193, 194.

On Tuesday morning, November 7, Poe called at Mrs. Whitman's; but she, having been alarmed, it is said, by his failure to keep his engagement the previous Saturday, which she distinctly ascribes to his having become intoxicated in Boston, refused to see him until noon, despite all the messages that he could invent. In the afternoon he again called, by appointment, and once more implored her to marry him at once and return with him to New York. He excused his excesses in Boston on the ground of his anxiety in respect to her decision, and on that and the following day continued to plead his cause with all his eloquent abandonment of language and manner. The details of the termination of this interview and of its consequences have been narrated by Mrs. Whitman herself with slight variations. The earliest account, so far as is known, is contained in a private letter of March, 1860. In this, after mentioning that Poe "had vehemently urged me to an immediate marriage," she continues as follows: —

"As an additional reason for *delaying* a marriage which, under any circumstances, seemed to all my friends full of evil portents, I read to him some passages from a letter which I had recently received from one of his New York associates. He seemed deeply pained and wounded by the result of our interview, and left me abruptly, saying that if we met again it would be as strangers. He passed the evening in the bar-room of his hotel, and after a night of delirious frenzy, returned the next day to my mother's house in a state of great mental excitement and suffering, declaring that his welfare for time and eternity depended on me. A physician, Dr. O. H. Oakie, was sent for by my mother, who, perceiving indications of brain fever, advised his removal to the house of his friend W. J. Pabodie, of this city, where he was kindly cared for until his recovery." [1]

Later and possibly more accurate accounts change some of these details and amplify others. In the interview of November 8, according to these, Mrs. Whitman showed Poe several letters, one of which especially moved him; on reading it, further confidential conversation being prevented by visitors, he took leave at once with a look of strange excitement, and made no reply to her invitation, "We shall see you this evening?" He did not, however, return, but sent a note of renunciation. On the next day when Poe called, he was so uncontrollable that his passionate appeals rang through the house. "Never have I heard anything so awful," records Mrs. Whitman, "awful even to sublimity. It was long before I could nerve myself to see him. My mother was with him more than two hours before I entered the room. He hailed me as an angel sent to save him from perdition. . . . In the afternoon he grew more composed, and my mother sent for Dr. Oakie.'" [2]

In consequence of this pitiable exhibition of

[1] Mrs. Whitman to ———. MS.
[2] Ingram, ii. 176.

Poe's state, and with the hope of helping him in what seemed to be a last struggle for life itself, Mrs. Whitman consented within a few days to a conditional engagement. Forced to be content with this, Poe, having on his side repeated the promise of reform that he had given to every woman whom he had known intimately, returned to New York on November 14, and on the same evening wrote to assure his *fiancée* that he had not dared to break his pledge.

In spite, however, of his success in so difficult and indeed desperate a wooing, he felt little of the happiness of an accepted lover. He arrived at Fordham safely, but so changed in outward appearance by the wear of the last fortnight that Mrs. Clemm declares, in a letter to "Annie," written two days later, he was hardly recognizable. All the previous night, according to the same authority, he had raved about this last lady, and the same day, November 16, he also wrote to her a letter which is inexplicable on the theory that he put any faith in the happy issue of his betrothal, since after giving the account, already quoted, of his suicidal attempt at Boston, he proposes to take a cottage for his mother and himself at Westford, where he might see her family every day and herself often, and concludes with a passionate appeal that she would come on to Fordham at once, if only for a week, saying, "I am so *ill* — so terribly, hopelessly *ill* in body and mind, that I feel I *cannot* live."[1] In his next letter, however, written four days later, to Edward Valentine, the brother of the first Mrs. Allan, and containing merely a request for the loan of $200 to start the "Stylus," he expresses a strong hope of surmounting his difficulties. On November 21, 22, and 24, and presumably on other dates, he wrote to Mrs. Whitman, warning her against his slanderers, particularly the women, begging her to be true to him, as his sole hope was in her love, and drawing golden anticipations of their worldly triumph. Meanwhile, on November 23, he had written to "Annie's" sister, already mentioned, in hardly less affectionate terms than to herself or Mrs. Whitman, protesting his love for "Annie" and imploring an answer to his former letter to the latter with a fervor amply indicated by a single line: "Her silence fills my whole soul with terror."[2]

With such conflicting and exhausting emotions, which happily have not been further disclosed by his confidants, Poe passed another fortnight. On December 20 he left Fordham to give the fifth lecture before the Franklin Lyceum of Providence. At the New York station he met a lady, who said to him, " Mr. Poe, are you going to Providence to be married?" "I am going," he replied, "to deliver a lecture on Poetry." Then he added, after a moment, "That marriage may never take place." His friend, Mr. Pabodie, in describing

[1] Ingram, ii. 194.   [2] Ingram, ii. 196.

this interview, states that "circumstances existed which threatened to postpone the marriage indefinitely, if not altogether to prevent it." [1] To these, which have not been divulged, Poe presumably referred. On reaching Providence he delivered the lecture, "The Poetic Principle," the same evening, December 20, to a large audience. He remained in the city, and still pleaded with Mrs. Whitman to be married and to return with him to Fordham. He was stopping at the Earl House, and there occasionally drank at the bar with some young men of the city. On Friday evening, December 22, he called at Mrs. Whitman's, partially intoxicated; but, says Mr. Pabodie, who was present, he was quiet and said little. The next morning he was full of contrition and profuse of promises for the future, and he persuaded Mrs. Whitman to appoint Monday evening for the ceremony. He then wrote to Dr. Crocker, engaging him to officiate, and to Mrs. Clemm, advising her to expect himself and his wife on Tuesday at Fordham. In the afternoon, however, Mrs. Whitman received a note from a friend, informing her that Poe had that morning again drunk at the bar of his hotel, and she therefore finally decided to break off the match. When Poe called, says Mrs. Whitman, "no token of the infringement of his promise was visible in his appearance or manner." [2] This

[1] Pabodie to Griswold, June 11, 1852. Gill, 224.
[2] Ingram, ii. 184, 185.

THE END OF THE PLAY.

circumstance, however, she disregarded, and carried out her predetermined plan. "Gathering together some papers," she says, "which he had intrusted to my keeping, I placed them in his hands without a word of explanation or reproach, and, utterly worn out and exhausted by the mental conflicts and anxieties and responsibilities of the last few days, I drenched my handkerchief with ether and threw myself on a sofa, hoping to lose myself in utter unconsciousness. Sinking on his knees beside me, he entreated me to speak to him, — to speak *one* word, but *one word*. At last I responded, almost inaudibly, 'What can I say?' 'Say that you love me, Helen.' '*I love you*.' These were the last words I ever spoke to him."[1] Mr. Pabodie, who had accompanied Poe on this visit, went with him to the train, in which he left at once for Fordham. About three weeks later he addressed a last letter to Mrs. Whitman, in respect to some slanderous misrepresentations of his conduct in this affair, which had been put in circulation; but to this, which he had first sent unsealed to "Annie," Mrs. Whitman made no reply, except, weeks afterward, indirectly by some "Stanzas for Music," published in "The Metropolitan" for February, and now included, in a revised version, in her "Poems" as "The Island of Dreams."

This episode has been narrated in minute detail because gross perversions of the facts were once

[1] Ingram, ii. 184, 185.

common, and are not yet entirely suppressed; and in the relation it has not been possible to ignore, as one would desire to do, the letters written by Poe, during this period, to Mrs. Whitman, "Annie," and her sister. If Poe's correspondence with other women — with Mrs. Osgood, for example, who terms his letters "divinely beautiful" — bore any resemblance to that of the last year of his life, fortune has been more than usually kind in destroying it. Not one word from these letters ought ever to have been published, but now it is too late to exclude them from the record. From this and other evidence it is plain that Poe, worn out by the ruin wrought on a romantic temperament by his unavailing struggle with poverty, insane indulgence, and secret disease, realizing now the hopelessness of his situation and oppressed by its loneliness, felt himself under an overpowering necessity of receiving human help, and sought for it with an ardor undisciplined by years, in whatever quarter there was any promise. He had made up his mind, moreover, to adopt Mrs. Shew's advice, and to try to save himself in what she had declared the only possible way, — marriage. A trivial incident — the anonymous exchange of a copy of verses — resulted in some slight relations between himself and a woman whose genius he had idealized, and he at once threw himself on her mercy. By his own declaration to Mrs. Whitman, hardly more than a week earlier he had been on the point of asking another woman to be his wife. Mrs. Whitman herself, notwithstanding her many virtues and admirable qualities of heart, so finely exercised in her lifelong devotion to Poe's memory, was eccentric, susceptible to romantic fancies and mystical moods. She was in particular a believer in occult spiritual influences, and by this approach to her weakness Poe made his persuasive appeal. Both in his letters to her and in the recorded fragments of their conversation, he rhapsodized about their affinities, as if that were the sure chord to respond to his touch. Poe may have believed in what he professed, but amid all his transcendental raptures, as well as in his vindication of his character and his absurd anticipations of their worldly triumph, as he called it, although his helplessness and real suffering are plain to see, it is futile to look for any unmistakable expression of the love man bears to woman, any passage that rings true with genuine devotion as does the single brief note written to his wife, Virginia. In all this correspondence there is a total and absolute absorption of his mind in his own affairs, — his injuries, distresses, and hopes; indeed, to one familiar with his modes of expression, it seems almost an accident that these letters were addressed to Mrs. Whitman. The language, confidential and studded with terms of endearment, is such as he habitually used both in written and spoken words to other women who he thought understood him. Clearly, so far as his need of sympathy, pity, consolation, was concerned, he put more trust in "Annie's" heart, just as he wrote to her with more freedom and besought her aid with more simplicity. He had selected Mrs. Whitman as the object of his marital determination out of admiration for her poems, had asked her hand at the first interview, and, finding himself opposed by private defamation, had urged his suit with eagerness and force; but he apparently never believed he would succeed, and in this fear he pressed for a conclusion. In fact Poe seems less absorbed in a woman than infatuated with an idea, — an idea which, originating in fancy, fostered by his idealizing faculty, made practicable by accident, and acted on from impulse, was now supported by the strongest worldly motives, since his reputation, ambition, and fortune were highly interested in the issue.

Besides these considerations, it must be remembered how plain and frequent in both Poe's acts and words at this period are the signs of a mind unstrung. To give but one additional instance, in judging the following passage to Mrs. Whitman, the only choice lies between Poe's insincerity or his practical insanity: —

"Was I right, dearest Helen, in my first impression of you? — you know I have implicit faith in first impressions — was I right in the impression that you are ambitious? If so, and *if you will have faith in me*, I can and will satisfy your wildest desires. It would be a glorious triumph, Helen, for *us* — for *you and me.* I dare not trust my schemes to a letter — nor indeed have I time even to hint at them here. When I see you I will explain all — as far, at least, as I dare explain *all* my hopes even to you. Would it *not* be 'glorious,' darling, to establish in America, the sole unquestionable aristocracy — that of intellect — to secure its supremacy — to lead and to control it? All this I can do, Helen, and will — if you bid me — and aid me." [1]

This, in the case of a man of Poe's years and powers, is either chicanery or irresponsible maundering. He merely let his pen run, as in nearly all these letters, which, to characterize them plainly, record the confusion and weakness of a mind abandoned to an emotional mood, and occupied only by self-pity, intellectual pride, or despair. That he has been thus revealed to the world in his weakest moments and most wretched abasement is the fault of his friends; but keeping in view his state of mind and body, the origin and course of his wooing, and the surrounding circumstances, one finds it least difficult to believe that if Poe was sincere in his professions he was self-deceived, and to agree with Mrs. Osgood, who, having herself been the object of similar sentiments from him, declared of his dead wife, "I believe she was the only woman whom he ever truly loved." [2]

[1] Poe to Mrs. Whitman, November 22, '848. Ingram, ii. 180, 181.
[2] Griswold, liii.

On reaching Fordham Poe found Mrs. Clemm, who had never favored the match, overjoyed to see him unaccompanied by a wife, and, were it possible, more devoted to himself. He set to work, and wrote several hours each day; but, in consonance with the view that has been taken, although doubtless bitterly aggrieved, he exhibited no regret at the event which he had always considered likely, and no fidelity to the woman whose loyalty to his memory in after years was almost ideal. On January 11, 1849, he wrote to "Annie" as follows: —

"In spite of so many worldly sorrows — in spite of all the trouble and *misrepresentation* (so hard to bear) that Poverty has entailed on me for so long a time — in spite of *all* this — I am *so, so* happy. . . . I need not tell you how great a burden is taken off my heart by my rupture with Mrs. W.; for I have fully made up my mind to break the engagement. . . . *Nothing* would have deterred me from the match but — what I tell you."[1]

Two weeks later he inclosed to the same correspondent a last letter to Mrs. Whitman, in which, after referring to the evil reports of him originating at Providence, he declared, "No amount of provocation shall induce me to speak ill of *you* [Mrs. Whitman], even in my own defense,"[2] — with directions to read it, seal it with wax, and mail it in Boston; and to this singularly indelicate act, which is excused only by the circumstance that

[1] Ingram, ii. 202.   [2] Ingram, ii. 185.

THE END OF THE PLAY. 327

"Annie's" confidence in him had been shaken by these same slanders, he added the dishonor of a hasty expression of his pique in words too violently in contrast with the line just quoted to escape notice.

"Of one thing rest assured, from this day forth I shun the pestilential society of *literary women*. They are a heartless, unnatural, venomous, dishonorable *set*, with no guiding principle but inordinate self-esteem. Mrs. Osgood is the *only* exception I know."[1]

Having thus freed himself of the affair, — for it is said that Mrs. Whitman's name never afterwards passed his lips, — Poe busied himself with literature, which, he wrote to Thomas, there was no seducing him from; and he adds, "Nor would I abandon the hopes that still lead me on for all the gold in California."[2] In the "Southern Literary Messenger" for February he published an unfavorable review of Lowell's "A Fable for Critics," and in "Godey's" of the same month "Mellonta Tauta," a revision of the introduction to "Eureka." He sent, but fruitlessly, "Landor's Cottage" to the "Metropolitan," whose short career was distinguished by some lines addressed to him by Mrs. Osgood, and also by Mrs. Whitman in indirect acknowledgment of his last letter; and with like ill success fifty pages of "Marginalia" (possibly the editor had discovered their second-hand character)

[1] Ingram, ii. 205.
[2] Poe to Thomas, February 14, 1849. MS. copy.

to the "Messenger," and "Critics and Criticism" to the "Whig." Poe was elated with his immediate prospects; and he had good reason, if there was no exaggeration in his statement that he had made permanent engagements with every magazine in America (except Peterson's "National"), including a Cincinnati magazine called the "Gentlemen's," at a minimum price of five dollars per Graham page. On February 6 he finished "The Bells," presumably the second draft, and the next day "Hop-Frog," a tale of grotesque humor out of Berner's Froissart, published in April in the "Flag of our Union," a Boston weekly. His only other publications that have been traced were the ghoulish lines "To Annie" (reprinted by Willis) and the sonnet "To my Mother," both in the same cheap Boston weekly, and, as it would seem, in April; and lastly, in "Sartain's Magazine" for March, "A Valentine," the anagrammatic poem to Mrs. Osgood. Perhaps "El Dorado," the only poem of which the first publication is unknown, belongs to this same period.

These various writings probably represent Poe's literary activity for some time before this spring, and this is certainly the case with the only noticeable pieces among them, "The Domain of Arnheim" and "Landor's Cottage," called its pendant. The latter closed the series of the landscape studies, which make as distinct a group in Poe's imaginative work as the tales of mystery, ratiocination, or conscience, since in these the sensuous element, which was primary in his genius, found its simplest and most unrestrained expression. The series had culminated, however, in "The Domain of Arnheim," in which the brilliancy and flood and glow of pure color are a mere reveling of the æsthetic sense; and so gorgeous is the vision and thrown out in so broad an expanse that, although only a description, the piece is as unique among works of imagination as is "The Black Cat" or "The Fall of the House of Usher." The landscape that the mention of the latter recalls, and much more the spectral woodland and tarn of "Ulalume," serve to measure by momentary contrast with the scenes of faëry in "Arnheim" the range of Poe's fantasy, and at the same time to bring out strongly the extent to which his work is dependent for its effect directly on the senses, however abnormally excited. In fact the impression made in the present case is solely spectacular. The landscape sketches, too, which belong to the dark period of Poe's career, afford some pleasant relief to the paltrinesses, the miseries, and debasements of his ordinary life. The idyllic sweetness of "Eleonora," the quiet beauty of "The Island of the Fay" and "Morning on the Wissahiccon," opened round Poe, as he was seen in his Philadelphia days, the only prospect beyond the mean walls of the newspaper office and the tenement house. Now in his yet more wretched years he was not deprived of his poet's birthright in the inheritance of nature; rather, as in this mythical "Arnheim," he indulged most purely his delight in the contemplation of loveliness for its own sake; and as he imagined the charming cottage of Landor just at the time when his letters exhibit him in his lowest spirits, it would seem that his country rambles still gave him an outlook on the things of beauty, of light and calm and joy. No life can continue in darkness and turmoil such as these past months would have been, had they been filled only with the incidents and passions of the written story. Of the bursts of sunshine and pauses of calm that checkered this portion of Poe's days, of the afternoons and frequent nights of summer whose beauty he drank in with senses dulled only by the lotus-flower, these landscape studies are the open secret.

While Poe was thus engaged a second female foe had arisen in the home of his Lowell friends in the person of a woman who had helped to relieve his necessities in 1847. She busied herself so successfully with disseminating the current slanders respecting him as to disturb the minds of the family, and to alienate, at least partially, the good-will of the head of the house. Poe, on being informed of this new misfortune, accounted for the gossip's hostility by saying that he had left her abruptly in consequence of her disparagement of "Annie," and added that he thought it hard that such a quarrel should prejudice him in the latter's mind. He was so far moved by the attitude assumed by her husband that he gave up a proposed visit to his house and the plan of settling near these new friends permanently, and he even professed to think it necessary that the correspondence should cease. He wrote, " I cannot and *will* not have it on my conscience that I have interfered with the domestic happiness of the only being in the whole world, whom I have loved at the same time with truth and with purity." [1]

Such an abrupt termination to one of the happiest friendships of his life was fortunately avoided. Poe was able to sustain his story, and after a few weeks the tale bearer, whose connection with his family seems to have been unbroken, wrote to him that she was about to publish a novel recording their relations in detail in such a way as to make his own character appear noble and generous, and that she would come on to Fordham at once to avail herself of any suggestions from him. What became of this novel, or what reception the lady's proposals met with, is unknown; but as in the sequel, even after Poe's death, she still busied herself in scandal, it is likely that there was no reconciliation.

In literary matters the spring had brought disappointment. The "Columbia" and "Union" failed; the "Whig" and "Democratic" stopped payment; the "Messenger," which was in Poe's debt, remained in arrears; another publication, with which he had engaged for ten dollars weekly,

[1] Poe to "Annie," February 19, 1849. Ingram, ii. 208.

was forced to decline contributions; with "Godey's" he had quarreled: and so, in his own words, he was "reduced to 'Sartain' and 'Graham,' both very precarious." His many engagements, on which he had built so hopefully a few months before, had dwindled away; and to add to his misfortunes he had again been seriously ill. "I thought," wrote Mrs. Clemm to "Annie," "he would die several times. God knows I wish we were both in our graves. It would, I am sure, be far better."[1] A deep gloom settled over his mind. He himself wrote to the same lady, in denying that this arose from his literary disappointments, — "My sadness is *unaccountable*, and this makes me the more sad. I am full of dark forebodings. *Nothing* cheers or comforts me. My life seems wasted — the future looks a dreary blank; but I will struggle on and 'hope against hope.'"[2] After this he visited his friends at Lowell, apparently in May, and there wrote the third draft of "The Bells;" he soon returned to New York, with the expectation of going South at once to try once more the old scheme, — the establishment of the "Stylus," for which he was now arranging a partnership with a Mr. Patterson, in accordance with which it would be published simultaneously in New York and St. Louis on January 1, 1850. He was delayed for some weeks, during which his despondency was marked and habitual. Before leaving Fordham, apparently led by

[1] Ingram, ii. 215.   [2] Ingram, ii. 214.

THE END OF THE PLAY. 333

the palpable signs of his danger, he wrote requests that Griswold would superintend the collection of his works, and that Willis would write such a biographical notice as should be deemed necessary. On June 29, having completed his arrangements for his journey, he went to New York in company with Mrs. Clemm, to pass the night at the house of Mrs. Lewis, the poetess, whose works he had lately reviewed, and with whom during the past year an intimacy of the old kind had sprung up. "He seemed very sad," wrote this lady, "and retired early. On leaving the next morning he took my hand in his, and, looking in my face, said, 'Dear Stella, my much beloved friend. You truly understand and appreciate me — I have a presentiment that I shall never see you again. I must leave to-day for Richmond. If I never return, write my life. You can and will do me justice.'"[1] Mrs. Clemm accompanied him to the steamboat, and on parting he said to her, "God bless you, my own darling mother. Do not fear for Eddy! See how good I will be while I am away from you, and will [sic] come back to love and comfort you."[2]

Poe stopped at Philadelphia, where he suffered a severe attack of *delirium tremens*, during which he was taken care of by Mr. John Sartain, the proprietor of Sartain's Magazine, who still remembers the visions about which he raved and the persistence with which he besought him for laudanum

[1] Ingram, ii. 220. [2] Ingram, ii. 221.

On recovering he proceeded to Richmond and there remained through July, August, and September, delivered his lecture on "The Poetic Principle," in Richmond and Norfolk, canvassed for the "Stylus," and enjoyed the society of his old and new friends. He stayed at the Madison Tavern, a once fashionable but then decayed hotel, and he visited much among his acquaintances, by whom he was well received, and, indeed, lionized. At Duncan's Lodge, especially, the residence of the Mackenzies, who had adopted his sister Rosalie, he was made at home; and at Robert Sully's, the artist whom he had befriended in his early schooldays, and at Mrs. Talley's, he passed many of those hours which he said were the happiest he had known for years. To Miss Susan Archer Talley, now Mrs. Weiss, who then looked on Poe with the romantic interest of a young poetess as well as with a woman's sympathy with sadness so confessed as his, is due the most life-like and detailed portrait of him that exists. Erect in stature, cold, impassive, almost haughty in manner, soberly and fastidiously clad in black, to a stranger's eye he wore a look of distinction rather than beauty; on nearer approach one was more struck by the strongly marked head, with the broad brow, the black curly hair brushed back, the pallid, careworn, and in repose the somewhat haggard features, while beneath the concealment of a short black moustache one saw the slight habitual contraction of the mouth and occasionally the quick, almost imperceptible curl of the upper lip in scorn — a sneer, it is said, that was easily excited; but the physical fascination of the man was felt, at last, to lie in his eyes, large, jet-black, with a steel-gray iris, clear as crystal, restless, ever expanding and contracting as, responsive with intelligence and emotion, they bent their full, open, steady, unshrinking gaze from under the long black lashes that shaded them. On meeting his friends Poe's face would brighten with pleasure, his features lost the worn look and his reserve its coldness; to men he was cordial, to women he showed a deference that seems always to have suggested a reminiscence of chivalry; and in society with the young he forgot his melancholy, listened with amusement, or joined in their repartees with evident pleasure, though he would soon leave them for a seat in the portico, or a walk in the grounds with a single friend. To the eyes of his young girlish friend he seemed invariably cheerful, and often even playful in mood. Once only was he noticeably cast down; it was when visiting the old deserted Mayo place, called The Hermitage, where he used to go frequently in his youth, and the scene was so picturesque that it is worth giving at length: —

"On reaching the place our party separated, and Poe and myself strolled slowly about the grounds. I observed that he was unusually silent and preoccupied, and, attributing it to the influence of memories associated with the place, forbore to interrupt him. He passed slowly by the mossy bench called the 'lovers' seat, beneath two aged trees, and remarked, as we turned toward the garden, 'There used to be white violets here.' Searching amid the tangled wilderness of shrubs, we found a few late blossoms, some of which he placed carefully between the leaves of a note-book. Entering the deserted house, he passed from room to room with a grave, abstracted look, and removed his hat, as if involuntarily, on entering the saloon, where in old times many a brilliant company had assembled. Seated in one of the deep windows, over which now grew masses of ivy, his memory must have borne him back to former scenes, for he repeated the familiar lines of Moore: —

> 'I feel like one
> Who treads alone
> Some banquet hall deserted,'

and paused, with the first expression of real sadness that I had ever seen on his face. The light of the setting sun shone through the drooping ivy-boughs into the ghostly room, and the tattered and mildewed paper-hangings, with their faded tracery of rose-garlands, waved fitfully in the autumn breeze. An inexpressibly eerie feeling came over me, which I can even now recall, and as I stood there, my old childish idea of the poet as a spirit of mingled light and darkness recurred strongly to my imagination." [1]

Poe talked with his young friend about his plans and hopes; about the restrictions on criticism which are imposed by personal friendship and editorial prepossessions, and from which even he could not wholly

[1] *Scribner's Magazine*, xv. 5, p. 712 (March, 1878).

THE END OF THE PLAY. 337

free himself; about his New York friends, the misconstructions his nature suffered under even among those who knew him, and other confidential topics that the charm of his listener and his own readiness to indulge in quick intimacies, beguiled him into. In particular it should be noticed that he showed her a letter from Griswold, accepting his commission to edit his works in case of his sudden death.

These reminiscences of quiet mornings in the grounds of Duncan's Lodge and of social evenings at the houses of various friends do not contain the whole story of this summer. Twice during this visit, it is said, Poe again suffered severe illness in consequence of intemperance, and though he recovered under kind and skillful care, he was told by his physician, Dr. Carter, that another such indulgence would probably prove fatal; and in the course of a long conversation in which Poe was moved to tears he convinced this gentleman of his earnest desire to overcome his temptations and of his unavailing struggle against them, though he had still, it seems, courage to keep up hope for the last trial.

During these months, too, he renewed his attentions to Mrs. Shelton and asked her hand in marriage. There is no room to doubt that in this act he obeyed worldly motives; for though there had been romantic passages between them in schooldays, there is no likelihood that these would have prevailed on Poe to unite himself with a woman who is described as of plain manners, older than himself, and with no attraction except wealth. It cannot have escaped attention that Poe uniformly attributed his ill-success in the world solely to his poverty; in later years especially this had become so settled a conviction in his mind that in his letters to " Annie," "I must get rich, get rich," is a refrain so constant as to seem the purpose he had most at heart; he needed money to secure his shattered health against the necessities of hard labor for a support precarious at best, and especially to establish the " Stylus," the scheme he pursued as a phantom. Mrs. Clemm believed that his motive was to provide a home and friends for herself. To her Mrs. Whitman wrote, "I think I can understand all the motives that influenced Edgar in those last days and can see how the desire to provide a home and friends for you, swayed him in *all*."[1] His engagement to Mrs. Shelton was commonly talked of, and is said to have been mentioned in the papers, greatly to his displeasure; and although Mrs. Shelton has denied that a formal agreement existed, and acknowledges only a partial understanding, she began a correspondence with Mrs. Clemm the first letter[2] of which is not to be explained on any other theory than that she meant to marry Poe. The most authentic indication of the actual state of affairs is Poe's letter to Mrs. Clemm, September

[1] Mrs. Whitman to Mrs. Clemm, April 17, 1859. MS.

[2] This letter, of which the author has a copy, is too private for publication.

18, 1849, in which, it will be noticed, his peculiar secretiveness is markedly illustrated by his directing her to address him under a fictitious name in Philadelphia.

[RICHMOND, VA.
TUESDAY, *September* 18, '49.

MY OWN DARLING MUDDY,

On arriving here last night from Norfolk I received both your letters, including Mrs. Lewis's. I cannot tell you the joy they gave me to learn at least that you are well and hopeful. May God forever bless you, my *dear dear* Muddy. — Elmira has just got home from the country. I spent last evening with her. I think she loves me more devotedly than any one I ever knew and I cannot help loving her in return. Nothing is as yet definitely settled —] and it will not do to hurry matters. I lectured at Norfolk on Monday and cleared enough to settle my bill here at the Madison House with $2 over. I had a highly fashionable audience, but Norfolk is a small place and there were two exhibitions the same night. Next Monday I lecture again here and expect to have a large audience. On Tuesday I start for Philadelphia to attend to Mrs. Loud's poems — and *possibly* on Thursday I may start for New York. If I do I will go straight over to Mrs. Lewis's and send for you. It will be better for me not to go to Fordham — don't you think so? Write immediately in reply and direct to Philadelphia. For fear I should not get the letter sign no name and address it to *E. S. T. Grey Esq*^{re}. *If possible* I will get married before I start, but there is no telling. Give my dearest love to Mrs. L. My poor poor Muddy I am still unable to send you even one dollar, — but keep [up heart — I hope that our troubles are nearly over. I saw John Beatty in Norfolk.

God bless and protect you, my own darling Muddy. I showed your letter to Elmira, and she says "it is such a darling precious letter that she loves you for it already."
Your own Eddy.

Don't forget to write immediately to Philadelphia so that your letter will be there when I arrive.

The papers here are praising me to death — and I have been received everywhere with enthusiasm. Be sure and preserve all the printed scraps I have] sent you and keep up my file of the Literary World.[1]

It has been stated that a disagreement arose between Poe and Mrs. Shelton in consequence of her expressed intention of keeping control of her property, and that he refused to give up her letters to him unless she would first surrender his; and this circumstance is alleged to be the basis of the scandalous story still circulated respecting Poe's levying blackmail on a woman and being beaten by her brother. Of the truth of this at any time in his life, there is no indication. Neither is there any evidence that any difference arose between the two at all. Poe is said to have himself written to Mrs. Clemm that the ceremony was fixed for October 17.[2] On any other supposition than that a practical engagement still existed, it is inexplicable that after Poe's death Mrs. Shelton should have gone

[1] Poe to Mrs. Clemm, MS.; where bracketed, MS. copy.
[2] Didier, 110.

THE END OF THE PLAY. 341

into mourning, as she did, or have written a letter of condolence to Mrs. Clemm, with whom she had no acquaintance, of such a character that the latter should have written to "Annie" regarding it, "I have received a letter from poor Elmira; oh, how you will pity her when you read it!"[1] Moreover, Poe's statement to his mother-in-law agrees with his promise to his friends at Richmond that he would return within two weeks, and with his expressed intention to reside thereafter in that city, although this would necessarily involve the abandonment of his plan in respect to the "Stylus," which his present partner in the enterprise, Mr. E. H. N. Patterson, in a letter dated August 21, proposed to issue, according to the plan, simultaneously in New York and St. Louis, on July 1, 1850.

In order to wind up his affairs in New York and to bring Mrs. Clemm to Richmond, as preliminaries of this marriage, Poe decided to go North. On the day before leaving, probably Saturday, September 29, he passed the evening at Mrs. Talley's, where he had a long conversation with her daughter, in which he spoke of his future, "seeming to anticipate it with eager delight, like that of youth," and, Mrs. Weiss adds, "he declared that the last few weeks in the society of his old and new friends had been the happiest that he had known for many years, and that when he again left New York he

[1] Mrs. Clemm to "Annie," October 17, 1849. Ingram, ii. 241.

should there leave behind all the trouble and vexation of his past life." [1] That night he spent with his friends at Duncan's Lodge, and sat late at his window, smoking and silent. The next day he passed in the city with some male friends, and late in the evening left Dr. Carter's office to take supper across the street, at Sadler's restaurant. There he met some acquaintances, who kept company with him until very late and then accompanied him to the boat, where they left him sober and cheerful. If, as seems probable, this was on Sunday night, he would have arrived in Baltimore late on Monday or early Tuesday. All that is known of his movements is that he called at Dr. N. C. Brooks's on an afternoon, partially intoxicated, and, not finding his friend, went away. It is reported, too, that he took the train to Philadelphia, but, being in the wrong car, was brought back from Havre de Grace in a state of stupor. On what foundation this story rests cannot now be determined. It is also said that he dined with some old military friends, became intoxicated, and while in that state was captured by politicians, who kept him stupefied, and made him vote at several places on Wednesday, election day. The basis of this tradition, too, is now lost. The only certain event after his call on Brooks, which, according to the hypothesis here made, was on Tuesday, is that on Wednesday, at some time after noon, he was recognized at

[1] Scribner's Magazine, xv. 5, p. 713 (March, 1878).

one of the rum-shops used for voting, Ryan's Fourth Ward Polls, by a printer, who wrote the following note: —

BALTIMORE CITY, *Oct.* 3, 1849.

There is a gentleman, rather the worse for wear, at Ryan's Fourth Ward Polls, who goes under the cognomen of Edgar A. Poe, and who appears in great distress. He says he is acquainted with you, and I assure you he is in need of immediate assistance.

JOSEPH W. WILSON.

To DR. J. E. SNODGRASS.[1]

Dr. Snodgrass called at Ryan's and had Poe taken to the Washington Hospital, where he was admitted, unconscious, at 5 P. M.; his relatives in the city were notified of his condition, and gave him such attention as was possible. He remained, except for a brief interval, in an alarming delirium, and on Sunday, about five o'clock, he died. The story of these last days, the catastrophe of "the motley drama," taken from contemporary documents, is as follows: —

BALTIMORE CITY MARINE HOSPITAL,
November 15, '49.

MRS. CLEMM,

MY DEAR MADAM,

I take the earliest opportunity of responding to yours of the 9th inst., which came to hand by yesterday's mail.

． ． ． ． ． ． ． ． ．

[1] *N. Y. Herald*, March 27, 1881.

But now for the required intelligence. Presuming you are already aware of the malady of which Mr. Poe died, I need only state concisely the particulars of his circumstances from his entrance until his decease.

When brought to the Hospital he was unconscious of his condition — who brought him or with whom he had been associating. He remained in this condition from five o'clock in the afternoon — the hour of his admission — until three next morning. This was on the 3d October.

To this state succeeded tremor of the limbs, and at first a busy but not violent or active delirium — constant talking — and vacant converse with spectral and imaginary objects on the walls. His face was pale and his whole person drenched in perspiration. We were unable to induce tranquillity before the second day after his admission.

Having left orders with the nurses to that effect, I was summoned to his bedside so soon as consciousness supervened, and questioned him in reference to his family, place of residence, relatives, etc. But his answers were incoherent and unsatisfactory. He told me however, he had a wife in Richmond (which I have since learned was not the fact), that he did not know when he left that city or what had become of his trunk of clothing. Wishing to rally and sustain his now fast sinking hopes, I told him I hoped that in a few days he would be able to enjoy the society of his friends here and I would be most happy to contribute in every possible way to his ease and comfort. At this he broke out with much energy, and said the best thing his best friend could do would be to blow out his brains with a pistol

— that when he beheld his degradation he was ready to sink into the earth," etc. Shortly after giving expression to these words Mr. Poe seemed to doze, and I left him for a short time. When I returned I found him in a violent delirium, resisting the efforts of two nurses to keep him in bed. This state continued until Saturday evening (he was admitted on Wednesday), when he commenced calling for one " Reynolds," which he did through the night until *three* on Sunday morning. At this time a very decided change began to affect him. Having become enfeebled from exertion he became quiet and seemed to rest for a short time; then gently moving his head, he said, " *Lord help my poor soul*," and expired!

This, Madam, is as faithful an account as I am able to furnish from the Record of his case.

. . . .

His remains were visited by some of the first individuals of the city, many of them anxious to have a lock of his hair.

. . . .

Respectfully yours,
J. J. MORAN, *Res. Phys.*[1]

The undistinguished funeral took place on Monday, October 8, and three days later Neilson Poe wrote an account of it to Mrs. Clemm: —

[1] Moran to Mrs. Clemm, MS. The omitted portions are of no interest. The different dates and additional circumstances given many years afterward by Dr. Moran, must give way to the statements here made when the event was fresh in his memory.

BALTIMORE, *October* 11, 1849.
MY DEAR MADAM:

. . . .

He died on Sunday morning, about five o'clock, at the Washington Medical College, where he had been since the Wednesday preceding. At what time he arrived in this city, where he spent the time he was here, or under what circumstances, I have been unable to ascertain. It appears that on Wednesday he was seen and recognized at one of the places of election in old town, and that his condition was such as to render it necessary to send him to the College, where he was tenderly nursed until the time of his death. As soon as I heard that he was at the College I went over; but his physician did not think it advisable that I should see him, as he was very excitable. The next day I called, and sent him changes of linen etc., and was gratified to learn that he was much better, and I was never so much shocked, in my life, as when, on Sunday morning, notice was sent me that he was dead. Mr. Herring and myself immediately took the necessary steps for his funeral, which took place on Monday afternoon at four o'clock. . . . The body was followed to the grave by Mr. Herring, Dr. Snodgrass, Mr. Z. Collins Lee (an old classmate) and myself. The service was performed by the Rev. William T. D. Clemm, a son of James S. Clemm. Mr. Herring and myself have sought, in vain, for the trunk and clothes of Edgar — there is reason to believe that he was robbed of them, whilst in such a condition as to render him insensible of his loss. . . .

Truly your friend and servant,   NEILSON POE.
MRS. MARIA CLEMM.[1]

[1] Neilson Poe to Mrs. Clemm. MS. The omitted portions are of no interest.

Shortly after Poe's death his remaining writings were published by the editors or friends who had copies. To mention only the first issue in each case, " Annabel Lee," the simplest and sweetest of his ballads, appeared in the New York " Tribune," " The Bells," that wonderful onomatopoetic experiment, in " Sartain's " for November, an essay " On Critics and Criticism" in " Graham's " for January, 1850, and in October following, " The Poetic Principle " in " Sartain's." The press had few notices of his loss; and, had it not been for the intense energy of Griswold's delineation of him in the " Tribune," a piece of writing that has the power of genius and cannot be forgotten while his memory lives, there would have been little to mark his death in contemporary papers. In consequence of this attack, however, Willis made a kind defense of his friend in the " Home Journal." Notwithstanding this incidental proof of Griswold's temper and predisposition toward Poe, the latter's papers, which contained ample materials for a biography, were put into his hands. After having edited two volumes of Poe's Works, Griswold prefixed his notorious memoir to the third volume, and at a later time published the fourth and last volume. The editing was poorly done, and in consequence there is at present no accurate or complete edition of Poe's works, since later editors have taken Griswold's work as a basis. The memoir aroused a stormy discussion; the poet's friends, Wilmer, Neal, and Graham, had already come to his defense; and since then many others of his acquaintances have come forward from time to time to tell whatever good they knew of him, so that there is at present no fund of personal reminiscence about any other American man of letters that can compare in fullness, detail, and variety with that regarding Poe.

The story that has now been told, in which has been substantially incorporated whatever knowledge of Poe was accessible, has shown, it is hoped, the folly of any summary view of his character. Where the fault lay those who are bold to take the scales of justice may determine; the simple fact is that Poe, being highly endowed, well-bred, and educated better than his fellows, had more than once fair opportunities, brilliant prospects, and groups of benevolent, considerate, and active friends, and repeatedly forfeited prosperity and even the homely honor of an honest name. He ate opium and drank liquor; whatever was the cause, these were instruments of his ruin, and before half his years were run they had done their work with terrible thoroughness — he was a broken man. He died under circumstances of exceptional ugliness, misery, and pity, but not accidentally, for the end and the manner of it were clearly near and inevitable. He left a fame destined to long memory, and about it has grown up an idealized legend, the elements of which are not far to seek; but in the first lines of the literary history of a young nation, the truth is better than a lie, however gilded, and in the case of genius, that so easily gathers romantic power over the heart and wins its devotion, candor is a social virtue. On the roll of our literature Poe's name is inscribed with the few foremost, and in the world at large his genius is established as valid among all men. Much as he derived nurture from other sources he was the son of Coleridge by the weird touch in his imagination, by the principles of his analytic criticism, and the speculative bent of his mind. An artist primarily, whose skill, helped by the finest sensitive and perceptive powers in himself, was developed by thought, patience, and endless self-correction into a subtle deftness of hand unsurpassed in its own work, he belonged to the men of culture instead of those of originally perfect power; but being gifted with the dreaming instinct, the myth-making faculty, the allegorizing power, and with no other poetic element of high genius, he exercised his art in a region of vague feeling, symbolic ideas, and fantastic imagery, and wrought his spell largely through sensuous effects of color, sound, and gloom, heightened by lurking but unshaped suggestions of mysterious meanings. Now and then gleams of light and stretches of lovely landscape shine out, but for the most part his mastery was over dismal, superstitious, and waste places. In imagination, as in action, his was an evil genius; and in its realms of revery he dwelt alone. Except the wife who idolized him and the mother who cared for him, no one touched his heart in the years of his manhood, and at no time was love so strong in him as to rule his life; as he was self-indulgent, he was self-absorbed, and outside of his family no kind act, no noble affection, no generous sacrifice is recorded of him. Many men, it is true, held him in kind regard, and many women, subjected by his romantic sentiment, remained loyal to his memory; but these winning attractions never overcame the subtle power within that made him unable to establish a natural human relation, to keep continuously on living terms with any one, except the inmates of his family. Solitary as he was, proud and selfish, how could he kindle his works with the vital interest of humanity? Other interests they have, but not this crowning one which is the supreme excellence of the works of men. Thus ever more remote from mankind ran the currents of his life and genius, interminably commingling, until their twin streams, glassing at last the desolation they had so often prophetically imaged, choked and stagnant in midway of their course, sank into the waste. The pitiful justice of Poe's fate, the dark immortality of his fame, were accomplished.

INDEX

OF THE PRINCIPAL NEWSPAPERS, PERIODICALS, AND PROPER NAMES MENTIONED IN THE TEXT.

[In consulting this index for any particular poem, story, or article by Poe, the references to the magazines he edited and the various collections of his writings published by himself should also be carefully looked up.]

ALEXANDER, W. C., concerning Poe's habits, 134.
Alexander's Weekly Messenger, 142.
Allan, John, adopts Poe, 15; attitude toward Poe, 22, 53, 54, 62; letter to Secretary of War, 42, 43; remarries, 56; death, 68.
Allan, Mrs. John, 14; her death, 38.
Arnold, Mrs., 3–5.
Arnold, Miss Elizabeth, first appearance on the stage, 4; her age, 6 *note*; marries David Poe, 8; birth of William and Edgar, 11; death, 13, 14.

BLACKWELL, MISS ANNA, 310.
Bliss, Elam, publisher of Poe's poems, 58.
Boscovich, 296.
Boston Gazette, appeal for Mrs. Poe's benefit, 10.
Bransby, Dr., Poe's description of, 18.
Briggs, C. F., 216; associated with Poe, 225; his opinion of Poe in letters to J. R. Lowell, 226–229, 235–239.
Broadway Journal, the, 225, 234, 235; Poe becomes proprietor of, 243; last issue of, 247.
Brooks, N. C., 54, 64, 108, 109.
Browning, Mrs. E. B., 219.
Bulwer, E. L., 91.
Burke, William, 20.
Burton, William E., as editor of the Gentleman's Magazine, 114; his quarrel with Poe, 126, 128–142.
Byron, influence on Poe, 33, 50.

CAMPBELL, MAJOR JOHN, 41.
Calderon, 122 *note*.
Carter, Dr., 337, 342.

Channing, W. E., 189.
Châteaubriand, influence on Poe, 51, 303.
Clarke, Joseph H., 19, 20.
Clarke, Thomas C., joins with Poe to publish the Stylus, 176, 182, 183; reminiscences of Poe's home, 188.
Clemm, Mrs., Poe makes his home with, 68; plan to start a boarding-house, 78, 79, 98, 99; on Poe's temperance, 135; head of Poe's household, 165; on Poe's home life, 301, 302.
Clemm, Virginia, 68; her marriage with Poe, 75, 78, 97, 98; her beauty, 166; illness, 167–170; death, 277.
Coleridge, S. T., 51, 91; influence on Poe, 93, 285.
Converse, Rev. F., 93.
Cooper, James Fenimore, 189.

DARLEY, F. O. C., to illustrate the Stylus, 180; reminiscences of Poe, 181.
Dawes, Rufus, 52; Poe's article on, 176.
Dewey, Dr. Orville, 257.
Dickens, Charles, 150, 198.
Didier, E., on Poe's marriage, 77 *note*.
Disraeli, influence on Poe, 85, 91.
Dollar Newspaper, the, 188, 189.
Dow, J. E., cares for Poe in Washington, 182.
Duane, William, his accusation against Poe, 204–207.
Duval, P. S., concerning Poe's learning lithography, 143 *note*.

EASTERN HERALD AND GAZETTE OF MAINE, 5.
Ellet, Mrs. E. F., 258, 262.

INDEX.

Ellis, Powhattan, 53.
Ellis, Col. Thomas H., 69.
Emerson, Ralph Waldo, 157.
English, Thomas Dunn, 265, 266.
Enquirer, The, 13.

FARADAY, 296.
Fay, Thomas S., his Norman Leslie reviewed by Poe, 86.
Fisher, E. Burke, 113.
Francis, Dr., 258.
Fuller, Margaret, 258, 262.

Gentleman's Magazine, the, character of, 114, 115; Poe's editorship, 115, 123-126; Graham assumes control, 143. *See* Graham's Magazine.
Gift, the, 186.
Gove, Mrs. Mary, 258; reminiscences of Poe, 272, 274.
Gowans, Wm., on Poe's habits, 108.
Graham's Magazine, 143; Poe's editorship of, 149, 160, 171, 196.
Greeley, Horace, his endorsement of Poe's note, 243.
Green, his company of players, 6, 7, 12.
Griswold, Capt. H. W., his letter recommending Poe, 40.
Griswold, R. W., relations with Poe, 171-175, 192, 195, 244, 245; description of Poe's home, 186, 187; engages to edit Poe's works, 337; his memoir, 347, 348.
Gwynn, Wm., 43, 44, 63, 64.

HALLECK, FITZ-GREENE, 189.
Hawthorne, N., 158; Poe's estimate of, 280.
Herschel, 83.
Hewitt, John H., 52; description of Poe, 68.
Hirst, 53 *note*, 241.
Hoffman, C. F., 312.
Hopkins, C. D., 6, 7.
Horne, Poe's praises of, 196.
House, Col. James, requests Poe's discharge from the army, 38, 39.
Howard, Lieutenant J., his letter recommending Poe, 40.
Hoyt, 241.

INDEPENDENT CHRONICLE AND UNIVERSAL ADVERTISER, 3.

KENNEDY, JOHN P., 65-77; concerning the reason of Poe's leaving the Messenger, 102.
Knickerbocker, the, on American criticism, 89.

LAFAYETTE, 3.
Laplace, 296.

Latrobe, J. H. B., reminiscences of Poe, 65-67.
Lawson, James, 258.
Lea & Blanchard, publishers of Poe's Tales, 116, 117, 164, 165.
Lewis, Mrs. S., 312; her last meeting with Poe, 333.
Longfellow, H. W., Poe's charges of plagiarism against, 124, 157, 231; Poe's estimate of, 159, 160; The Waif, 224, 230; his opinion of Poe's criticism, 232.
Lord, W. W., 232.
Lowell, J. R., Poe's letters to, 176 *et seq.*; his sketch of Poe, 207, 222; meeting with Poe, 234.
Lynch, Miss Anne C., 258.

MAGRUDER, ALLAN B., reminiscences of Poe, 54, 55.
Massachusetts Mercury, 4.
McIntosh, Miss Maria, 310.
Meunier, Mme. L., translates Poe's Tales, 283.
Mirror, the, on Poe's criticisms, 87, 88; advertises the Penn, 175; Poe assistant editor, 218; Poe's libel suit against, 266.
Moore, Thomas, influence on Poe, 51.
Moran, Dr. J. J., account of Poe's death, 343-345.
Morell, Voyages of, Poe's indebtedness to, 106.

NEAL, John, 44.

OAKIE, DR., 317.
Opal, the, 189.
Osgood, Mrs. F. S., 259-263.

PABODIE, W. J., 317, 319.
Paulding, J. K., 106.
Penn Magazine, the, cause of Poe's trouble with Burton, 135-137; prospectus, 145-148; scheme of, revived, 160, 175. *See* Stylus.
Pioneer, the, 177, 183.
Poe, Edgar Allan, parentage, 1-14, date of birth, 11 *note;* adopted by John Allan, 15; at school in England, 16-19; youthful characteristics, 20-23; at the University of Virginia, 25-28; in Boston, 30-36; in the army 37-39; misstatements concerning his age, 53; at West Point, 54-57; rupture with Mr. Allan, 62, 69; in Baltimore, 64-74; first evidences of intemperance, 72, 73; in Richmond, 74-103; marriage, 75, 78, 97, 98; as a critic, 86-91, 153, 160, 266-271: poetic theory, 91-94, 159; goes to

New York, 104; to Philadelphia, 108; employed by Burton, 115; quarrel with Burton and discussion of habits, 126, 128-142; employed by Graham, 149; aim and method in narration, 152; household, 165-167; wife's illness, 167-171; plans for the Stylus, *see* Stylus; trip to Washington, 181-183; as a lecturer, 195; goes to New York, 199; on the Mirror, 218; lectures before N. Y. Historical Society, 223, 224; on the Broadway Journal, 228, 247, 248; before the Boston Lyceum, 241-243; estimate of his poetry, 249-257; his acquaintance with the New York literati, 257-263; removal to Fordham, 262; home life at Fordham, 271-276; his wife's death, 277; his illness, 278, 279; his lecture, Eureka, 284, 285; his opinion of Eureka, 285, 300, 301, 312; trip to Richmond, 311; his love affairs, 308-327; despondency, 332; last trip to the South, 333; his proposed marriage with Mrs. Shelton, 337-341; departure for New York, 341, 342; last illness, 343, 346.

WORKS. AL AARAAF (1829), 47 *note*; estimate of, 48-52; *Annabel Lee*, 347; *Assignation, The*, 81, 232; *Automatic Chess Player, The*, 96, 97; *Bells, The*, 302-304, 328, 347; *Berenice*, 70, 80, 81, 232; *Black Cat, The*, 189; *Bon-Bon*, 85, 232; *Bridal Ballad*, 240; *Business Man, The*, 240; *Cask of Amontillado, The*, 275; *Catholic Hymn*, 240; *City of the Sea*, 240; *Coliseum, The*, 240; CONCHOLOGIST'S FIRST BOOK, THE, 109-113; *Conqueror Worm, The*, 186, 232; *Critical History of American Literature*, 215; *Critics and Criticism*, 328, 347; *Devil in the Belfry, The*, 246; *Diddling considered as one of the Fine Arts*, 240; *Domain of Arnheim, The*, 328-330; *Dream, A*, 240; *Dreamland*, 207; *Duc de L'Omelette, The*, 80, 240; *El Dorado*, 328; *Eleonora*, 168-170, 332; *Epimanes*, 80; *Estelle*, 301; *Eulalie*, 240; EUREKA, first planned, 280; elaborated, 283, 284; publication of, 285; estimate of, 286-301; *Fairyland*, 123, 241; *Fall of the House of Usher*, 120-122; *Four Beasts in One*, 246; *Flaccus*, 186; *Gold Bug, The*, 188, 189; *Hans Pfaall*, 70, 83; *Hop Frog*, 328; *How to write a Blackwood Article*, 240; *Island of the Fay, The*, 240; *Israfel*, 240; *Julius Rodman*, 125, 126;

King Pest, 80, 240; *Landor's Cottage*, 327; *Landscape Garden, The*, 240; *Lenore*, 186, 240; *Ligeia*, 118-120; *Lionizing*, 232; *Literary Life of Thingum-Bob*, 220, 240; *Literati of New York, The*, 263, 268; *Loss of Breath*, 80, 246; *Man Who was Used Up, The*, 189, 240; *Marginalia*, 221, 263, 275, 301; *Masque of the Red Death, The*, 240; *Mellonta Tauta*, 327; *Mesmeric Revelations*, 214; *Metzengerstein*, 80; *Morella*, 80, 232; *Morning on the Wissahiccon*, 189; *MS. Found in a Bottle*, 83, 240; *Murders in the Rue Morgue*, 150, 189, 283; *Mystery of Marie Roget*, 176; *Mystification*, 246; *Never Bet the Devil your Head*, 240; *Notes upon English Verse*, 179, 186; *Oblong Box, The*, 220, 246; *Our Amateur Poets*, 186, 189; *Our Contributors*, 189; *Oval Portrait, The*, 232; *Pæan*, 186; *Peter Snooks*, 232; *Philosophy of Composition, The*, 263; *Philosophy of Furniture*, 232; *Pit and the Pendulum, The*, 186, 232; *Poetic Principle, The*, 311, 320, 334, 347; *Poets and Poetry of America, The*, 172, 195; POEMS (1831), 58-61; *Politian*, 70; *Power of Words, The*, 240; *Premature Burial, The*, 232; *Purloined Letter, The*, 221; *Quacks of Helicon*, 154; *Rationale of Verse, The*, 186, 312; RAVEN AND OTHER POEMS, THE (1845), 248-257; *Raven, The*, 221, 222; *Romance*, 240. *Science*, 240; *Shadow*, 80-82, 232; *Silence*, 123, 240; *Sleeper, The*, 232; *Some Words with a Mummy*, 246, *Song* ("I saw thee"), 241; *Spectacles, The*, 246; *Spirits of the Dead*, 123; *Tale of Jerusalem, A*, 80, 240; *Tale of the Ragged Mountains, A*, 207, 246; TALES (1845), 239 *note*; *Tales of the Folio Club*, 80-85; TALES OF THE GROTESQUE AND ARABESQUE (1840), 115; TAMERLANE AND OTHER POEMS (1827), 30-36; *Tell-Tale Heart, The*, 185, 240; *The 1002 Tale*, 222; *Thou art the Man*, 220; *Three Sundays in a week*, 232; *To* —— ("The bowers whereat"), 241; *To Annie*, 328; *To F*——, 232; *To Ianthe in Heaven*, 123; *To M. L. S*——, 280; *To My Mother*, 328; *To the River* ——, 123, 241; *Travels in Arabia Petræa*, 104, 105; *Ulalume*, 281-283; *Valentine, A*, 328; *Valley of Unrest, The*, 241; *William Wilson*, 122, 240; *Why the Little Frenchman Wears his Hand in a Sling*, 240.

Poe, David, 1, 2, 6, 7; his marriage, 8; uncertainty about his death, 12, 18.
Poe, Gen. David, his character, 2, 3.
Poe, George, 79.
Poe, Neilson, 75; his account of Poe's death, 346.
Poe, William, 11, 14.
Poe, Rosalie, 13, 14, 334.
Preston, James C., recommends Poe for West Point, 41, 42.

REID, MAYNE, 165; reminiscences of Poe's home, 187.
Royster, Miss S. E., reminiscences of Poe, 24, 311; Poe's proposal of marriage to, 337, 341.

SARTAIN, JOHN, 333.
Saturday Evening Post, the, 143, 149, 172.
Saturday Museum, publishes a sketch of Poe, 181; attack on Griswold of, 195.
Saturday Visiter, 65.
Schlegel, 96, 97.
Shapley, R. F., 301.
Shelton, Mrs. S. E., *see* Royster, Miss S. E.
Shew, Mrs. M. L., 275; intimacy with Poe, 277–279, 302, 304–307.
Smith, Mrs. E. O., 258.
Snodgrass, Dr. J. E., Poe's letters to, 127 *et seq.;* has Poe taken to the hospital, 343.
Snowden's Lady's Companion, 176.
Southern Literary Messenger, 70; Poe's editorship of, 74–100.
Spirit of the Times, the, charges Poe with plagiarism, 189.

Stanard, Mrs. Jane Stith, 23.
Stoddard, R. H., on the date of Poe's birth, 11 *note*.
Stylus, the, 176; plans for, 180, 186, 284, 332.

THOMAS, CALVIN F. S., 30, 36.
Thomas, F. W., 161; Poe's letters to, 161 *et seq*.
Thompson, J. R., 311.
Thomson, Sir William, 296.
Tomlin, John, 190.

UNITED STATES MILITARY MAGAZINE, 143.

VALENTINE, EDWARD, 319.
Virginia Patriot, 13.

WALTER, MISS, 242.
Ward, Thomas, 186.
Watson, Henry G., 227.
Weiss, Mrs. S. A., reminiscences of Poe, 334–337.
White, T. W., 70; relations with Poe, 100–103.
Whitman, Sarah H., 62; Poe's love affair with, 308–327.
Wilmer, Lambert A., 65; intimacy with Poe, 68, 69; on Poe's habits, 135; Poe's accusation against, 191, 192; defends Poe, 347.
Willis, N. P., 197, 218; on Poe's lecture, 224; on Ulalume, 281; defense of Poe by, 347.
Worth, Lieut. Col. W. J., letter of, recommending Poe, 40, 41.

YANKEE AND BOSTON LITERARY GAZETTE, THE, 44–47.

GEORGE E. WOODBERRY was an American man of letters in his own right. A frequent contributor to the *Atlantic Monthly* and the *Nation*, he served as literary editor of the *Boston Post* before moving on in 1891 to begin a thirteen-year tenure as Professor of Literature at Columbia University. His works include an impressive array of critical biographies, literary essays and poems.

R.W.B. LEWIS, Professor of English and American Studies at Yale University, is the author of *The American Adam* and *Edith Wharton: A Biography*.

WITHDRAWN

818.309　Woodberry, George
WOO　　　Edward, 1855-1930.

Edgar Allan Poe.

$34.95　　　　　　　　　5/12/99

DATE			

LONGWOOD PUBLIC LIBRARY
MIDDLE COUNTRY RD
MIDDLE ISLAND NY 11953

04/27/1999

BAKER & TAYLOR